The Cherokee Syllabary

*American Indian Literature
and Critical Studies Series*

The
CHEROKEE
SYLLABARY

*Writing the
People's Perseverance*

ELLEN CUSHMAN

University of Oklahoma Press

Norman

Also by Ellen Cushman
  The Struggle and the Tools: Oral and Literate Strategies in an Inner City Community
    (Albany, N.Y., 1998)
  (co-ed.) *Literacy: A Critical Sourcebook* (Boston, 2001)

Parts of chapter 1 first appeared in *Wicazo Sa Review* 26(1) (Spring 2011). Parts of chapter 2 first appeared in *Written Communication* 28(3) (July 2011) and are reprinted by permission of SAGE Publications, Inc. Part of chapter 4 was first published in *Ethnohistory* 2010 57(4).

Library of Congress Cataloging-in-Publication Data

Cushman, Ellen, 1967–
  The Cherokee syllabary : writing the people's perseverance / Ellen Cushman.
    p. cm. — (American Indian Literature and Critical Studies series; v. 56)
  Includes bibliographical references and index.
  ISBN 978-0-8061-4220-3 (cloth)
  ISBN 978-0-8061-4373-6 (paper)
  1. Cherokee language—Writing. 2. Cherokee language—Alphabet.
  3. Cherokee language—Grammar. I. Title.
  PM781.C87 2011
  497'.55711—dc23

                                                                      2011018380

The Cherokee Syllabary: Writing the People's Perseverance is Volume 56 in the American Indian Literature and Critical Studies Series.

The paper in this book meets the guidelines for permanence and durability of the Committee on Production Guidelines for Book Longevity of the Council on Library Resources, Inc. ∞

CONTENTS

FIGURES

Tables

Preface

Ꭱ Ꭰ Ꮃ Ꮵ Ꮐ Ꮽ Ꮺ Ꮅ Ꮑ Ꮌ Ꭹ Ᏹ Ꮟ Ꮲ Ꭳ Ꮇ
Ꮄ Ꭽ Ꮼ Ꮰ Ꮤ Ᏼ Ꮈ Ꭿ Ꮝ Ᏺ Ꮁ Ꭺ Ꮷ Ꮍ Ꮞ
Ꮠ Ꮯ Ꮘ Ꮗ Ꮜ Ꮖ Ꮓ Ꭷ Ꮸ Ꮢ Ꮒ Ꭶ Ꮩ Ꭸ Ꮣ
Ꭼ Ꮻ Ꭲ Ꭴ Ᏸ Ꮂ Ꮫ Ꭻ Ꮶ Ꮙ Ꮔ Ꮎ Ꮆ Ᏻ Ꮴ
Ꮧ Ꮾ Ꮪ Ꮥ Ꮳ Ꭵ Ꮕ Ꮦ Ꮚ Ꮀ Ꮡ Ꭾ Ꮨ Ꮋ
Ꮭ Ꮬ Ꮹ Ꮉ Ꮮ Ꮏ Ꮿ Ꮱ Ꮊ Ꮛ

This simple list of characters in the Cherokee writing system provides a modern starting point for a story that began nearly two centuries ago. This book revisits that story to gain a better understanding of the mysteries of this writing system. These eighty-five characters arranged in the original order of Sequoyah's syllabary are re-created with the font face ᏗᎪᏪᎵ/Digoweli/Digohweli, roughly meaning papers, book, or writings. This font maintains a good measure of the visual information found in the original syllabary. Sequoyah's syllabary is the first indigenous writing system, invented by a Cherokee during a time when Cherokees faced tremendous pressure to adopt Anglo ways, the English language, and alphabetic writing. Within the span of a few years, Cherokees were able to read and write in Sequoyan, without print or mass education. This book seeks to unfold the mysteries of how and why it was so easily learned and to address other pressing questions.

Before my computer could reproduce this font, before I could read these eighty-five glyphs or understand their history, workings, and importance and what they actually mean to Cherokee identity, I had hung a huge Cherokee syllabary chart next to my office desk when I taught at the University of California, Berkeley writing program from 1997 to 2000. I recall feeling proud and curious, looking forward to the time when I would be able to explore all those nagging questions. Why so many characters? How is this learned? Why these shapes? Where can I find samples of writing in Sequoyan? Is it even still used? What does it all *mean*?

When a student would ask me about that poster of the Cherokee syllabary, I could offer only the briefest description. I knew it was important, but why and how eluded me. If a student or colleague asked for a deeper explanation, I quickly changed the subject. Though the syllabary chart had great symbolic value for me, I also knew what I didn't know. My ignorance of the syllabary pressed against the symbolic weight of the poster, fueled my wonder, and imbued me with a hopeful determination to delve into its mysteries someday.

My mother had heard the Cherokee language growing up and remembered how her grandfather prayed every morning to the east with the Cherokee he knew. With gestures and softly uttered phrases she would try to re-create the prayers for me. Then her hands would fall into her lap and she would say with a deep sigh, "But I don't know what it all meant and he's gone now. Go get me some sassafras."

We lived in the woods of upstate New York, where she and Dad raised seven children after they left the U.S. Navy. They had met during their service. Mom was raised in Joplin, Missouri, by way of Pryor, Oklahoma, where her father, grandparents, aunts, and uncles had been allotted land. For her, serving in the navy had been a way to get through nursing school in Texas. She missed her family, but seven children and hard times allowed no visiting, only gifts sent at Christmas.

Having been raised away from Cherokee speakers by a mother who was still fiercely Southern Baptist in the face of my father's Catholicism and living under the tacit mandate that Cherokees don't claim the tribe until the tribe claims you, we children knew who we were and what we were not. Mother encouraged all of us to enroll as citizens of the Cherokee Nation when we were old enough to understand what voting meant, and so I did. She kept her two Cherokee family names her entire life and would sign all her documents "Virginia Lee Drew Cushman."

When my position and stability finally made it possible to start the study of writing that I had always wanted to do, I began earnest research on the Cherokee language and identity. My first task was to reestablish connections with the Cherokee Nation. In 2004 I taught Michigan State University undergraduate and graduate students, and together we created online interactive histories for the Cherokee Nation website. Since then, I have twice taught for the Co-Partner Johnson O'Malley (JOM) Program. In 2008 Chief Chadwick Smith honored me with an appointment to the Sequoyah Commission, working alongside former principal chief Wilma P. Mankiller and Drs. Richard Allen, Les Hannah, Lynda Dee Dixon, and Tom Holm.

I suspect that there are thousands of Cherokees like me, citizens who grew up away from the tribal centers, perhaps with some degree of knowledge and connection with the Cherokee Nation and family in Oklahoma, and who are interested in knowing more about our writing system. Of the 296,087 Cherokee Nation citizens, roughly 90,000 still live in the fourteen-county Cherokee Nation jurisdiction, which means that more than two-thirds of the tribe's citizens live away from the tribal core (Allen 2010). The number of these citizens who are Cherokee speakers, readers, and writers is alarmingly low.

To English speakers, whose first writing system is of course the alphabet, the Cherokee syllabary may seem complex and hard to learn. Laid out in Sequoyah's arrangement, it looks a bit like a Cherokee periodic table of language elements. Many English-speaking Cherokees share my interest and pride in the syllabary and wonder how it came to be, how it works, and why it still matters. As answers to these questions are developed in these pages, my hope is that Cherokee speakers, readers, and writers will find their understandings about its functionality and development confirmed. I also hope that English-speaking Cherokee citizens may find instructional value in awareness of how the syllabary works, enabling us to learn the language more strategically.

The story of the evolution of the Cherokee writing system is an important facet of Cherokee perseverance as a tribe and as a people. Historians and scholars in American Indian studies will find in these pages compelling evidence of the ways in which a writing system can resist and accommodate the forces of empire. Literacy scholars will find ample evidence of a tradition of meaning-making that enriches our histories of American literate practices. Linguists and writing systems scholars will be asked to reconsider the ways in which a writing system might represent language. To characterize the evolutionary story of the Cherokee syllabary, I needed to inquire into areas of interest to scholars in a range of fields.

In these ways this book stems from personal and professional questions, gaps in understandings, and the felt need to address the distance separating peoples, histories, and disciplines. Meaning-making with various tools, within cultures, and as an articulation of identity has been a central focus of my research for some time (see Cushman 1998, 2005, 2008; Cushman et al. 2001). Using ethnohistorical methods to trace the invention and continued use of the Cherokee syllabary, the present work results from five years of archival data collection. I interpreted and analyzed artifacts and then triangulated the results through cross-reference to additional print resources as well as observation, interviews, and language study with Cherokee Nation employees and citizens. As one slice of language revitalization efforts, the Cherokee Nation offers online language classes and language materials free to the public, in the hope that its employees and citizens will take advantage of them and integrate spoken Cherokee and Sequoyan into daily interactions. By enrolling in these classes, studying Sequoyan dictionaries and workbooks, and attending language immersion classes whenever possible, I have developed adequate proficiency in the written language and a very modest measure of speaking ability, though I have far to go before achieving anything like fluency.

The results of this analysis illustrate the story of the evolution of the Cherokee syllabary presented here. This book provides instruction in the mysteries, nature, and workings of Sequoyan within the larger themes of sovereignty, identity, and the mediation of cultural change. Yet this story is only a beginning, lending itself to further studies of the precise linguistic features of Sequoyan as well as the concerted ongoing efforts to teach, learn, and use it within the Cherokee Nation. This book and future studies that will spring from it signal a qualified hope that the Cherokee language and writing system will exist beyond this generation.

Acknowledgments

This work has been made possible through the support of many research libraries, librarians, and museums: the Northeastern Oklahoma State University Archive, the University of Tulsa, the Smithsonian Institution's National Anthropological Archives, and the Thomas Gilcrease Museum. Special thanks to the many librarians, directors, and curators who have facilitated this work: Jerry Dobbs at the Sequoyah Cabin in Sallisaw, Oklahoma; Kay Calkins and I. Marc Carlson at the University of Tulsa; Duane King, Michelle Maxwell, and volunteers at the Thomas Gilcrease Museum in Tulsa, Oklahoma; and Dolores Sumner, the Special Collections librarian at Northeastern Oklahoma State. Yale University, Cornell University, Ohio State University, Saginaw Valley State College, and the University of Wisconsin, Madison, have contributed materials for study.

Michigan State University's Office of Research and Development has supported this work through a research leave grant and sabbatical. Many colleagues at Michigan State University deserve my thanks, with special acknowledgment for chair Kitty Geissler and associate chair Laura Julier for their flexibility, support, and direction; Susan Krouse, former director of the Native American Studies program; and Mindy Morgan and Rocio Guispe-Agnoli, whose discussions and support have been appreciated.

Many thanks for the generous readings and suggestions provided especially by Richard Allen of the Cherokee Nation and for the insights offered by John Ross, Ed Fields, Durbin Feeling, Dr. Neil

Morton, Dr. Shelley Butler Allen, Jeff Edwards, Anna Huckaby, Bobbie Gail Smith, Denis Springwater, Benny Smith, Jim Carey, Sue Thompson, Wade Blevins, Travis Owens, Bonnie Kirk, Tonia Williams, Ben Phillips, and Roy Boney. Sammy Still of the United Keetoowah Band and Wyman Kirk and Harry Oowasowee of Northeastern Oklahoma State University have shared invaluable stories and language resources and have facilitated this work tremendously.

My sincerest gratitude goes to Chief Chad Smith, who appointed me to the Sequoyah Commission; to Shelley Butler Allen and Imogene Alexander, who asked me to teach in the JOM Co-Partner Program; and to Donna Gourd, who invited me to work on the Cherokee Lifeways curricular project. I am deeply honored and humbled by their invitations. Wilma P. Mankiller has been an inspiration to me ever since my mother proudly introduced me to her in 1987 as *MS.* magazine's woman of the year and continues to inspire me. I am sincerely grateful for the opportunity I had to work with her on the Sequoyah Commission and for her many kindnesses.

For their general encouragement, thoughtfulness, and support for my work, my gratitude goes to Tom Holm, Lynda Dee Dixon, Leslie Hannah, Kathryn England-Aytes, Rose Hodges, Rosemary Cushman, Bill Cushman, and Mike Rose. Many thanks to Chris Harvey of LanguageGeek.com, who provided insights into the Unicode font design and workings as well as a version of the Digohweli font that included the original shape of Sequoyah's shorthand characters used here. For suffering through drafts of chapters and providing incisive readings that have helped strengthen the arguments, Richard Allen, Albert Wahrhaftig, Rex Hauser, Violet Oliver, Gail Perkins, and Keith Rodgers all deserve my heartfelt thanks.

Finalmente, muchas gracias a mi familia cubana, Félix Sr., Esther, Adibys, y mi esposo, Félix González Goenaga, sin cuyo cariño este libro no sería posible.

GᎪ hᏚᏉ GᎪ
(thank you all/everyone thank you)

A NOTE
ABOUT CONVENTIONS

Names of important Cherokee figures are written in transliterations of Cherokee and standardized according to their most frequent spelling.

The "h" at the end of Sequoyah is conventional and helps English speakers to pronounce the slight aspiration at the end of his name. Sequoyah is often referred to in the historical documents quoted here by his English name, George Guess, with various spellings, such as Gist, Guyst, and Guess.

George Lowrey's last name has been spelled Lowry, Lowery, and Lowerey in historical documents.

Inali has also been spelled Inoli by Anna Gritts Kilpatrick and Jack Kilpatrick.

Cherokee phrases are presented first in the Cherokee syllabary then in a Roman alphabet transliteration, followed by rough translations. For instance: ᏣᏫᏯ ᏗᎪᏪᎵ /tsalagi digowelv/ 'Cherokee writing system, writing, books, and lessons.'

The phonemic versions use the following rules. Vowels are represented as *a, e, i, o, u,* and *v* and sound as they do in Spanish except for *v,* which is pronounced with a nasalized sound similar to *un* in French. The *ts* sounds like the English /j/ as in "juice," and the *qu* sounds like /gw/ as in "guava." While *tl* doesn't exist in English, it can be approximated with a /cl/ sound as in "click." Aspirations in Cherokee are written with an *h* in the transliteration. Other consonant sounds are mostly similar to English.

Unless otherwise noted, translations are my own.

The Cherokee Syllabary

INTRODUCTION

Peoplehood, Tools, and Perseverance

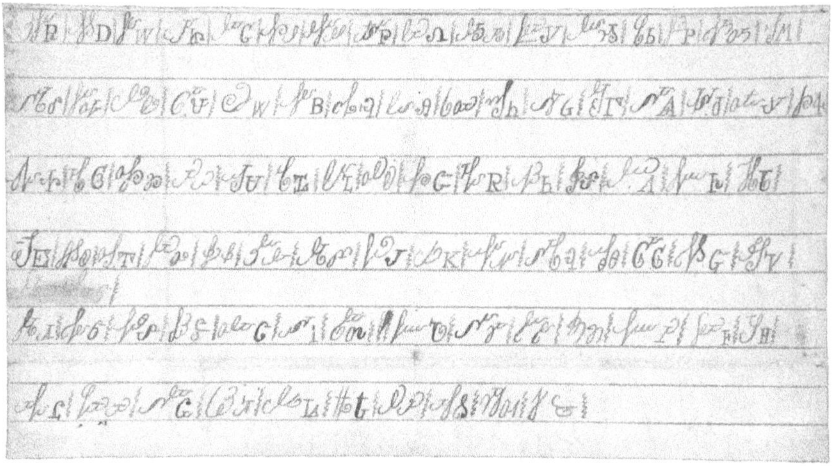

Figure I.1. Sequoyah's original arrangement of the syllabary from the John Howard Payne papers, circa 1839. Courtesy of Gilcrease Museum, Tulsa, Okla.

The Cherokee writing system invented by Sequoyah and formally introduced to the Cherokee tribal council by him and his daughter in 1821 became widely used by the tribe within the span of a few years. Figure I.1 shows the eighty-six characters of the Cherokee syllabary in Sequoyah's original writing. This unsigned manuscript "was attributed to Sequoyah by Jack Kilpatrick and may have been written for John Howard Payne in 1839" (Walker and Sarbaugh 1993: 79). Note that the original eighty-six characters or glyphs are separated by borders, with the longhand version of the glyph on the left and the shorthand on the right. To eyes trained to read and write the alphabet, this system seems complex, difficult to reproduce, and inefficient. Yet an entire people learned to read and write with it within the span of five years after its introduction, and it has been in continued use by Cherokees since that time.

Writing systems in general have been lauded for their instrumentality in preserving culture, building civilizations, and codifying historical events. "A cornerstone of the Western intellectual heritage," Konrad Tuchscherer and P. E. H. Hair (2002: 427) write, "is a fervent belief in the power of the written word to transform man and society. In this tradition, the existence of writing serves as a hallmark for civilization." Considerable scholarly attention has focused on the social and intellectual consequences of the alphabet as a cornerstone of Western intellectual heritage (Goody 1977; Ong 1982; Havelock 1986; Olson 1994). While much of the scholarship presumes alphabetic literacy as its subject, some studies have placed a growing emphasis on equally important writing systems (Christin 2002; Glassner 2003; Houston 2004). When it includes mention of the Cherokee syllabary, this line of scholarship has tended to do so in passing as related to other syllabaries such as the Vai (Tuchscherer and Hair 2002) or in larger taxonomies of all representational systems (Gelb 1963; Hill 1967; DeFrancis 1989).

THE CHEROKEE SYLLABARY: A WRITING SYSTEM IN ITS OWN RIGHT

At times scholars have misrepresented the Cherokee syllabary altogether. Linguist Henry Rogers (2005: 247) suggests that "visually, many of the Cherokee symbols are drawn from upper case Roman letters. Others are alterations of Roman letters or invented symbols." Like Rogers, Johanna Drucker (1997: 38) mentions the syllabary as an example of a problematic borrowing of letters from the alphabet: "The most extreme example of this [borrowing] is perhaps the 19th Century invention of the Cherokee script by Chief Sequoyah, who merely used the alphabet as he might have any other set of written marks and arbitrarily assigned them the values of sounds in the Cherokee language." Basing their claims on the print version of the syllabary, Rogers and Drucker certainly were not aware that Sequoyah (who was never a chief) invented, introduced, and taught the writing system in manuscript form seven years before print arrived on the scene. In fact, the syllabary in script as produced by Sequoyah himself had absolutely no Roman letters or any relation whatsoever to the Roman alphabet (Walker and Sarbaugh 1993).

Scholars have also tended to see the Cherokee syllabary through an alphabetic lens, a perspective that privileges alphabetic writing systems and contributes to "great divide" theories that posit intellectual differences between oral and literate cultures.[1] The alphabetic bias leads some scholars to believe that the alphabet, which works through letter-sound correspondence, is the best, most efficient, and most intellectually rigorous form of writing. As Harris (1986: 39) notes, "By comparison with this alphabetic ideal, syllabic writing is automatically seen as something more primitive and clumsy. . . . To say that a syllabary is a system of characters each of which stands either for a vowel or for some fixed combination of consonants and vowels is already to describe what a syllabary is in alphabetic terms." The very terms used to describe the instrumentality of the Cherokee syllabary, which are based on an alphabetic bias, may have obscured the ways in which the syllabary actually works.

So the mysteries of the Cherokee syllabary remain. Here is a writing system quickly, easily, and widely adopted in manuscript form by a people without print or mass education that continues to be used today by Cherokee speakers. But the nature of this system has not been understood. How was it so easily learned? What cultural values might be lost on modern Cherokee scholars and language learners who use the alphabet as a baseline for comparison? And what factors facilitated persistent use of the syllabary across nearly two centuries of sweeping social upheaval and cultural change? The answers to these questions matter a great deal.

While the Cherokees are one of the largest tribes in the United States, the Cherokee Nation estimates that only a few thousand speak, read, and write the Cherokee language. Of these few thousand speakers, a 2001 census by the Cherokee Nation found no one under the age of forty who spoke the language daily (Morton 2009). This alarming statistic coincides with another important challenge facing Cherokees. The language is one of four pillars of Native peoplehood: language, history, religion, and place. Its loss would spell the ruin of an integral part of Cherokee identity. Despite the decline in the number of Cherokee language speakers, Cherokees are unique in having developed a completely indigenous writing system. The syllabary may have helped the language remain in existence, because it includes distinctive logics. This book traces the historical development of the Cherokee syllabary to demonstrate the ways in which it has served and continues to serve as a tool for the perseverance of the tribe as a people.

PEOPLEHOOD AND TOOLS

In his report on the conditions of American Indians submitted to the War Department in 1825, Thomas McKenney likens Sequoyah to Cadmus, the man credited with the introduction of the Phoenician alphabet to the Greeks: "Like *Cadmus*, he has given to his people the alphabet of their language. It is composed of eighty-six characters, by which, in a few days, the older Indians, who had despaired of deriving an education by means of the schools, and who are not included in the existing school system . . . , may *read and correspond!*" (McKenney 1825: 102; original emphasis).

Samuel Worcester (1828b: 330), a minister who worked closely with Cherokees from 1827 to 1859, also describes the syllabary as an alphabet, comparing it to a writing system that he knew his readers would value and appreciate. Even as he recast this historical achievement in terms of alphabetic literacy to show outsiders the great efforts that Cherokees had undertaken to become a "civilized" tribe, Cherokees were using this writing system daily to unify their tribe, codify their laws and government, and form a national and distinctive cultural identity as a people.

Peoplehood includes the four pillars of Cherokee life that have allowed the tribe to persist through times of displacement, removal, war, disease, and sweeping social change. As Robert Thomas argues, "People who had survived difficult circumstances 'over the long haul' had four features in common: (1) a unique language . . . ; (2) a distinctive religion . . . ; (3) a tie to a particular geographic area . . . ; [and] (4) a sacred history which defined the group as an enduring people, a chosen people, and often with a sacred destiny" (quoted in Fink 1998: 121). These four aspects of peoplehood—language, religion, land, and sacred history—remain intact today. When Cherokees use the syllabary, several aspects of peoplehood emerge and mark a distinctive Cherokee identity apparent to insiders and outsiders alike. As Thomas notes (quoted in Fink 1998: 121), "These four features function as symbols of a people's identity, constant reminders of who they are and that they live under perpetual social and cultural threat. Further these features as activities establish boundaries, define membership, set up standards of judgment about the commitment and behavior of one's fellows and so on." For Cherokees, using this unique writing system served two purposes simultaneously. On the one hand, it offered a means for solidifying Cherokee perspectives through representation of the language in writings such as daily correspondences, traditional stories, religious practices, and legal and governmental documents. On the other hand, it symbolized their intellectual abilities and civilized culture to outsiders, acting as an important indicator of their sophistication and equality to whites.

Any number of Native material tools might be seen as working to enact peoplehood. Among the Cherokees, wampum belts, crystals, foods, medicines, pipes, weapons, and more could be understood as useful tools in both signifying and practicing peoplehood. In their book *Power and Place: Indian Education in America,* Vine Deloria and Daniel Wildcat (2001: 63) offer one way to understand how certain tools can work in support of Native peoplehood and knowledge-making. Though their case in point is educational practice, they're very much interested in establishing an indigenous stance toward knowledge-making:

> Modern science tends to use two kinds of questions to examine the world: (1) "How does it work?" and (2) "What use is it?" These questions are natural for a people who think the world is constructed to serve their purposes. The old people might have used these two questions in their effort to understand the world, but it is certain that they always asked an additional question: "What does it mean?"

An indigenous epistemology provides the necessary posture toward an object to reveal its meaningful properties: its structure, place, and particular elements. Technologies were used in ways that honored the relationship of living things to each other, so a writing system, as a tool, would have had to represent a holistic understanding of the world, our relationships to it, and our relationships to each other. As Deloria and Wildcat (2001: 62) indicate, "Tribal people in using their instruments did not simply extend the scope of their own capabilities, but enhanced their abilities through the addition of powers inherent in the relationships they had with other living things." Inventing these glyphs in the ways he did, Sequoyah brought forth and enhanced the particular force of the spoken word. His art and craftsmanship reveal not only his understanding of the ways in which representational systems work but how he related the whole of his system to this ancient language and the Cherokee perspective. The relational experience implicit in the Cherokee writing system demands more than just linking glyph to sound; it demands an understanding of Cherokee perspectives, values, and ways of structuring and experiencing the world.

To indigenize this writing system and attempt to free it from the alphabetic bias, then, involved a shift in the terms that are typically used to describe reading and writing: letters, literacy, literate, and the alphabet. These words, so taken for granted in discussions of reading and writing, are no longer useful for describing the Cherokee writing system, if indeed they ever were. The etymologies of these words link them to one writing system alone: "letters" refers only to alphabets; "literacy" denotes working fluently with letter-sound correspondences; to be "literate" is to be fluent with letters or to be lettered, from the Latin *literatus*; and "alphabet" (from the first two Greek letters, *alpha* and *beta*) means the whole set of letters. In this book I use the words "letter," "literacy," and "alphabet" only in reference to the Roman alphabet, never when describing the Cherokee writing system. Rather than using this constellation of terms that link reading and writing to the letter, this book uses a constellation of terms showing the relationship of reading and writing in Cherokee to image, design, and language.

The terms "glyph" and "character" describe each individual mark in the Cherokee syllabary, reflecting the ways in which they were created, designed, and redesigned for print and how they work instrumentally. A glyph is a meaningful mark on paper that is also a building block of all fonts. Characters are marked or engraved signs that represent sound and semantic meaning as they do in Chinese. I use "reading" and "writing" to represent meaning-making activities, including the Cherokee writing system. The Cherokee writing system as a whole is a "syllabary" and possibly a "morphographic system"; while each glyph in the writing system represents sound units, it also potentially represents additional important linguistic information, depending on the order of the syllables. Instead of replacing the word "literate" with "syllabarate," I use the phrase "fluent in Sequoyan" to describe a person who uses the Cherokee writing system well. This book changes the terms of the discussion, rather than understanding the Cherokee writing system through an alphabet-centric perspective (Harris 2009), an alphabetic lens (Baca 2008), or a value system that maintains a hierarchy of signs (Cushman 2010). The goal is to understand the Cherokee writing system in its own right, situate it within the matrix of peoplehood, and reveal its connection to the tribe's perseverance.

PRESERVATION, PERSEVERANCE, AND INVENTING TRADITIONS

In 1821 the Cherokee tribal council agreed that Sequoyan script was of use to the nation. As Theda Perdue (1994: 120) notes, "The single aspect of Cherokee culture change from which we can document extensive grass-roots support is adoption of the syllabary. The masses, in fact, embraced the Cherokee syllabary far more readily than did the official leadership of the nation. What does this mean?" Perdue argues that Cherokees' rapid mastery of the syllabary is evidence of an "affirmation of themselves as a people" (122). What does it mean that the syllabary came to be so quickly and widely adapted to everyday life among Cherokee speakers? Precisely how has the Cherokee syllabary affirmed Cherokees' sense of peoplehood from its inception to its present use? And in what ways might it have helped Cherokees to persevere?

As one tool important to a tribe, this writing system has allowed Cherokees to protect, enact, and codify Cherokee knowledge and perspectives. It has enabled the Cherokees to weave foreign ideas about governments and religions into the fabric of everyday language and life: the massive social change in the tribe was made in—if too rarely on—Cherokee terms. As Tom Holm, Diane Pearson, and Ben Chavis (2003: 18) note, "The occurrence of syncretic change is especially interesting. American Indian peoples have taken foreign ideas, institutions, material goods and filtered them through the matrix of peoplehood, and given them meaning within their own cultures and societies." From its design to its instrumentality to its remarkable adaptability to new technologies, the syllabary as a tool has contributed in no small measure to the tribe's perseverance. People have frequently suggested how and in what ways it has done so but rarely analyzed the topic, in part because those who study culture sometimes seek to understand it as a static, well-bounded object to preserve.

The problems with studying the nexus of cultural preservation, new tools, and identity formation are made clear by Marxist historian Eric Hobsbawm (Hobsbawm and Ranger 1983), anthropologist James Clifford (2001), and cultural studies theorist Ileana Rodríguez (2001). Some anthropologists would have tribes *preserve* their cultures and meaningful objects, enclosing them in vacuum-packed, climate-controlled containers, sealed off from everyday practice and protected from contamination by outsiders. Academics who subscribe to the idea of culture preservation tend to believe that continuity with the past without contamination from outside influence is the best way to ensure the sanctity of tradition.

Hobsbawm (Hobsbawm and Ranger 1983: 2) argues that many traditional Native cultures are created, or invented, in factitious ways. In times of rapid change a tribe will invent tradition in an "attempt to structure at least some parts of social life . . . as unchanging and invariant"; however, "the peculiarity of 'invented' traditions is that the continuity with [the past that they establish] is largely factitious." This places cultures, especially American Indian cultures, in quite a bind. In trying to persevere in cultural practices, tribes select artifacts, knowledge bases, stories, and practices. When these selections represent a continuity of practice over time, Hobsbawm argues, then tradition remains intact. "Where the old ways are alive, traditions need be neither revived nor invented" (8). Hobsbawm's idea calibrates tradition to a zero-sum baseline: a culture either has tradition because it continues throughout history or no longer has it and has to invent it from recollections, ancient artifacts, or anthropological accounts.

When the selection of artifacts, knowledge bases, stories, and practices represents a revival of old ways that have disappeared from practice, then we see the emergence of "invented traditions," which belong to three types: "a) those establishing or symbolizing social cohesion or the membership of groups, real or artificial communities, b) those establishing or legitimizing institutions, status or relations of authority, and c) those whose main purpose was socialization, the inculcation of beliefs, value systems, and conventions of behavior" (Hobsbawm and Ranger 1983: 9). These traditions are invented to serve as markers of group identity, to establish legitimate institutions, and to create a group of like-minded followers of the tradition. The upshot of such invention of tradition is the formation of a fictionalized tribal identity that is ultimately inauthentic.[2]

One shortcoming of Hobsbawm's understanding of tradition as preserved and static rests in its inability to account for the emergence of new technologies, their influence on traditional practices, and the ways in which culture itself has permeable boundaries that allow these influences (Rosaldo 1989). In short, his theory would place almost all attempts to persevere in cultural ways by American Indians in the realm of invented tradition and therefore consider them "factitious." Extending the logic of his categories, a tribe can only preserve an authentic tradition in the medium in which it was first created. Thus Sequoyah would be understood as inventing an inauthentic tradition with his creation of the syllabary because he developed a written script for a language that was previously only spoken. No matter how the syllabary works, Hobsbawm's thinking goes, it is an invented tool and thus neither traditional nor authentic. Using this logic, authentic Cherokee knowledge and cultural practices would have remained unwritten, because writing is a technology introduced by Westerners. The problem here is that cultural change cannot be described using a notion of cultural preservation. It's too rigid a concept to account for ways in which tribal cultures adapt to new sign technologies and materials for meaning-making.

In response to Hobsbawm's theory, anthropologist James Clifford finds that tradition is always seen against its antithesis: the popular, the novel, the routine, or the low. Rather than using this notion of tradition, Clifford (2001: (479), following Stuart Hall, prefers to see the idea of tradition as more like articulation:

> In articulation theory, the whole question of authenticity is secondary, and the process of social and cultural persistence is political all the way back. It is assumed that cultural forms will always be made, unmade, and remade. Communities can and must reconfigure themselves, drawing selectively on remembered pasts. The relevant question is whether, and how, they convince and coerce insiders and outsiders, often in power charged, unequal situations, to accept the autonomy of a "we."

Cultural perseverance, then, would be viewed as a place where Native cultures, for example, enact part of their sovereignty—a process that allows them to name who they are, what practices count, what structures govern, and what technologies allow for adaptation. Authenticity is not the question for Clifford, because cultural articulation focuses on the political acts of social and cultural persistence. Thus Clifford might see the Cherokee Nation's attempts to use the Internet to teach online language classes as a reconfiguration in which new technologies and popular cultural artifacts are developed in an ongoing process of cultural formation. For Clifford, the real focus of anthropologists should be on how popular technologies and knowledge products help cultures do their work of tradition-making in order to convince others to accept the autonomy of the group.

The point here is that the use and impact of meaning-making technologies must be incorporated into understandings of knowledge, cultural tradition, and identity. "In whichever theoretical instance we choose," cultural studies theorist Ileana Rodríguez (2001: 57–58) finds, "it is clear that tradition cannot be discussed separately from the subject that bears it; from the technologies that inform the logic of its production; from the mediations or spaces where hegemony refunctionalizes everything to actualize or modernize it." Rodríguez would have us understand how the medium indicates cultural persistence in itself and in its continued use. As an articulated tradition, the Cherokee syllabary shows the cultural perseverance of the tribe because the culture has been permeable, adaptive, and stabilized by its own reconfigurations.

Finally, cultural preservation does not work well to describe the ongoing struggle to remain because it is an absurdity for many Cherokees. "You can't pickle our ways!" one quipped. Richard Allen, policy analyst for the Cherokee Nation, says: "Cultural preservation? Sounds like you're putting it on a shelf in a jar with formaldehyde." Preserving culture the way some anthropologists would like to makes many Cherokees uneasy because it does nothing to characterize the growth of the community through generational learning and exchange. Worse yet, it objectifies cultural artifacts, taking them out of their contexts, relationships, and reasons for use and rendering them meaningless.

Rather than preserving culture, Cherokees sometimes speak of persevering. Former principal chief of the Cherokee Nation Wilma Mankiller (2002: 55) asserts that generations before us have done "what we could in our time and it is now up to them [this generation] to make sure our life ways are continued. If we have persevered, and if we are tenacious enough to have survived everything that has happened to us to date, surely 100 years or even 500 years from now, the future generations will persevere and will have also have [sic] that same sort of tenacity, strong spirit, and commitment to retaining a strong sense of who they are as tribal people." Perseverance has been a hallmark of Cherokee spirit and an indicator of the ways in which the tribe maintains its cultural identity through a notion of peoplehood. Cultural perseverance best characterizes the integrity of the language and writing system while accounting for continued traditional practice and innovation with new tools across generations.

WHY THIS BOOK AND WHY NOW?

Sequoyah's invention of the Cherokee syllabary was remarkable for many reasons, including the ones that anthropologist James Mooney (1892: 63–64) outlines: "The Cherokee syllabic alphabet . . . made the Cherokee at once a literary people, and has probably contributed more than any other thing to elevate them." Writing scholars and historians alike have applauded the invention of the syllabary as an impressive achievement for Cherokees, but it has not typically been viewed from the Cherokees' perspective. Though the syllabary is not an alphabet, scholars like Mooney have tended to view it through the lens of alphabetic literacy. When seen from this perspective, it appears to have "several defects, which seriously impair its usefulness" (63), especially to those whose first language is English. Unfortunately, many have misunderstood the importance and nature of this system because they have used alphabetic literacy as a baseline for comparison.

Even though "the extraordinary persistence of peoplehood is a study in and of itself," as Holm et al. (2003: 18) note, too few have taken up this call, especially in relation to American Indian ways of writing. Until quite recently ethnohistorians and literacy scholars alike have neglected the study of American Indian graphic representations, in part because "true writing" was long held to include only alphabetic-based inscriptions of sound. As Frank Salomon and Sabine Hyland (2010: 2) note, "An illogical but habitual corollary was that systems using other principles, or conveying information in ways other than verbal equivalence, were considered less worthy of study. These languished, defined only by what they were not: namely, not a part of the grand genealogy of 'letters' as enshrined in the humanities."

As an initial step toward correcting this alphabet-centrism, the scholarly journal *Ethnohistory* recently published an entire special issue dedicated to both "understanding the properties of inscriptions outside the canonical terrain of writing" and developing a richer "media historiography that places the originality of New World 'graphism' into the complexity of mixed-media situations evolving round the edges of the transatlantic empires" (Salomon and Hyland 2010: 6). Two recent historiographies have helped chart the direction of initial research on American Indian reading and writing. Mindy Morgan's *The Bearer of This Letter: Language Ideologies, Literacy Practices, and the Fort Belknap Indian Community* (2009) shows how a tribe comes to resist the imposition of alphabetic literacy and the written representation of words altogether. In like fashion, Margaret Bender's *Signs of Cherokee Culture: Sequoyah's Syllabary in Eastern Cherokee Life* (2002) presents the results of an ethnographic study of Cherokee language and literacy in the Qualla Boundary in North Carolina. These two books take important steps toward a fuller understanding of the current issues and ideologies surrounding American Indians' present-day use of imposed or indigenous writing systems. Hence the present book embarks on its journey with the good company of scholars from across disciplines and nations onboard.

This study takes the Cherokee syllabary into its sight, calculating the angle by using the star of identity and the horizon of culture. While biographies of Sequoyah have chronicled his life and the process of inventing the syllabary (Foreman 1938; Kilpatrick and Kilpatrick 1965; Walker and Sarbaugh 1993; Hoig 1995) and ethnographies have studied its everyday use (Mooney 1900; Olbrechts 1931; Witthoft 1948), they have not examined how the syllabary works as a writing system. *The Cherokee Syllabary* broadens the historical lens as it follows the development of the syllabary and its circulation among Cherokees from 1821 to the present.

This book also seeks to reach students of the Cherokee language, an audience that includes general readers among the Cherokee people as well as linguists. Only a small fraction of the 296,087 Cherokee citizens in the three federally recognized bands and over 700,000 self-identified Cherokees know the language (U.S. Census 2003). The 1990 United States census (1994: 874) shows 6,259 speakers of Cherokee in Oklahoma, with a total of 9,285 for the entire country. The 2000 census (U.S. Census 2003: 5) indicates a slightly larger number: 6,528 Cherokee speakers in Oklahoma and a total of 12,009 speakers around the country. These numbers seem high, however, especially in light of the findings of a 2001 Cherokee Nation survey of more than three hundred Cherokees in small towns and cities in Oklahoma. Of those surveyed, only fifty used the Cherokee language—and no one under the age of forty spoke the language on a daily basis (Morton 2009). Without younger generations learning Cherokee and more adults practicing it openly, the future of the language is at risk. Overall, these demographics suggest that, while the Cherokee language is fairly healthy when compared to other Native languages, its future as a living language is uncertain, perhaps even threatened.

Though linguistic research has done much to make apparent the structure, meaning, and sound of the Cherokee language, the syllabary has not been understood by linguists to be central to continued language learning. Linguists focus on the spoken language (Holmes and Smith 1976; Pulte 1985; Scancarelli 1992, 1994; Montgomery-Anderson 2007) and have tended to underestimate the syllabary because of its imperfections in representing the sounds of the language. Thus they have missed the ways in which the syllabary can sometimes represent sound, structure, and meaning. For students of the Cherokee language, this book will be an instructional resource that reveals linguistic information that the Cherokee syllabary originally codified but that is too often lost for English speakers who approach the syllabary using an alphabetic lens. From its design to its instrumentality to its remarkable adaptability to new technological environments, the syllabary has been a tool used for the tribe's continued existence.

THE DEVELOPMENT OF SEQUOYAN

The creation of the Cherokee writing system, its rapid adoption, and its continued use all illustrate ways in which it mediates cultural change and encodes linguistic identity. The story of its evolution tracks alongside events in American history from the early 1800s to the present day, a history that moves from a small cabin outside of Fort Loudoun, Tennessee, through westward emigrations and removals. The evolution of Sequoyan has occurred well beyond and mostly outside of Sequoyah's lifetime as a gift that continues to help Cherokees codify our religious beliefs, knowledge of place, language, and sacred histories.

While alphabetic literacy, print, and now digital literacies are widely recognized as primary tools to educate citizens and build nations, this book demonstrates how reading and writing in a script other than the Roman alphabet became a vehicle for and symbol of tribal sovereignty. The Cherokee writing system indicated to outsiders that the tribe was a civilized nation within the United States, even as it ensured the steadfast continuance of traditional knowledge and language. When it moved to print, Cherokees developed a literary legacy through the production of millions of pages of religious tracts, newspapers, educational materials, laws and constitutions, almanacs, and books. As it did so, manuscript writing also maintained a

strong foothold in the day-to-day life of Cherokees, who used longhand to organize meetings, write letters, create books of plants and
incantations, and keep business records.

The breadth and depth of Sequoyan in the nineteenth century
indicates the growth and resurgence of the Cherokee Nation after
the Trail of Tears and Civil War, commenting on and facilitating the
continued perseverance of the tribe. While the public production of
Sequoyan in print came to a standstill after allotment and tribal
government dissolution in the early 1900s, the continued use of Sequoyan in manuscript form took place out of public view, demonstrating Cherokees' ever-present, quiet tenacity, persevering in traditional ways.

When Sequoyan again reappeared in public in the late 1960s, it
facilitated everyday acts of self-determination and grew into a central facet of the Cherokee Nation's current educational mission under
the leadership of Chief Chad Smith and instructional guidance of
his wife, Bobbie Gail Smith, a fluent Cherokee speaker, reader, and
writer. Cherokee tribal sovereignty has been facilitated by the invention and development of the syllabary, the public and private
uses of Sequoyan, and the policies and initiatives of the Cherokee
Nation as a political body separate from and intricately connected to
the tribal body.

The story of the development of the Cherokee writing system from
script to print to digital media parallels and comments upon the
social and cultural challenges that Cherokees have faced in the last
century and a half. Since its inception, the Cherokee writing system
has been a coalescing force for the tribe in both its instrumentality
and symbolic weight. The internal logic and structure of the syllabary itself inscribed Cherokee lifeways so well that it afforded the
tribe a viable alternative to the imposition of alphabetically based
writing systems. Sequoyan provided the means for creating a rich
and varied corpus of intellectual, religious, and governmental documents that unified the tribe through cultural change as it presented
a socially acceptable face. Today that legacy has been foundational
in efforts to address what is arguably the most important challenge
faced by the nation and tribe: the battle against language erosion.
Sequoyan enters the battle in every theater, produced in multiple
media, for every generation, in K–12 schools and Northeastern State

University, in Cherokees' nationwide efforts to educate adults, and via the Internet. The story of the Cherokee writing system includes by turns the mystery of how it works, the tale of Cherokees' resilience, and an account of a tenacious and ongoing struggle to mediate cultural change.

To tell this story, I proceeded from an analytical framework that helped to recover instrumental, meaningful, and historical aspects of the Cherokee syllabary. Galen Brokaw (2010: 124) offers a dialogic model of media in which tools for meaning-making can be described by both their technical attributes and the values associated with them: "any given form of media develops in dialogic relationship to the ideological institutions with which it is associated. The dialogic model of media . . . [does not] attribute socio-political and economic transformations solely to a secondary medium or to ideological institutions, but rather to both of them in their interrelationship as it evolves over time." Within a dialogic model of media, any tool used for meaning-making can be understood by characterizing its evolutionary process over time to show its transformations. These transformations will emerge from their mutually sustaining relationship with the values and practices attached to them. In other words, the historical process by which a writing system develops also "influences the nature of the medium and its associated institutions" (125). Cherokee tribal institutions of peoplehood and everyday acts of perseverance emerge in the mutually sustaining relationship with Sequoyan and the various material forms it has taken.

More specifically, writing systems scholar Florian Coulmas (2003: 33) describes three principles to guide such a linguistic study of writing systems: "These are the principle of autonomy of the graphic system, the principle of interpretation, and the principle of historicity." The principle of autonomy provides insight into the structures of writing systems by analyzing them in terms of "functional units and relationships" (34). Such a perspective yields information on the instrumental workings of the writing system, the "basic operational units of the system," and the "well-formed sequences of these units" (34). The principle of interpretation provides that writing systems must also be understood in terms of the linguistic information that they codify. "Writing systems are structured in such a way that they map onto other levels of linguistic structure, those of phonetic, phonemic, morphophonemic and lexical representation in particular" (34). Writing systems facilitate interpretation and meaning-making by representing specific aspects of languages. Finally, the principle of historicity attempts to account for language change: "How are writing systems adjusted to the languages they represent, and how does writing a language affect its development?" (35). The various material forms that writing systems have taken suggest the ways in which systems adjust not only to the languages they represent but also to the historical exigencies that influence the various material forms that they can take.

Ethnohistorical methods have been used to understand these instrumental, interpretive, and historical dimensions of Sequoyan because they proved well suited to blending anthropological and historical approaches to evidence.[3] At their most basic, ethnohistorical methods bridge the study of history with anthropological research on current values, practices, and beliefs (Wood 1990: 81). While this methodology has primarily been used in studies of American Indian tribes (Axtell 1979; DeMallie 1993), William Simmons (1988: 10) broadens this by defining ethnohistory as:

> a form of cultural biography that draws upon as many kinds of testimony as possible—material culture, archaeology, visual sources, historical documents, native texts, folklore, even earlier ethnographies—over as long a time period as the sources allow. One can't do this without taking account both of local-level social history and the larger-scale social and cultural environments that affected that history. This kind of holistic, diachronic approach is most rewarding when it can be joined to the memories and voices of living people.

Over the past five years I've used ethnohistorical methods as I collected several forms of data, including artifacts such as reproductions and observational notes of archival pieces, public documents printed in Sequoyan, and several material artifacts that included the writing system as well as interviews with Cherokees in northeastern Oklahoma, observations on current uses of the writing system, and participant-observation in online Cherokee language classes. Simmons is correct to say that this approach is most rewarding when it can be joined to the voices and living memories of Cherokees today.

Those voices not only provide helpful corrections of my translations but also help explain the historical significance of various artifacts.

Though a handful of Cherokee syllabary artifacts and translations appear in this book, the bulk of the writing is of necessity in English. The irony of writing a book on the Cherokee syllabary using almost exclusively the English alphabet has not escaped me. Indeed, this work has drawn me to many untranslated documents, to develop and test language materials based mostly on the syllabary and to outline another book based on the findings that appear in chapters 1 through 3. Much more can and should be said on this topic, especially in Cherokee, and my hope remains that scholars and Cherokee language users and teachers will take up this topic in future work.

Many of the questions raised in the preface about the nature, workings, and importance of the syllabary are explored in this book, but many questions remain: How do Cherokee language learners and speakers teach and get taught in communities? What reading and writing practices in Sequoyan are used in homes and small communities, by whom, and for what purposes? To date, my access has been predominately to programs sponsored by the Cherokee Nation and public uses of Sequoyan. Though I have had some experiences with private uses of the syllabary and the Cherokee language in a Cherokee Baptist church and in homes, I do not yet have enough evidence to provide answers. And these questions matter a great deal if we hope to create a fuller understanding of the blend of implicit and explicit instruction used to ensure fluency in the Cherokee language and writing system.

This book situates the Cherokee syllabary in the center of the peoplehood matrix to afford a better understanding of how this writing system has allowed Cherokees to protect, practice, and codify everyday life, traditional knowledge, and cultural practices. Chapter 1 demonstrates that Sequoyah was quite aware of the tradition he was inventing and had political and cultural reasons for creating this writing system. The chapter reexamines historical accounts of his invention of the syllabary to reveal his trial-and-error process over the decade it took to create the system. In the end he designed the writing system to be easily learned by Cherokee speakers. Chapters 2 and 3 are dedicated to illustrating the linguistic and design features that made it so. Chapter 2 explores how this writing system works linguistically, and chapter 3 considers how its original design and arrangement might have contributed to the ease with which Cherokees learned the 86-character system. These chapters present findings that begin to recuperate some of the design and linguistic logics informing this writing system.

Chapters 4 through 6 examine the development of the Cherokee syllabary from script to print. Scholars have been tempted to think that the print version of the Cherokee writing system departed significantly from the handwritten one and have credited Samuel Worcester with the design of the printed syllabary. Chapter 4 presents visual analysis of the glyphs coupled with evidence from primary sources to correct these misunderstandings: Sequoyah and Cherokees who used the system in shorthand were largely responsible for the development of the print version of the syllabary. Chapter 5 explores the role that Elias Boudinot played as the first editor of the first American Indian newspaper, the *Cherokee Phoenix*. He helped to move the syllabary from script to print, and this new technology served as an important identity marker for the Cherokee Nation as distinct from the tribe. The story of the *Cherokee Phoenix* brings to light the very real difficulties faced in using a national publication as a vehicle for statecraft.

Chapter 6 discusses the Cherokee Nation in the period from 1840 to 1920, marked by the destructive removal, Civil War, and allotment as well as the eras of cultural reconstruction and resurgence that followed. This chapter presents the broad sweep of Cherokee print and script as manifested in primers, four newspapers, religious materials, and social documents, including letters, announcements, tribal histories, and descriptions of medicines. During a time of immense social change, dislocation, and cultural upheaval, the Cherokee syllabary unified the tribe through communication in a shared language, codified laws and the workings of religious institutions, and became a symbolic representation of Cherokees to outsiders.

Chapters 7 and 8 locate the Cherokee writing system in modern times to illustrate how Cherokees continue to invent linguistic resources through bilingual programs developed in the 1970s and online language classes and games today. Chapter 7 opens with a brief history of the Cherokee Nation's resurgence in the 1970s with the Indian Self-Determination Act. Excerpts from rare bilingual-education materials and the *Cherokee Nation Newsletter* and interviews with key players who led efforts to revitalize language use are featured in this chapter.

Chapter 8 revisits the evidence and findings of previous chapters in light of the Cherokee Nation's most recent efforts to address language erosion. The Cherokee syllabary figures centrally in this mission because it is known to carry linguistic information, to be highly adaptable, and to be useful in unifying Cherokees across dialectical and geographic distances. The legacy of the Cherokee syllabary presented in this book reveals the instrumental logics and cultural value of this writing system, with the hope that such findings can both correct the scholarly record and facilitate the awareness of Cherokee language learners.

The origin of the Cherokee writing system was unique, unlike other writing systems that had thousands of years and hundreds of scribes refining the characters, glyphs, and letters (Christin 2002). As the brainchild of one man, Sequoyah, the Cherokee writing system developed in calculated response to an ever-increasing presence of white people and their letters. The arduous and systematic process by which Sequoyah systematically developed it reveals the social pressures that Cherokees faced at that time, a topic discussed in the next chapter.

CHAPTER 1

Sequoyah and the Politics of Language

A handwritten note in English, undated and unsigned, in the John Howard Payne papers seems to have accompanied the copy of the syllabary chart that Sequoyah created for John Howard Payne (fig. I.1): "Now I will write for you the alphabet, friend John. It is the best I can do in the way of writing. But it is good to talk with when anything good has been found out. I think it is equal to the method of reading that you know. (Here comes the alphabet.)"[1] A second note in English is signed by Sequoyah:

> We have met and see one another friends and brothers. I am extremely glad to see you friends and brothers, and I am glad for what you have seen. Make every effort to complete it, for all can see what is going on, it is clear to every one. There is no doubt of its success–do not forget it–that which you will hear of me my brothers and friends. What is coming is wonderful when I think of it.
>
> It has only been fourteen years since we who are called Cherokees have learned to read. I am thankful that the people have slowly understood how much labor it has cost me.

Payne had visited the Cherokees to research a book he was writing in 1835 (Bass 1932). The handwriting of this first document seems similar to that found on the second document, signed by Sequoyah. The reference to "fourteen years" in that note places it roughly

Parts of this chapter originally appeared in *Wicazo Sa Review* 26(1) (Spring 2011).

between 1832 and 1835. Sequoyah seems to have been grateful that others were beginning to recognize his efforts in developing the syllabary and the "labor it has cost me." This second document was originally included with the John Ross papers before being moved to the Payne papers and then finally to the Sequoyah file in the Gilcrease Museum collection. Its archival route suggests that this was included as part of Ross's papers originally procured by the museum.[2]

In 1832 Ross wrote a letter to Sequoyah to be delivered to him in the Arkansas Territory by way of their mutual friend Charles Vann. Ross had given up hope that Sequoyah would come to New Echota to claim the medal that the Legislative Council of the Cherokee Nation had awarded him in 1824 for having developed the syllabary. Ross's letter describes the extent to which the creation of the syllabary had helped the tribe develop a literary canon and had been easily learned by young and old and states that Sequoyah served as a model for all nations that might begin to create their own writing systems (January 12, 1832, in Moulton 1985: 1:235). Sequoyah is believed to have completed the syllabary by 1818 or 1819 (Foreman 1938; Walker 1969; Hoig 1995). The document signed by Sequoyah indicates that it was written roughly "fourteen years since . . . Cherokees have learned to read," which would correspond to 1832, when Ross wrote this letter to Sequoyah. Sequoyah's gratitude and his observation that "the people have slowly understood how much labor it has cost" may have been in response to Ross's listing of all the ways in which the syllabary had helped Cherokees. Finally, Sequoyah's letter was originally filed as part of the John Ross papers held by the Thomas Gilcrease Museum, which indicates that it was in Ross's possession, even if not addressed directly to him.

Remarkably, both of these documents in regard to the syllabary were written in English. Most historians and biographers agree that Sequoyah knew little to no English. Mooney (1900: 109) claims that he never learned the language: "Having nearly reached middle age before the first mission was established in the Nation, he never attended school and in all his life never learned to speak, read or write the English language" (see also Bass 1932; Foreman 1938; Walker 1969; Hoig 1995). Those who had interviewed Sequoyah always did so with an interpreter present and found, as John Stuart (1837: 21) did, that "he did not speak one word of the English language." Cherokees who represented the tribe to outsiders in English describe Sequoyah as knowing at least some words in English. Chief Charles Hicks (1825: 554–55), a contemporary of Sequoyah, describes him: a "native Cherokee without any education whatever and scarcely understands the English language." And Wahnenauhi (1966: 198), a granddaughter of George Lowrey, who was Sequoyah's cousin and close companion, says that "Sequoyah did not speak the English language, and understood only a few words, of which he could make but little use." According to these accounts of Sequoyah's abilities in English, he surely would not have been able to pen the two missives discussed above. Yet one seems to accompany the demonstration of the syllabary for John Howard Payne in 1839, and the other, signed by Sequoyah, may have been written in reply to John Ross in 1832.

If these are indeed letters written by Sequoyah as this evidence suggests, then he knew English. Indeed, he may have been literate in English and may have had good control of letter-sound correspondence. Or he may have had a scribe in the family who wrote in English for him, such as his nephew who attended missionary school or his cousin George Lowrey, who was bilingual and interpreted for him during the John Howard Payne interview (Bass 1932; Walker 1969). Regardless of the form it took, Sequoyah had deeper exposure to English literacy than previously believed. This stands to reason: by all accounts of his development of the script, he had at least seen and held documents that were written in English, including letters exchanged between whites, his nephew's spelling book, his sister-in-law's Bible, and scraps of paper along the road.

Admitting the possibility that Sequoyah could have had some English literacy or at least some understanding of letter-sound correspondence, his development of the Cherokee syllabary and his steadfast refusal to speak English might be understood as even more potent acts of perseverance than previously thought. These letters suggest that Sequoyah had a more complex relationship to the English language and Roman alphabet than commonly believed. What has been described as mere ignorance of English might instead have been Sequoyah's choice to avoid the ever-increasing influence of English-speaking settlers and their Roman alphabet in Cherokee daily life. At the very least, these two letters raise questions: What story of language perseverance and peoplehood does Sequoyah's life tell? What relationship to English literacy might have Sequoyah wanted when he created the syllabary—and why? The tale of his respectful studies of the Cherokee language and resistance to outside influences in the ten years it took to invent this writing system should be examined.

SEQUOYAH'S EARLY LIFE

Sequoyah grew up near the British Fort Loudoun not far from the Little Tennessee River. His father was an English-speaking white man who had apparently been captured by the Cherokee and remained with them for six years, and his mother was a Cherokee woman whose uncle had been a chief in Echota. Once freed, his father moved to Virginia and then Kentucky, where Sequoyah visited him in later years and was warmly received as family (Mooney 1900: 108–109).[3] Sequoyah's mother raised him in the Overhill town near Tuskegee, just outside of Fort Loudoun, where the young man traded furs and dairy products as he got older (Hoig 1995: 5). Showing a talent for drawing, metalwork, and designing with his hands at an early age, Sequoyah created a refrigerator for the milk of his mother's cows by building a small house over a spring (Phillips 1870: 542). He developed considerable skill with tools on his mother's farm through silver working and blacksmithing. Sequoyah repurposed British and French coins into silver ornaments that Cherokees wore well—gorgets, nose rings, armbands, earrings, and chains—and designed and made his own bellows for his work as a blacksmith (Phillips 1870: 543; Hoig 1995: 17–20). "From a very early age, he has possessed a natural talent for drawing, and very far surpasses any man in his nation in the art," Captain John Stuart (1837: 21) wrote in his contemporary description of Sequoyah. "He can also draw rough portraits, a circumstance which, connected with his fondness for drawing, contributed very much toward inducing him to attempt the formation of a type for his language" (quoted in Foreman 1938: 37). These design skills that Sequoyah developed in his early life became foundational to his imaging of the syllabary.

Sequoyah's early life also brought him into contact with whites and the English language. Trading furs and milk with people at the fort and his father's brief presence in his early life seem to have had little impact on Sequoyah's facility with or interest in the ways of whites. Wahnenauhi tells a story of Sequoyah's first extended meeting with whites and English literacy. At the age of seventeen, Sequoyah, George Lowrey, and a third cousin, John Leach, were inseparable friends who went out on a hunting trip (Wahnenauhi 1966: 196–97):

> With several others of the Tribe, they met with a Company of white hunters; this accidental meeting proved to be quite an important, as well as pleasing incident to the Indians, as it was the means of changing the life-purpose of at least two of them. Lowrey was the only one of his party who spoke the English Language and this he did very imperfectly. . . . The whites and Indians camped near each other, ate and smoked together, and spent several hours in pleasant intercourse. . . . [One of the hunters] had with him a small book which he showed and explained to them; Lowrey acting as Interpreter for both parties—the Indians were filled with astonishment at the new and interesting things they had learned; and soon after separating with the white hunters they decided to return home. For the first time in their lives, Lowrey and Sequoyah felt an intense and longing desire for improvement.

As a teenager, Sequoyah apparently had no skills in speaking English, let alone reading or writing it. This first encounter with a book and a group of white hunters seems to have made a lasting impression, at least insofar as George Lowrey passed it on to his granddaughter, who lived with him. She is known to have seen Sequoyah on several occasions (Wahnenauhi 1966: 182). In this exchange, Sequoyah may have learned the mechanics of one product of English literacy: how books work and what they contain.

John Howard Payne's 1835 interview with Sequoyah, which was transcribed in Cherokee and then translated into English by George Lowrey, reveals another interesting example of Sequoyah's contact with English literacy. Sequoyah's silver work was well regarded and sought out by prominent Cherokees. He wanted to begin signing his work, particularly the larger pieces that he was designing. "One day he called on Mr. Charles R. Hicks, to write his name for him on paper in English; and upon his silver ornaments he would engrave the copy; especially upon the gorgets & arm bands that they might be known as his work. With a piece of pointed brimstone he imitated the writing of Mr. Hicks on the silver and then cut it in with a sharp instrument" (Payne quoted in Bass 1932: 11–12). As Sequoyah "imitated" each letter of his name, it's possible that he began to recognize letter-sound correspondence at least in principle, if not precisely which letters stood for which sounds of his own name. His imitation could have worked on the visual level as well, as he copied the shapes and designs of the letters of his name. In these ways he might have become acquainted with the workings of the alphabet and developed a rudimentary understanding of English literacy.

This makes some sense given the historical context. Sequoyah's interactions with whites were frequent from a very young age, if not always pleasant. Because they had joined forces with the French to fight British enemies during the Revolutionary War, the Cherokees in the Overhill towns, where Sequoyah was raised, faced the ill feelings of early settlers (Mooney 1900: 109–12). Sequoyah grew up in a time of increasing land cessions to whites, deeper encroachment of settlers and missionaries into Cherokee territory, and a rapidly shifting economy (McLoughlin 1974, 1984). In 1816 Sequoyah was one of several Cherokees who signed a treaty with a group of whites led by Major Andrew Jackson ceding lands in Tennessee, for which the Cherokees were to be reimbursed; this was perhaps Sequoyah's first encounter with the future president, who went on to orchestrate the Cherokee removal. Having learned to sign his name in English from Chief Hicks, Sequoyah signed his name to this treaty as George Guess, his English name. During these years Sequoyah had access to English literacy and had seen its importance firsthand; he understood the need to be able to sign his name in English. He was witnessing an era of increasing social change, land loss, and negotiation with whites, all mediated to varying degrees by the English language and Roman alphabet. And he was inventing a writing system that, as he later observed, was "equal to the method of reading" of whites.

Between 1810 and 1820 Sequoyah lived in Wills Valley, between the Cherokees who had chosen to emigrate farther west to what is now Arkansas and the Cherokees who remained in Tennessee and Georgia (Mooney 1900; Bass 1932). During this period he had set himself to earnest pursuit of the development of the Cherokee writing system. He seems to have understood the potential use of

English literacy, though he revealed little if any knowledge of the English language, and also understood something of the instrumental workings and shapes of letters. Sequoyah had achieved some prominence in the tribe as a principal person who was allowed to treat on behalf of the rest of the people. As he immersed himself in the process of inventing this writing system, he did so in isolation from whites and fellow Cherokees.

THE SYSTEMATIC PROCESS OF CREATING THE SYLLABARY

While historians debate the dates, Sequoyah's work took place roughly between 1809 and 1821 (Mooney 1900: 109). It seems that the whole creation of syllabary had unfolded over at least a decade before Sequoyah and his daughter demonstrated it to leaders of the Cherokee Nation in 1821, when the tribal council acknowledged its usefulness as a Cherokee script. Sequoyah had been studying and practicing for years before deciding upon the best representational system. According to Wahnenauhi (1966: 198), "He was convinced that if a written language was beneficial to one people, it would be equally so to another so he determined to make this for his people, the Cherokees."

Writing systems can sometimes take hundreds of years and thousands of people to create (Fischer 2001; Christin 2002; Rogers 2005). All writing systems use a mark, design, letter, or character (signifier) that is meant to represent the object, event, word, sound, or image (signified). The complexity of creating a writing system lies in deciding upon the best combinations of signifiers and signifieds out of thousands of possible permutations. The creation of the Cherokee syllabary took detailed study and trial and error to determine the best possible relations between signifiers and what they represented. A reexamination of how this writing system was created offers insight into the instrumental and ideological nature of the system itself.

The story behind the creation of the syllabary reveals an interesting invention process in creating a sign system uniquely tailored to the Cherokee language. The variance in these accounts allows us to understand the ways in which Sequoyah seems to have tested representational properties of sign systems. Samuel Lorenzo Knapp interviewed Sequoyah in 1828 with two bilingual interpreters, John Maw and John Rogers, because Sequoyah publicly only spoke and wrote in Cherokee. According to this source, Sequoyah first became aware of the ways in which writing worked as a technology when he saw a letter taken from a prisoner during a warring adventure. According to Knapp (1829: 32), "The warriors expressed their amazement at the white man's ability to put talk on a piece of paper, send it any distance, and have it understood by others. It was an art, they said, that was beyond the reach of the Indian, but Sequoyah disagreed. Taking up a flat stone, he began making marks on it with a pin. When he finished he told his friends that he had written in making a symbol for every word." In 1828 the editors of the *Cherokee Phoenix* wrote a similar story about the creation of the syllabary in which Sequoyah corrects the mystification of several young men who were admiring the ability of whites to talk on paper: "After silently listening to their conversation for awhile, [Sequoyah] . . . said, 'You all are fools; why the thing is very easy; I can do it myself.' And, picking up a flat stone, he commenced scratching on it with a pin; and after a few minutes read to them a sentence, which he had written by making a mark for each word" (quoted in Hoig 1995: 32–33).

These accounts reveal Sequoyah's initial understandings of the ways in which sign systems worked without needing to understand the precise instrumental relation between a specific signifier (here a mark) and signified (a spoken word). Without knowing the form or content of the letters that he saw others reading, he deduced the logic of the signifier/signified relation and may have been trying to use a mark as a representation of a whole word. Sequoyah demonstrated an understanding of the representational properties of writing systems, even if he didn't understand the precise relationships between letters and sounds. Written marks, he reasoned, can represent spoken language. This much he could have learned from writing his name on the silver work he had created as well. He demonstrates a rough conception of writing systems: when each word is represented in a symbol, it can be delivered to anyone else across time and space: mystery solved.

While it is not altogether clear whether Sequoyah had seen writing demonstrated by whites in a hunting party or by prisoners of war, it is certain that he and others in his tribe had contact with white people's literacy artifacts. The ways in which the writing system worked initially puzzled Cherokees. But for Sequoyah, who had mechanical and design experience, the mystery of its instrumentality was easily understood in general if not in particular. He did not need to know English to see the power that the written word had for those who used it and wanted similar power for his own people on their own terms. So he set out to test his theory of how a writing system works. As Knapp (quoted in Hoig 1995: 36) notes, "Sequoyah at first sought to make a character that would represent a sentence. Then he tried using symbols for every word. He produced thousands of them, but he soon realized that that method was much too cumbersome." Thus Sequoyah first tried to create a writing system in which symbols would represent every sentence and then, when that failed, every word.

This process would indeed have been daunting. One "word" in Cherokee can be an entire sentence, with each syllable representing semantic units of meaning. For instance, the Cherokee word for goodbye is ᏙᏓᏓᎪᎲᎢ /dodadagohvi/, roughly translated 'until we [two or more] meet each other again.' This is both one word and one sentence and thus might be represented by a single image. But if the speaker is talking to a single person, it's ᏙᎾᏓᎪᎲᎢ /donadagohvi/, roughly, 'until we [you and I] meet again,' with only one syllable marking the change in the number of people present. Developing one symbol for every sentence and/or word would have been confusing and inefficient: how could it show subtle changes in the structure of the word and sentence in a single image?[4] Sequoyah would have needed to develop thousands of symbols to represent the meaning of the phrases as well as some way to distinguish subtleties between verb and noun phrases.[5] To his credit, he understood that a semiotic representation was taking place and roughly understood how one form of representation worked, but he apparently did not settle quickly upon what precisely was being represented and by what placeholder.

In other accounts of his development of the syllabary, it appears that Sequoyah tested a different signifier/signified relation, with images as signifiers and objects for the signified. In a conversation with John Alexander, a merchant who met with him and recorded the meeting in his diary, Sequoyah recounted his creation this way: "when in the company of several other young Cherokee men, he drew the figure of a horse. The idea struck him that an alphabet would permit them to talk by use of these symbols. . . . He talked with others about it, asking if there was anyone in the nation who could make such characters. Here was no one who could do so, so he gave up his aimless sketches and began to work on his idea" (quoted in Hoig 1995: 32). Sequoyah tried a pictographic system in which, for example, an image of a horse would represent the animal itself. This makes sense given his early abilities and talents in drawing. As he attempted to make image-based characters for the words in Cherokee, Sequoyah's "aimless sketches" of figures and forms might have reminded Cherokees of ancient petroglyphs and perhaps would not seem aimless to them: Cherokees had carved pictographs into rocks for thousands of years. Pictographs are not as efficient as other sign systems, however, and would require tremendous collaboration to create—hence Sequoyah's question about who in the nation could make these. With so many ways of writing possible, and without knowing precisely how other sign systems work, the complexity and enormity of his undertaking began to become apparent to Sequoyah. He set aside his work with pictographs.

Sequoyah next began to distinguish between the sounds of the language and tried to represent them first with images. Historian Stan Hoig (1995: 35) quotes Knapp's interview with Sequoyah on this point at length:

> From the cries of wild beasts, from the talents of the mocking bird, from the voices of his children and companions, he knew that feelings and passions were conveyed by different sounds, from one intelligent being to another. The thought struck him to try to ascertain all the sounds in the Cherokee language. His own ear was not remarkably discriminating, and he called to his aid the more acute ears of his wife and children. He found great assistance from them. When he thought that he had distinguished all the different sounds in their language, he attempted to use pictorial signs, images of birds and beasts to convey these sounds to others, or mark them in his own mind.

Here Sequoyah seems to have linked the sound of the language as the signified with an image, a pictorial sign as signifier. This pictographic system also proved impossible, however: as the images began to multiply into the thousands, he couldn't remember what sound was being represented by which image because he had to use so many images to reflect these sound units "without any regard to appearances" (35). But Sequoyah had solved half of the puzzle: he had decided, finally, to represent the sounds of the language.

Sequoyah eventually broke down the sounds of the Cherokee language further into syllables and began to represent these sounds in script. With more work, he eventually found "that eighty-six distinct characters would be necessary. To make so many distinct figures differing so much in their shape, as to be easily distinguished from each other, and, at the same time, to be easily and quickly made with a pen on paper, was a matter of much difficulty" (Hoig 1995: 22). His characters developed for pen and paper were flowing, artistic in their flourishes, with sweeping strokes and overlapping shapes (fig. I.1). When seen through an alphabetic lens, these characters in script appear numerous and difficult to learn, a point explored in the next two chapters. Suffice it to say here that Sequoyah had finally created a Cherokee writing system, though not without considerable personal cost.

INTRODUCING THE INVENTION

For nearly a decade Sequoyah had systematically developed and set aside drafts of writing systems in a monastic pursuit of the one he finally settled upon. In his interview with John Stuart (1837: 21), Sequoyah explained that few of his contemporaries understood, supported, and helped him: "No one had the least confidence in the success of his [Sequoyah's] project, and thought him to be laboring under a species of mental derangement on that subject." He labored on, despite the lack of support and confidence in his success. His friends and family had nearly given up on him and tried to convince him to abandon the project. "He was laughed at by all who knew him," Stuart continues, "and was earnestly besought by every member of his family to abandon a project which was occupying and diverting so much of his time from the important and essential duties which he owed his family" (21). Though apparently alone for most of his efforts, Sequoyah worked relatively quickly, with limited resources, and in isolation from outsiders, his friends, and his family.

Sequoyah persisted this way for over a decade. "Sequoyah often wandered away alone avoiding everyone," Wahnenauhi (1966: 197) writes; "at such times he was absent for hours, no one knew where." She describes how a hunter had once seen Sequoyah in the woods, "seated on the ground, playing like a child with pieces of wood that he had chopped from a tree. . . . He was often seen this way, always making odd little marks, sometimes on rocks, using paint rocks as pencils, and sometimes with his knife cutting them on wood" (197). Sequoyah seemed like a man possessed to his family and other Cherokees, so focused on trying out various representational systems by using whatever materials he could muster. His family members tried to divert his attention from these ways and bring him back to ball games and more daily pursuits and even thought he might be "in communication with the Spirits." But he simply ignored the neglect of his friends and the "annoying sarcasm of opponents," staying true to his mission (198). Sequoyah persevered in his pursuit of the invention of a writing system, though logographs and pictographs had failed him and he had little support from his family and tribe.

While Sequoyah was in the process of creating the syllabary, his friend Turtle Fields paid him a visit. As George Lowrey tells it (quoted in Bass 1932: 15–16), Turtle Fields told Sequoyah that his friends thought that this pursuit was a waste of time, that Sequoyah was making a fool of himself, and that his friends were losing their respect for him. Sequoyah made clear to Turtle Fields his motivation for undertaking this enormous project. "If our people think I am making a fool of myself, you may tell our people that what I am doing will not make fools of them. They did not cause me to begin and they shall not cause me to give up. . . . What I am doing will not make our people the less respected, either by themselves or others." Understanding that his people were more concerned about their own appearance to outsiders, Sequoyah explained that he would take responsibility for his actions upon himself, especially if he was not successful in the end. He only hoped that what he was doing would make his people more respected "by themselves and others." The Cherokees who were concerned about his actions did not cause him to undertake this journey and did not need to worry about taking responsibility for his actions. Rather, Sequoyah undertook this arduous process because he was motivated by white people's literacy, their ownership of such a powerful tool, and the respect that such ownership garnered. If whites could have a writing system that so benefited them, filling them with self-respect and earning the respect of others, then Cherokees could have a writing system with all this power as well. But first Sequoyah had to convince the others that his syllabary worked.

A writing system in itself represented a foreign intrusion, which would certainly have made the invention a tough sell to some Cherokees (Foreman 1938: 38). He had completed the writing system and used it for some time to keep books and accounts for his transactions as a blacksmith before he could even convince his neighbors and family members to learn it. According to Payne ([1835] 1932: 16), "He made several copies of it, & sent for some of his neighbors, and gave them the copies & taught them how to use his alphabet; so that shortly it got about and several persons found that they could form words and note them down & read them off again." Sequoyah had become a teacher to his neighbors, who in turn had begun to find the syllabary useful for their daily needs and communications.

Before long Sequoyah's daughter volunteered to learn the syllabary and "soon became able to write and read with ease and fluency anything the father would write. This began to open the eyes of the family and some of the neighbors, but did not prove to be entirely satisfactory" (Stuart 1837: 22). Finally, after Sequoyah had taught his daughter to write and given several demonstrations to neighbors and friends, a more public meeting was held in Echota to test the utility of the system. Traveling from their home on the Coosa River, Sequoyah and his daughter arrived at the council meeting and were separated from each other. Once out of earshot of his daughter, Sequoyah was asked to write what was dictated to him; his daughter was brought back into the council house. She was given the script and read it to the group. By the end of the council meeting everyone had been shown the utility of the system, and several pledged to learn it (22).

Even after the 1821 council meeting where some were convinced of the usefulness of the syllabary, others proved harder to persuade.

According to Wahnenauhi (1966: 199), "It was not received by the people generally, until after many experiments, it was proved beyond a doubt that Sequoyah had indeed devised a most wonderful invention." In one experiment Sequoyah had demonstrated the writing system in a court. "He had a suit in the Indian Court held at Chatouga," Payne ([1835] 1932: 18) writes. "He wrote down a statement of his case. When he got there, he read his statement, instead of speaking; and all the people were amazed. This was about a year after the invention was completed." Sequoyah created the ultimate demonstration of the writing system, as Wahnenauhi (1966: 199) recounts: "He sent a letter to some friends, who had removed to the Arkansas Territory, and on receiving a reply, all doubts were forever banished." Sequoyah had managed to re-create the very process that had mystified the Cherokee hunting party a decade earlier, though this time with a completely unique writing system.

Sequoyah's perseverance, inventiveness, and discipline, coupled with his abilities in art and drawing, all seem to have contributed to his ability to delve into the ways in which representation works. His work with multiple media, as a silversmith, portrait artist, and first-rate draftsman, honed his talents for observation. He abandoned representational systems that would have been too difficult to continue developing and reproducing, suggesting that he was considering the ease of learning, efficiency in application, and potential for dissemination. He also had his people's well-being in mind, hoping to build their self-esteem and pride. Rather than believing that writing was an art or magic resting in the hands of colonists and their armies, Sequoyah understood that it was a relatively simple instrument that could help the members of his tribe communicate with each other.

Sequoyah considered the best ways to represent meaning, invented a system completely distinct from the one he saw in use among settlers, and created a writing system without having any formal schooling, literacy, or printed materials. His process itself is a study in Cherokee perseverance. This decade-long work ended up creating a brand-new writing system that allowed and still allows Cherokees to carry forward the mutually sustaining relationships of our language, religion, place, and history.

Though Sequoyah may not have known precisely how the Roman alphabet worked at the time when he created the syllabary, he did understand its general principles and lasting effects. The Roman alphabet had helped to make possible rapid westward colonialist expansion. Armies, warriors, and settlers could communicate across distances. They had books of ideas and knowledge. Writing, he saw, facilitated the colonists' war efforts and takeover of land. It was used in treaties, one of which he signed. English literacy had been used to codify trade agreements and treaties made by the Cherokees, British, and colonists since 1730 (Rozema 2002). Sequoyah had seen the impact of this technology on the face of the land, had understood how Cherokees marveled at the mystery of it, and had determined not to let Cherokees continue demeaning themselves by believing that it was magic only whites had. He wanted to prove to whites and to Cherokees themselves that such power was within the Cherokees' reach.

Understanding how writing systems work in the abstract, Sequoyah defined a unique, completely Cherokee relationship between signifier and signified through systematic trial and error. As these examples suggest, he considered, tried, and developed logographic (character represents word) and pictographic (image represents word) systems before settling upon his final system (character represents sound). That is, he knew enough about the Roman alphabet and alphabetic literacy to choose not to use it for the Cherokee language. The Cherokee writing system would be by, for, and of Cherokees.

Sequoyah seems to have had no interest in modeling his writing system after the alphabet, so mysteries about the Cherokee syllabary remain. If Sequoyah purposely avoided the influence of English literacy, the only model of writing available to him, then in what ways might the Cherokee writing system work differently than previously believed? In another words, if the alphabetic bias (Harris 2009) leads people to believe that the Cherokee syllabary works through character-sound correspondence, the way an alphabet works through letter-sound correspondence, then what other relations might exist between character and glyph that have been underappreciated? And another mystery: the writing system that Sequoyah developed in manuscript was complexly elegant and seemingly difficult to learn (see fig. I.1). Given the complexity of these original manuscript forms, how did the entire tribe gain fluency with this script, with no mass education or print?

The first phase of the development of the syllabary produced a unique manuscript form of a writing system that was developed in self-imposed isolation from the influence of the Roman alphabet. Sequoyah's outright resistance to the Roman alphabet and English language was present not only in the stories of his life and the process of invention of the writing system but also in its very workings and designs, as the next two chapters illustrate.

CHAPTER 2

THE SYLLABARY
AS WRITING SYSTEM

As described in chapter 1, interviews with Sequoyah and historical accounts handed down by those close to him reveal something about his systematic process of creating the syllabary. Sequoyah chose a character-syllable correspondence for his writing system and purposely avoided any influence of the Roman alphabet in his original manuscript form. W. A. Phillips (1870: 544) writes that Sequoyah "seems to have disdained the acquirement of the English language. Perhaps he suspected first what he was bound to know before he completed his task, that the Cherokee language has certain necessities and peculiarities of its own. It is almost impossible to write Indian words and names correctly in English. The English alphabet has not capacity for its expression." Phillips is partially right. Although Sequoyah had some degree of English literacy and understanding of the alphabet, his disdain for the alphabet and use of the language was manifest in his creation of the syllabary.

While chapter 1 illustrates the ways in which Sequoyah came to match sound to character, this chapter explores the implications of this matching more closely in order to determine why such a pairing might have been chosen over all the others. A systematic analysis of just a fraction of the linguistic information potentially carried by each character reveals the immense functionality of this writing system. The earliest stage of development of the syllabary

Parts of this chapter originally appeared in *Written Communication* 28(3) (July 2011).

actually assured that its use-value would be recognized quickly and its meaning-making potential would be put to use in day-to-day correspondences and writings. As history shows, this was in fact what happened after the invention was introduced to the tribe: reading and writing took hold in many facets of daily public and private reading and writing activities.

The entire Cherokee Nation was said to have become literate within the span of just a few years after the introduction of Sequoyan in the longhand arrangement (see fig. I.1); children as well as adults learned it quickly and easily (Knapp 1829; Mooney 1900: 110). Phillips (1870: 546), writing about learners' acquisition of the syllabary in an article for *Harper's Monthly*, notes:

> The astonishing rapidity with which it is acquired has always been a wonder, and was the first thing about it that struck me. In my own observation, Indian children will take one or two, at times, several, years to master the English printed and written system, but in a few days can read and write in Cherokee. They do the latter, in fact, as soon as they learn to shape letters. . . . It is not too much to say that a child will learn in a month, by the same effort, as thoroughly, in the language of Sequoyah, that which in ours consumes the time of our children for at least two years.

In a letter to Sequoyah (January 12, 1832, in Moulton 1985: 1:235) John Ross describes the extent of the rapid and easy dissemination of the syllabary as a contribution to the welfare of the nation: "The old and the youth find no difficulty in learning to read and write in their native language and to correspond with their distant friends with the same facility as the whites do." Granted, as Ross and Phillips point out, the nation was speaking primarily Cherokee at the time and by all accounts it is easier for someone who has heard the language spoken since childhood to learn the syllabary. Even some Cherokee speakers who are fluent in the spoken language today still grapple with memorizing the syllabary, however, and rely on the printed chart to help them recall which glyph corresponds to which syllable.

The quick dissemination of the syllabary without the aid of print, mass education, or abundant writing materials remains significant. Anthropologist Willard Walker (1969: 150) finds that Sequoyah's achievement was one of the most noteworthy intellectual tours de force in American history: "Equally remarkable, however, was the fact that within a few years, thousands of tribal Cherokees became literate in their native language. People wrote letters, kept accounts, and copied the sacred songs and curing formulas. A weekly newspaper called The Cherokee Phoenix was printed by a Cherokee national press as early as 1828." This rapid dissemination occurred without mass education or print and was based on the scripted version of the syllabary, not the one that is most commonly seen in print. "It has been estimated that Cherokees were 90 percent literate in their native language in the 1830's" (151). Given the high reading and writing rates of Cherokees in the early 1800s, a change in the form and arrangement of the characters seems to have had little initial impact on learners' facility with Sequoyan.

Unfortunately, scholars and the general public alike have long misunderstood the Cherokee writing system, comparing it to the English alphabet when such a comparison makes little sense. To his credit, Phillips (1870: 544) understood that the Roman alphabet has little capacity to represent the Cherokee language. Perhaps because of its instrumental failings and/or because of his disdain for the English language, Sequoyah recognized that the alphabet would not do justice to the Cherokee language.

Sequoyah worked from an indigenous view of writing and seems to have appreciated the ways in which writing tools could represent levels of meaning-making potential. This chapter introduces the standardized version of the Cherokee syllabary to suggest the ways in which its arrangement may have obscured its original instrumental workings. The remainder of the chapter illustrates the linguistic information potentially represented by each character to demonstrate that the Cherokee language requires a writing system that speakers can use to represent underlying morphological elements. Because of this, the Cherokee syllabary can potentially do more than simply represent sound with each character written.

NEVER AN ALPHABET AND
NOT JUST A SYLLABARY

The first issue of the *Cherokee Messenger* opens with a "Translation of Genesis into the Cherokee Language" and includes the "Cherokee Alphabet" pictured in figure 2.1.[1] This was a reprint of the syllabary as it had been standardized for print in an early issue of the *Cherokee Phoenix*. By the 1840s the new arrangement of the syllabary had become standardized in part through these two publications. Just under this title, two complete sets of characters are included: "Characters as Arranged by the Inventor" and "Characters Systematically Arranged with the Sounds" (fig. 2.1), assuming, of course, that Sequoyah's arrangement had no system.

The second arrangement includes the equivalent English phonetic sound of the syllables next to each character, with a key at the bottom that demonstrates the vowels and consonants in Cherokee as represented by sounds in English. For instance, "a as *a* in *father*, or short as *a* in *rival*" and "g nearly as in English, but approaching to k."

The characters were "systematically arranged" in a way that mimics the way English alphabetic writing is ordered and taught. Though it is not an alphabet, calling the syllabary a "Cherokee Alphabet" had a rhetorical effect for settlers, political leaders, and reformers, who perceived Cherokees as more civilized because of this "alphabet."[2] The rearrangement of characters rests on conventions similar to those used in alphabetic literacy primers that organized spelling and vocabulary lessons around consonant-vowel combinations. The vowels are listed in alphabetic order and the combinations are roughly arranged alphabetically, except for the *d/t* combinations, which can sound similar in Cherokee. The arrangement in print versions of the syllabary should have had little impact on people's abilities to learn it. In fact, given the ways in which this standardized version is keyed to the alphabet, it should have made learning Cherokee much easier for those whose first language was English. But that was not the case.

For English speakers, this standardized arrangement of the syllabary may have drawn too much attention to the sounds of characters, diverting attention from the ways in which the syllabary actually represents much more than sound. Mooney (1892: 63) describes how difficult it was for English speakers to learn the Cherokee syllabary through the standardized syllabary chart: "The syllabary, however, has several defects which seriously impair its usefulness. A number of the characters are so nearly alike that they can scarcely be distinguished even in the most carefully written manuscript. There is no logical connection of characters denoting related sounds—as *tsa*, *tse*,

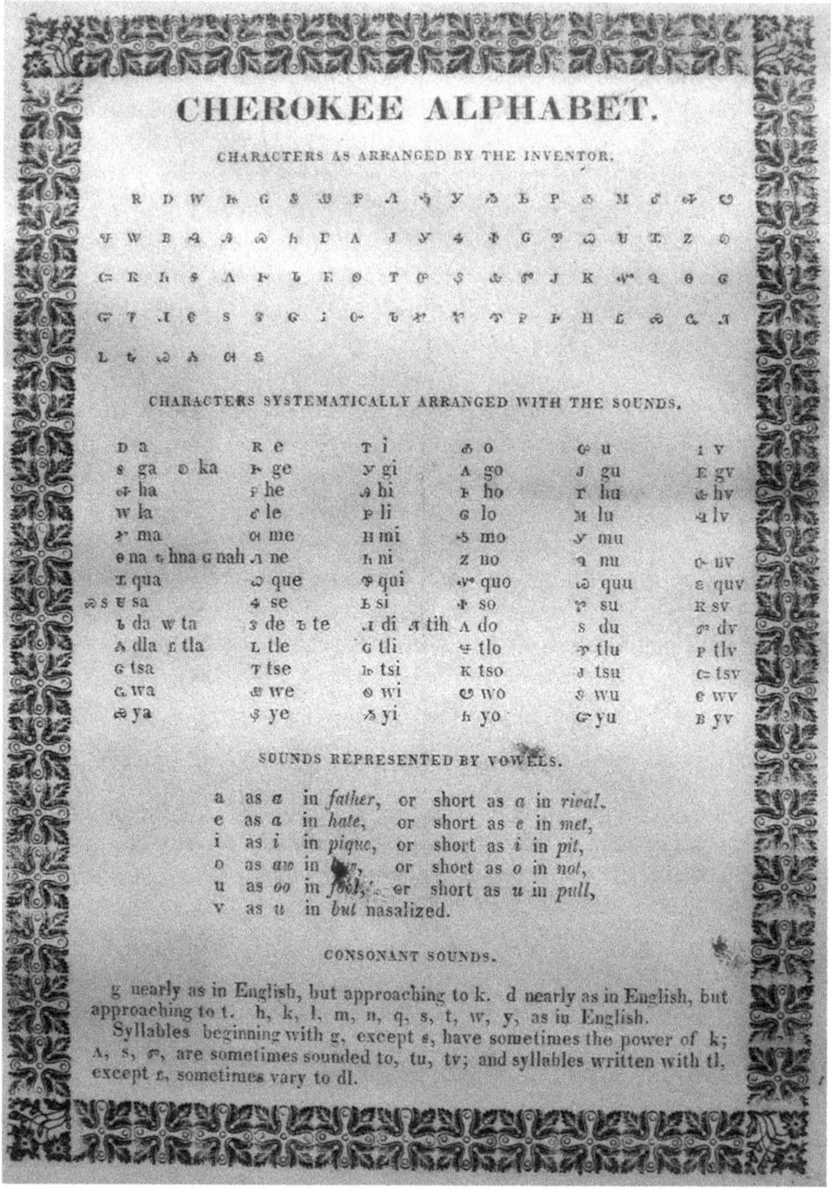

CHEROKEE ALPHABET.

CHARACTERS AS ARRANGED BY THE INVENTOR.

R D W Һ G S Ꮃ Ᏸ Ꭱ Ꭰ Ꮴ Ᏹ Ꭰ Ꮮ Ᏼ Ꮲ Ꮒ Ꮻ Ꮇ Ꮷ Ꮼ Ꭴ

Ꮙ W Ᏼ Ꮃ Ꮃ Ꮱ Һ Ꮁ Ꭺ Ꮳ Ꮴ Ꮴ Ꮝ Ᏻ Ꮲ Ꮑ Ꭴ Ꮓ Ꭶ

Ꮐ Ꭱ Һ Ꮞ Ꭺ Ꮁ Ꮃ Ꭼ Ꮎ Ꮏ Ꭴ Ꮝ Ꮧ Ꮢ Ꭻ Ꮶ Ꮼ Ꮖ Ꭷ Ꮐ

Ꮐ Ꮳ Ꮮ Ꭼ Ꮝ Ꮓ Ꮐ Ꮧ Ꮎ Ꮒ Ꮯ Ꭲ Ꮄ Ꮲ Ꮲ Ꮅ Ꭽ Ꮱ Ꮦ Ꭰ Ꮑ

Ꮮ Ꮔ Ꮰ Ꭺ Ꭶ Ꮝ

CHARACTERS SYSTEMATICALLY ARRANGED WITH THE SOUNDS.

D a	R e	T i	Ꮬ o	Ꮕ u	i v
Ꭶ ga Ꮗ ka	Ꮁ ge	Ᏹ gi	Ꭺ go	Ꭽ gu	Ꭼ gv
Ꮤ ha	Ꮁ he	Ꭺ hi	Ꮵ ho	Ꮁ hu	Ꮴ hv
Ꮃ la	Ꮄ le	Ꮅ li	Ꮇ lo	Ꮈ lu	Ꮴ lv
Ꮄ ma	Ꮑ me	Ᏸ mi	Ꮋ mo	Ᏻ mu	
Ꭴ na Ꮏ hna Ꮐ nah Ꮑ ne	Ꮒ ni	Ꮓ no	Ꮔ nu	Ꮕ nv
Ꮖ qua	Ꮗ que	Ꮙ qui	Ꮚ quo	Ꮝ quu	Ꮢ quv
Ꮜ s Ꮄ sa	Ꮞ se	Ꮟ si	Ꮠ so	Ꮡ su	Ꮢ sv
Ꮧ da Ꮴ ta	Ꮥ de Ꮦ te	Ꮧ di Ꮨ tih Ꭰ do	Ꮩ du	Ꮫ dv
Ꮪ dla Ꮬ tla	Ꮮ tle	Ꮮ tli	Ꮯ tlo	Ꮰ tlu	Ꮱ tlv
Ꮳ tsa	Ꮴ tse	Ꮵ tsi	Ꮶ tso	Ꮷ tsu	Ꮸ tsv
Ꮹ wa	Ꮺ we	Ꮻ wi	Ꮼ wo	Ꮽ wu	Ꮾ wv
Ꮿ ya	Ᏸ ye	Ᏹ yi	Ᏺ yo	Ᏻ yu	Ᏼ yv

SOUNDS REPRESENTED BY VOWELS.

a   as *a* in *father*, or short as *a* in *rival*.
e   as *a* in *hate*, or short as *e* in *met*,
i   as *i* in *pique*, or short as *i* in *pit*,
o   as *aw* in *law*, or short as *o* in *not*,
u   as *oo* in *fool*, or short as *u* in *pull*,
v   as *u* in *but* nasalized.

CONSONANT SOUNDS.

g nearly as in English, but approaching to k. d nearly as in English, but approaching to t. h, k, l, m, n, q, s, t, w, y, as in English.
Syllables beginning with g, except s, have sometimes the power of k; Ꭰ, Ꮝ, Ꮢ, are sometimes sounded to, tu, tv; and syllables written with tl, except Ꮮ, sometimes vary to dl.

Figure 2.1. The "Cherokee Alphabet," initially published in issue 1 of the *Cherokee Phoenix* (February 21, 1828) by Samuel Worcester, with its "characters systematically arranged with the sounds," and republished in the inaugural issue of the *Cherokee Messenger* in 1844.

43

tsi, etc.—and finally each character commonly requires several strokes in the making." The Cherokee syllabary seems devilishly complex to learn for those raised with English as their first language. As Mooney noted, characters resemble each other and require several strokes, sometimes seeming to show no "logical" connection between the characters and related sounds. Though the Cherokee writing system is difficult to learn for people whose first language is English, it carries its own cultural logics, meanings, and values that abide today, if we view it outside of the alphabetic lens.

In *Signs of Cherokee Culture: Sequoyah's Syllabary in Eastern Cherokee Life*, Margaret Bender (2002) presents results of her qualitative fieldwork in Cherokee, North Carolina. She explores how Cherokees used and learned the syllabary. In the instructional materials presented in her study, the syllabary is taught as a sign system, using the same arrangement made popular by Worcester: with eighty-six characters and seemingly without any logic behind the character-sound relationship. Bender finds that the syllabary is often very difficult to learn and memorize both for Cherokees whose first language is English and for Cherokees who first language is Cherokee:[3]

> For most of my consultants, mastery of the entire writing system came later, when the person became a responsible adult member of a particular parish. Not every member of the community followed this progression, however, and the total number of adults literate in the syllabary remains small. Literacy in the syllabary is a specialization, not a matter of basic adult competency. (101)

Even for adults who are fluent in the spoken Cherokee language, learning the syllabary today is not easy, requires the aid of the syllabary chart, and takes considerable time and study. Certainly, the Cherokee writing system does not always show a perfect phonetic correspondence between glyph and syllable (Mooney 1892; Scancarelli 1994; Bender 2002), but it has fewer exceptions to the rules of its practice than English does. Despite this consistency in character-sound correspondence and its arrangement keyed to an alphabetic order, the Cherokee writing system is not easy to learn from this standardized version.

My own experience both as a Cherokee language learner and as a participant-observer of English-speaking Cherokee language learners in five years of online language classes and immersion classes in Tahlequah has revealed that the syllabary organized in this fashion vexes learners. They have a difficult time finding the right character because first they have to locate the sound according to alphabetical order and the English sound system. Spelling becomes the arduous task of first relying on English transliterations then locating the correct syllabary character within the alphabetic order (Cushman 2011a). Rather than having a direct correspondence between characters and Cherokee sounds, Worcester's arrangement inserts alphabetic sound systems and orthographies as intermediary steps that learners must go through to locate the correct character. Two problems emerged with the standardization of the syllabary chart: first, knowledge of the English writing system interferes with learning Sequoyan (for example, the habit of expecting "R" to sound like /r/ as in "Robert" hinders Cherokee learners from reading it in its Cherokee sound /sv/); second, the original learners of this system were all fluent Cherokee speakers who were learning to read and write in their first language. These problems with the standardized syllabary chart rest in its visual and aural arrangement of the characters, as demonstrated below.

What instrumental and interpretive logics might Sequoyan have that become apparent when it is viewed as a writing system in its own right? Writing systems scholar Peter Daniels suggests that the Cherokee syllabary should be understood as possibly representing morphemic units of the language. Daniels (2009: 36) compares the world's writing systems to reveal their origins and offers a fresh perspective on three important and functionally similar writing systems, Mayan, Chinese, and Sumerian: "there were three known independent ancient origins of writing . . . all of which served societies that had developed some degree of urbanism, and that the three languages involved were similar in basic structure: most of the morphemes are just a single syllable." Morphemes are the smallest meaningful units of a language. If each syllable in a language has meaning, then syllabic-based writing systems in those languages might also be carrying linguistic information in each character.

Cherokee is what linguists call a polysynthetic language, in which words can consist of a high number of morphemes. Thus one word in Cherokee can be an entire sentence in which each syllable uttered has meaning (e.g., the Cherokee word for good-bye is a sentence: ᎠᏙᎳᏓᎪᎯ /donadagohvi/ 'until you and I meet again'). Each Cherokee verb phrase is a complete sentence that has specific rules governing where syllables can be used. In their simplest form, verb phrases can include prefixes, verb roots, and suffixes. These verb phrases paint pictures of the action unfolding, potentially showing who, what, where, and when in one word. This polysynthetic structure of Cherokee lends itself well to a writing system in which each grapheme represents not just sound but also the potential underlying morphological elements of the language.

Bender (2002: 122) has proposed something similar. As her research suggests, perhaps "the syllables are actually syllable-long morphemes with stable semantic meanings." When Cherokee speakers are writing and come across a word in which syllables have been elided in everyday speech, they try "to find a morphological or semantic justification for the otherwise arbitrary choice of syllabary characters in consonant clusters" (124). In her interviews and observations, she finds that "as far from being arbitrary as was possible, the syllabary was treated as though it had a direct, tangible connection to meaning" (122). My own research bears out this understanding.

When asked to translate Cherokee speech into writing, some native speakers of Cherokee will repeat the elided word over and over, slotting in all the possible consonant/vowel combinations until they find the correct vowel to replace the one that has been elided. Sometimes they might say aloud how the meaning changes with each of the consonant/vowel arrangements; or they might say Ꮬ /tla/ 'no' (as in that syllable doesn't work) or just shake their heads. As Bender (2002: 129) notes, "This [practice] implies that the choice of spelling is a meaningful one that provides semantic (and possibly even grammatical) information."[4] In this process of finding the correct vowel to replace the one that has been elided, Cherokee speakers work to find meaning in the words rather than simply the sound of the syllable.

More to the point, a number of Cherokee readers and writers with whom I've spoken and a handful who are not fluent in the spoken or written language indicate that all of the syllables do mean something to them when they write. Though they may not explicitly say that each syllable has morphemic information, they demonstrate this linguistic knowledge implicitly as they offer me on-the-fly language lessons. In a passing conversation with Benny Smith, a well-known Cherokee historian and fluent speaker who is also a professor emeritus and former dean at Haskell Indian Nations University, he explained that every syllable imparts meaning and/or functions grammatically. He recited a typical Cherokee conversational response to the question ᎠᏎᏍᏗ /tohitsu/ 'how are you?' "Sure, you could say ᎣᏍᏓ /osda/ like most do, but it's really ᎠᎣᏍᏓ /gosda/ for 'I am good, doing fine,' ᎰᏍᏓ /hosda/ for 'you are good,' and ᎣᏍᏓ /osda/ for 's/ he or it is good.' Every part means something." If every syllable means something, then each glyph potentially represents sound and meaning together.

Five years ago on a visit to Tahlequah on Labor Day weekend, I struck up a conversation with two sisters who were basket weavers, showing and selling their work at the Cherokee Heritage Center. When I mentioned that I was a Cherokee citizen just learning the language, one asked me my name: "ᏚᎠ ᏍᏣᎠᎠ?" /gado detsadoa/ 'What your name?'

When I replied, "Ellen ᏍᏣᎠᎠ" /ellen detsadoa/ 'Ellen your name,' they responded with gales of laughter. As I stood there half smiling, pretty sure I had just become the butt of a joke I didn't get, they tried to explain. One sister pointed to herself and said, still trying to hold back a smile, "Ellen ᏔᏫᎠᎠ" /ellen daquadoa/ 'Ellen my name.' Then she pointed to her sister and said, "Cheryl ᏚᏔ" /cheryl dudoda/ 'Cheryl her name.' Still not catching on, I said "Oh, your name's Ellen too?" This caused more laughter: "No, no, it's different for each of us. You'll learn! You'll learn!" In one of my first conversation classes, we learned how to answer the question "What is your name." The prefixes for verb phrases differ according to who is speaking, such as ᏔᏫᎠᎠ /daquadoa/ 'my name is,' ᏍᏣᎠᎠ /detsadoa/ 'your name is,' and ᏚᏔᏔ /dudoda/ 'her name is.' In my interaction with the sisters, I was using the wrong subject prefix. Notably, this was pointed out to me by someone whose first language is Cherokee and who does not read and write in Sequoyan, as I learned later. She was demonstrating knowledge of the morphological character of the language, showing that she was able to distinguish the meanings of three different prefix syllables in these verb phrases, even without being well practiced with Sequoyan.

Though space does not permit me to cite the many times when Cherokee language speakers (some of whom are not versed with Sequoyan) have corrected me, this evidence suggests that some Cherokees may tacitly understand the language on a morphemic level. This understanding allows them to correct my Cherokee at the syllabic level, especially when I incorrectly use prefixes and affixes in verb phrases. For some Cherokees, this knowledge exists independently from a working knowledge of the syllabary.

One final example of this tacit knowledge of the morphemic structure of Cherokee: I recently attended a conference held by the Cherokee Nation in which dozens of native Cherokee speakers and all other participants were given tote bags and stainless steel water bottles that sported the Sequoyan phrase ᎠᎹ ᏍᎹᏗ /ama galudi/ 'water it's liked.' But some of the first-language speakers who are Cherokee National Living Treasures for their teaching in Cherokee Nation programs and the Immersion School frowned in apparent confusion at the spelling and broke into a discussion. "It's missing something. What's it supposed to say?" Then they started saying the word *galudi* over and over, slotting in syllables under their breath and aloud. "It's like 'they like it,' ᏍᎹᎾᏗ /galuquidi/ or something," one offered, trying to link it to a recognizable message by adding another syllable to the verb. When one of the most respected elders offered his interpretation of it as 'water they like,' explaining that the bottle connects to an important ceremony for Cherokees, the participants nodded. When a Cherokee National Living Treasure for language instruction suggested that maybe it was missing a character, the elder nodded.

The verb phrase on the water bottle had been contracted to sound like speech, the way that "do not" becomes "don't" in English. But in English little information is lost by the missing "o" in the reduction of "not" and elision of the two separate words. In Cherokee, though, important semantic information was missing for speakers who were looking for the second part of the verb phoneme for 'like': ᏊᎾ /lv(u) qui(quo)/. This verb was necessarily reduced in the context of spoken language but made little semantic sense in the context of written language (for example, 'I like water' would be ᎠᎹ ᎠᏯᏊᎾᏗ /ama

agilvquidi/ and 'you like water' would be DᎧᎻ ᏩᏒᎥᏫ /ama
tsalvquidi/).[5] When one of the speakers offered the missing character, all were satisfied with the message on the bottle. These fluent
speakers recognized that two characters made up essential information for this verb phrase: with one of the missing, the verb didn't
sound right, alerting them to missing semantic information.

This pattern of evidence suggests that this writing system involved
more than merely the relation between glyph and syllable; if the
glyph and syllable work so well together, then a different arrangement and shift in the appearance of each glyph from script to print
would not have deterred learners. Learning Worcester's rearranged
system would have been just as easy for native speakers and perhaps easier for English-speaking learners. Sequoyah arranged the
syllables differently and the print version of these glyphs keeps much
of the scripted design intact (more on that next chapter), which suggests that this writing system is more than simply a syllabic one. It
stands to reason that more than one form of representation within
the system could have facilitated its rapid uptake by individuals and
transference from one tribal member to the next.

Sequoyah's writing system not only matches sound units to characters but at times can also match meaningful units (morphemes) to
glyphs. Thus the syllabary carries with it another way of mapping
the Cherokee worldview: it represents the sounds of the language
and potentially entire ways of constructing meaning in single words
that portray scenes of action. If this is the case, Sequoyan is not just
a syllabary but can also work at times like a morphographic system,
in which each written syllable can potentially carry sound and semantic information. This inscription process might suggest how such
a complex system spread throughout the Cherokee tribe so easily
and rapidly. To illustrate, it's necessary to move beyond qualitative
descriptions of the encoding/decoding process of today's Cherokees
to a linguistic examination of each character.

ANALYSIS OF THE CHEROKEE
WRITING SYSTEM

Linguistic study of the Cherokee language confirms that each of the
syllables carries semantic meaning and/or grammatical function.

Tables 2.1 to 2.6 show a digital reproduction of each individual row of Sequoyah's syllabary as he reportedly reproduced it for John Howard Payne (see fig. I.1 for the whole syllabary). To translate these, each of Sequoyah's glyphs was searched in two Cherokee dictionaries (Feeling 1975; Montgomery-Anderson 2007), the Cherokee Nation's online word list (http://www.cherokee.org/AboutTheNa tion/Wordlist.aspx), the language lessons from Ruth Holmes and Betty Sharp Smith (1976), and notes from the Cherokee Nation online language classes taught by teacher and native speaker, reader, and writer Ed Fields. The translations of the first row of Sequoyah's syllabary are presented in table 2.1 according to their English phonetic equivalent and its grammatical and/or semantic function. The remaining rows are shown in tables 2.2 to 2.6.

Although the goal of this analysis was to explore the potential information that each character might codify, these tables are neither exhaustive nor comprehensive. They should be understood as an initial attempt to explore meaning potentials. These tables were reviewed by a small number of language speakers, but more analysis and work to determine additional meaning potentials are warranted. It should also be noted that these tables do not mean that *only* these meanings are associated with each character. It is not possible to take the syllables on this chart and combine them to form meaningful words in Cherokee. Instead these tables should be understood as identifying just a small sample of latent meanings when each character is used in particular contexts.

It is also important to note that these tables are the result of my analysis. Though Cherokee language speakers, some of whom have no fluency with Sequoyan, can isolate meaningful units of language, they would not itemize the language this way, isolating units into potential meanings. Meaning for Cherokee speakers in almost all instances derives from multiple contexts of use in ways illustrated below.

Isolating syllables as I do in the tables would likely be seen by Cherokees as artificial and atomistic and certainly as the academic exercise that it is. But it is useful to demonstrate the ways in which Sequoyan can work instrumentally and move readers beyond reading the Cherokee writing system through an alphabetic lens, which views this system as working only on a character-sound basis. By demonstrating potential meanings of Cherokee morphemes in this

Table 2.1. Grammatical Function and/or Meaning of the First Row of Sequoyah's Syllabary Produced for John Howard Payne

Character and Sound	*Grammatical Function and/or Meaning*
Ꭱ /e/	Frequently used as verb prefix and suffix and as a pronoun (Feeling 1975: 89); indicates third person as noun and verb prefix (Feeling 1975: 89) .
Ꭰ /a/	Indicates human, as in *asgaya* 'man' or *ageya* 'woman' or *ani* 'people' (Feeling 1975: 307).
Ꮃ /la/	Root of *nula* 'hurry' and 'come here' (Feeling 1989:148); root of interrogatives *ha la* 'what? how much? how many?'; *ha la ya* 'when? how far?' (Holmes and Smith 1976: 259); *hadla* 'where? where to?' (Holmes and Smith 1976: 260).
Ꮵ /tsi/	Root for *uwetsi* 'child', *etsi* 'mother,' and *uwetsi* 'egg'; can also be first-person singular pronoun subject 'I,' as in *tsiwoni* 'I speak' (Feeling 1975: 134) .
G /nah/	Rarely used, this character does not appear in the Cherokee font provided by the Cherokee Nation and is replaced here with an alphabetic Times New Roman "G." This character was dropped from the syllabary when it moved to print.
Ꮽ /wu/	Root for 'west,' as in *wudeligv* and 'biggest,' as in *wutanv* (Feeling 1975: 189)
Ꮺ /we/	Root for *uwetsi* 'child' or egg; can also be verb suffix that reverses action (Feeling 1975: 188), as in *dahnawesgvi* 'he was undressing' (Feeling 1975: 283).
Ꮅ /li/	Root for *lisi* 'grandmother' (Holmes and Smith 1976: xx), *ayoli* 'child,' and *unalii* 'friend' (Holmes and Smith 1976: 149; Feeling 1975: 317); with *du* acts as root of the verb 'to want,' as in *uduliha* 's/he/it wants it' (Holmes and Smith 1976: 26).
Ꮑ /ne/	Shows relation when used as a prefix to nouns, as in *gvnetsi* 's/he is her/his child' (Feeling 1975: 315); used as an ordinal for numbers (Feeling 1975: 147) as in *taline* 'second' (Feeling 1975: 230–33); shows specified action, as in *gado hadvne* 'what are you doing?' (Feeling 1975: 246).
Ꮍ /mo/	Infrequently used; appears to be a variation of *ma* 'salt,' as in *amohi* 'in salt' (Feeling 1975: 309); also used to translate English words, as in *Mosi* for 'Moses' (common).
Ꭹ /gi/	Pronoun for passive construction, as in *eginiquotiha* 'you and I are being seen' (Feeling 1975: 300–301); used as pronoun for 'ourselves,' as in *ginvsa* 'you and I alone'; also the root of 'to be,' as in *asgaya yigi* 'man is not' (Feeling 1975: 305).

Table 2.1.—*continued*

Character and Sound	Grammatical Function and/or Meaning
ꮂ /yi/	Negates verbs, meaning 'not,' as in *yigoliga* 'I don't know,' and *doyi*, 'outside,' literally 'not here' (Feeling 1975: 86).
Ꮟ /si/	Interjection meaning 'wait!'; adverb meaning 'yet' or 'still' (Feeling 1975: 153, 342); also a verb suffix meaning 'final,' as in *dagowonisi* 's/ he will speak' (Feeling 1975: 288)
Ꮅ /tlv/	Word meaning 'no,' variation of *tla*; negative adverb (Holmes and Smith 1976 263).
ꮟ /o/	Possessive and reflexive pronoun meaning 'mine,' 'my,' or 'me,' as in *oginali* 's/he and I are friends' (Feeling 1975: 317) and *ogvsa* 'they and I are alone' (Feeling 1975: 327); also a prefix for verbs meaning 'exclusive' and suffix meaning 'repeatedly' (Feeling 1975: 150).
Ꮇ /lu/	Root for the verb 'arrive,' as in *wigalugi* 's/he/it arrived here' (Montgomery-Anderson 2007: 149, 253, 317).

Crop of figure I.1 courtesy of Gilcrease Museum, Tulsa, Okla.

Table 2.2. Grammatical Function and/or Meaning of the Second Row of Sequoyah's Syllabary

Character and Sound	Grammatical Function and/or Meaning
Ꭷ /le/	Root of coordinating conjunction *ale* 'and,' 'but,' 'or' (Feeling 1975: 38, 343).
Ꮂ /ha/	Verb suffix meaning 'x is part of y' (Feeling 1975: 129) or 'x is being done to y' reflexively (Feeling 1975: 255–64); verb prefix showing 'you'/'it' reflexivity, as in *hahlviha* 'you're tying it up' (Feeling 1975: 258); verb suffix indicating present tense.
Ꮼ /wo/	Root of verb 'to speak,' as in *tsiwoni* 'I speak' and the noun *nvwodi* 'medicine' (Feeling 1975: 249; Holmes and Smith 1976: 304–305).
Ꮰ /tlo/	Root of the verb 'to cry,' as in *dunatloyilvi* 'where they cried' (Montgomery-Anderson 2007: 475) and *atlohiha* 'to cry' (Feeling 1975: 223).
Ꮺ /ta/	Noun root meaning 'two,' as in *tali* 'two' (Holmes and Smith 1976: 262–63; Feeling 1975: 156).
Ꮃ /yv/	Combined with *a* to form root of noun meaning person, as in *ayvwi* 'person' (Feeling 1975: 310) and *tsiyvwi* 'I originate' (Holmes and Smith 1976: 304).

Table 2.2.—*continued*

Character and Sound	*Grammatical Function and/or Meaning*
Ꮅ /lv/	Root of *dikalvgvi* 'east' (Feeling 1975: 200; Holmes and Smith 1976: 260) and *kalvi* 'month' (Feeling 1975: 210; Holmes and Smith 1976: 260).
Ꭾ /hi/	Verb prefix for second-person singular, 'you,' as in *hiwoni* 'you speak' (Feeling 1975: 129).
Ꮝ /s/	Verb suffix indicating a question, as in *hiyvwiyas?* 'Are you an Indian?' (Holmes and Smith 1976: 76); also noun prefix showing relation, as in *sgidoi*, meaning a sibling speaking of a brother or sister of the opposite sex (Holmes and Smith 1976: 164).
Ᏺ /yo/	Pronoun for passive construction, as in *uyodea* 's/he/it is itching' and *uyohuseha* 's/he/it is losing it' (Feeling 1975: 185); and *uyo* as in 'poor, wicked, mean, evil, miserable' (Holmes and Smith 1976: 266).
G /mv/	Worcester deleted this character. See page 93 for further explanation.
Ꮀ /hu/	Root for *gohusdi* 'something' (Feeling 1975: 121, 219).
Ꭺ /go/	Verb prefix for first-person singular, as in *goliga* 'I understand it' (Feeling 1975: 121); also root of the tenth power in numeric system, as in *nvksgo saquu* 'four-tens and one' (forty-one).
Ꮷ /tsu/	Noun and verb suffix question marker (Feeling 1975: 135; Holmes and Smith 1976: 203); also verb prefix meaning specific past time (Feeling 1975: 243).
Ꮍ /mu/	Rarely used except for words borrowed from English (Montgomery-Anderson 2007: 95).
Ꮜ /se/	Reportative and future progressive verb suffix, as in *atlisei* 's/he/it was reportedly running' and *atlisesdi* 's/he/it will be running' (Feeling 1975: 242).

Crop of figure I.1 courtesy of Gilcrease Museum, Tulsa, Okla.

Table 2.3. Grammatical Function and/or Meaning of the Third Row of Sequoyah's Syllabary

Character and Sound	*Grammatical Function and/or Meaning*
Ꮡ /so/	Noun prefix that acts as an adjective meaning 'another' or 'additional one' when used with *i*, as in *soi* (Feeling 1975: 154).
Ꮭ /tli/	Root of *gitli* 'dog' and *utli* 'away' (Montgomery-Anderson 2007: 475); root of the verb 'running,' as in *atli* 's/he/it is running' (Feeling 1975: 251).

Table 2.3.—*continued*

Character and Sound	Grammatical Function and/or Meaning
Ꮙ /qui/	Subject and object prefix for transitive verbs (Feeling 1975: 279–81).
Ꮚ /que/	Subject and object prefix for transitive verbs (Feeling 1975: 279–81).
Ꮦ /sa/	'First' and root of number 'one' (Feeling 1975: 151; Holmes and Smith 1976: 261).
Ꮖ /qua/	Noun prefix for 'myself,' as in *aqua dageyu gahlquasgo* 'I love myself' (Holmes and Smith 1976: 77); verb prefix for 'I,' as in *aquanvta* 'I know.'
Ꮓ /no/	Verb suffix showing previously noted action (Feeling 1975: 245).
Ꭶ /ka/	Interjection meaning 'now' (344) or 'listen to this!' or 'attention!' or 'enough!' or 'come on!' (Montgomery-Anderson 2007: 139); at the end of a word means that the speaker is counting on a yes answer (Holmes and Smith 1976: 130).
Ꮳ /tsv/	Adverb suffix meaning 'extremely' or 'exceptional'; also root of *tsvsa* 'yourself' (Feeling 1975: 138).
Ꭱ /sv/	Noun prefix that seems to mean 'late,' 'last,' 'end of day,' as in *svhiyeyi* 'evening' and *svhi* 'yesterday' (Feeling 1975: 155); also a reflexive verb suffix in the past tense, as in *aquadadvquusvi* 'I forgot myself' (Feeling 1975: 298).
Ꮒ /ni/	Interjection meaning 'look!'; also verb prefix meaning lateral position, 'already,' or previously noted action (Feeling 1974: 147).
Ꮤ /ga/	When used with *i* shows quantity, as in *iga* 'day' or *igada* 'some' or *igati* 'height' or *hala iga* 'how many?' (Feeling 1975: 131); verb prefix for third-person singular and plural (Feeling 1975: 90); verb prefix meaning 'since' (Feeling 1975: 90).
Ꭺ /do/	Verb suffix meaning 'here' and 'there' (Feeling 1975: 86), 'stasis,' 'well,' or 'fine' (Feeling 1975: 156).
Ᏻ /ge/	Suffix used to mark a question (Feeling 1975: 347); verb prefix for first- and third-person singular (Feeling 1975: 90), as in *geloha* 's/he/it is feeding him/her/it.'
Ꮼ /da/	Verb prefix indicating future tense (Feeling 1975: 66) or motion toward the speaker (Feeling 1975: 250); root for 'good' when used with *s*, as in *osda* 's/he/it is good'; also used as a reflexive pronoun for verbs, as in *gadaquotihi* 'I see myself' (Feeling 1975: 296).

Crop of figure I.1 courtesy of Gilcrease Museum, Tulsa, Okla.

Table 2.4. Grammatical Function and/or Meaning of the Fourth Row of Sequoyah's Syllabary

Character and Sound	Grammatical Function and/or Meaning
E /gv/	Verb prefix for third-person singular, as in *gvhnv* 's/he/it is alive' (Feeling 1975: 126); also *ga* plus *a* becomes *gv*, which means 'since' (Feeling 1975: 255).
Ꮻ /wi/	Verb prefix indicating position or motion away from speaker (Feeling 1975: 244).
Ꭲ /i/	Verb prefix indicating repetitive action (Feeling 1975: 241) and 'again' (Feeling 1975: 251); verb suffix indicating future tense (Feeling 1975: 289); noun meaning 'self' as locative and agent (Feeling 1975: 131); verb prefix meaning the exact opposite of an action, as in *sdudi* 'close' and *sduidi* 'open' (Feeling 1975: 327); locative suffix for noun phrases meaning 'place of': for example, *gitli* 'dog' becomes *gitlii* 'dog place' (Feeling 1975: 308).
Ꝍ /u/	Verb prefix for third-person subject (Feeling 1975: 320).
Ᏸ /ye/	Noun prefix indicating something nonfactual and verb prefix for negative or conditional 'if' (Feeling 1975: 189).
Ꮗ /hv/	Noun and verb suffix used to form a question (Feeling 1975: 131); verb ending meaning 'but' (Feeling 1975: 294).
Ꮷ /dv/	Verb, noun, and adjective suffix indicating the affirmative (Feeling 1975: 295).
Ꮣ /gu/	Verb prefix for third-person singular, as in *guhisdiha* 's/he is accusing her/him' (Feeling 1975:125).
Ꮶ /tso/	Root for the number 'three' and all ordinals (Feeling 1975: 228–33); verb prefix meaning 'relative' (Feeling 1975: 134) and noun prefix also showing relation, as in *tsosdadahnvtli*, 'my fellow brother' (Holmes and Smith 1976: 165).
Ꮖ /quo/	Root for the number 'seven' (Feeling 1975: 227).
Ꮔ /nu/	Verb prefix meaning 'already,' as in *nugahnanoi* 'it had already rained' (Feeling 1975: 245).
Ꮎ /na/	Interjection meaning 'here' (Feeling 1975: 146, 344); pronoun suffix meaning 'that,' 'those,' and 'what about *x*?' (Feeling 1975: 146).
Ꮈ /lo/	With *i* as a verb suffix means repetitive (Feeling 1975: 284), as in *uwonisiloi* 's/he reportedly spoke over and over.'
Ꭻ /yu/	Root meaning 'really' and 'very' when used with *do* or 'truth' when used with *du* (Feeling 1975: 86).
Ꮟ /tse/	Verb prefix indicating a negative command, as in *hesdi tsenvnili* 'quit/stop, let's you and I not hit him'; also as an 'again' imperative, as in *tsenvniga* 'Let's you and I hit him again.'

Crop of figure I.1 courtesy of Gilcrease Museum, Tulsa, Okla.

Table 2.5. Grammatical Function and/or Meaning of the Fifth Row of
Sequoyah's Syllabary

Character and Sound	Grammatical Function and/or Meaning
Ꮜ /di/	Noun prefix indicating plural and distant position (Feeling 1975:79).
Ꮖ /wv/	Affix meaning 'only' or 'just,' as in *awvsasv* 'by myself' or 'alone' and *dowvno* 'now what?' (Montgomery-Anderson 2007:150).
Ꮣ /du/	Root of numbers 'eleven' through 'nineteen' (Feeling 1975: 334–35); also transitive verb prefix indicating a subject-object relation (Feeling 1975: 281); *duli* is root for the verb 'to want,' as in *aquoduliha* 'I want it' (Feeling 1975: 291).
Ꮥ /de/	Verb prefix for plural object (Feeling 1975: 77, 241), as in *degvniha* 'I'm hitting them [inanimate].'
Ꮬ /tsa/	Verb prefix for second-person singular (Feeling 1975: 134); noun prefix meaning 'who,' 'that,' or 'which' (Feeling 1975: 242).
Ꭵ /v/	Verb suffix indicating past tense when used with *i* (Holmes and Smith 1976: 328; Feeling 1975: 186); *vv* 'yes' (Holmes and Smith 1976: 6).
Ꮕ /nv/	Root of the number 'four,' *nvgi* (Feeling 1975: 227), and 'brain,' as in *unvtsida* 'her/his/its brain' (Feeling 1975: 311).
Ꮼ /te/	Interrogative verb suffix (Feeling 1975: 293).
Ꮉ /ma/	Root for 'water' and 'salt'; also in *kamama* 'butterfly' (Feeling 1975: 195) and *kamama* 'elephant' (Feeling 1975: 200).
Ꮡ /su/	Root for the number 'six,' as in *sudali* (Feeling 1975: 227).
Ꮏ /tlu/	Root for verb 'to split,' as in *tastluyasga* 's/he/it is splitting it' (Montgomery-Anderson 2007: 370).
Ᏸ /he/	Root for 'happy,' as in *haliheliga* 'you are happy'; also used in future tense of some transitive verbs, such as *unehesdi* 's/he/it will have a liquid in hand' (Holmes and Smith 1976: 324).
Ꮵ /ho/	Verb prefix for second-person singular (Feeling 1975: 129); varies with pronunciation rules.
Ꮊ /mi/	Root for *gagami* 'cucumber'; also used for English words, such as *mitsigani* 'Michigan' (common).

Crop of figure I.1 courtesy of Gilcrease Museum, Tulsa, Okla.

Table 2.6. Grammatical Function and/or Meaning of the Sixth Row of
Sequoyah's Syllabary

Character and Sound	Grammatical Function and/or Meaning
Ɫ /tla/	Adverb meaning 'no, not' on its own; also negates verbs to mean 'never' and nouns, as in *tla gohusdi* 'nothing' or *hla ilvtlv* 'nowhere' (Feeling 1975: 130).
⟨ɔ /ya/	Root meaning 'person,' as in *agasya* 'man' (Feeling 1975: 318), and 'pure' or 'real' (Feeling 1975: 310), as in *ayvwiyai* 'pure person,' 'Indian.'
Ꮐ /wa/	Verb prefix indicating movement away from the speaker (Feeling 1975: 241, 244).
Ꭷ /ti/	root of verb 'to see,' as in *aquotiha* 's/he/it sees her/him/it' (Feeling 1975: 299).
Ꮮ /tle/	Part of the root for 'revenge' (Montgomery-Anderson 2007: 232; Feeling 1975: 161), as in *utlega* 's/he took revenge' (Feeling 1975: 161).
Ꮏ /hna/	Verb suffix meaning just finished in the recent past (Feeling 1975: 285); also root for *uhna* 'there.'
Ꮕ /quu/	Noun and verb suffix meaning 'only,' 'just,' 'still' (Feeling 1975:129).
Ꮪ /dla/	Root of the verbal 'opening,' as in *udlanvda* 'there's an opening'; *udlanvda de ha* 's/he has time [opening in her/his schedule]'; and also of the verb 'disbelieve,' as in *udla sitveha* 's/he's disbelieving' (Feeling 1975: 161).
Ꮝ /me/	Used for English words, as in *meli* 'Mary'; most words that include /m/ sounds are borrowed from English (Montgomery-Anderson 2007: 42).
Ɛ /quv/	Perhaps an elision of or verb prefix for 'I' when preceded by a vowel (Feeling 1975: 277).

Crop of figure I.1 courtesy of Gilcrease Museum, Tulsa, Okla.

way, I hope to show that this polysynthetic language requires a writing system that speakers can use to represent implicitly meaningful elements of the language.

A final caveat: these tables by no means exhaust the meaning potentials of each character. They only demonstrate that each character can potentially relate to various kinds of meaning. Depending upon its location in the verb or noun phrase and the context of other words, a character may activate one potential meaning over another.

For example, the character Ꮖ /ha/ in the verb phrase below functions as a reflexive pronoun for the future tense: 'you are tying it up,' but the same character Ꮖ /ha/ at the end of the verb phrase means that the action is happening in the present: ᏆᏜᎢᏆ /halviha/ (Feeling 1975: 258).

This analysis simply lays out the syllables and glyphs to show that each glyph represents not just a sound unit but a grammatical function and/or semantic meaning as well. The arrangement of Sequoyah's syllabary does not appear to reveal any manifest logic in the types of linguistic information that each glyph imparts. Similar analysis that involved reading Sequoyah's syllabary (see fig. I.1) from top to bottom and in columns showed no discernible logic in the semantic meaning and grammatical function of these glyphs. They may be arranged in order of frequency of use in day-to-day speech, but further research is needed to substantiate this preliminary finding. While it does stand to reason that "there is a mnemonic pattern structuring Sequoyah's list," my analysis and Bender's work have yielded no concrete evidence of a mnemonic pattern that would organize the "specific content that is associated with each character" (Bender 2002: 124). But this analysis does provide initial and necessary evidence for Bender's claim that a correlation might exist between each syllable and meaning. The Cherokee writing system includes both phonemic and morphemic information.

HOW THE CHEROKEE WRITING SYSTEM INDICATES MEANING

As noted above, the glyphs for each syllable can potentially indicate sound as well as semantic and grammatical information and thus impart elements of the Cherokee worldview. Hence the sounds of each syllable are the most superficial level of representation. If the syllabary does have the ability to represent morphographic elements as this analysis suggests, then learning the syllabary would indeed aid in cultural perseverance because the glyph could potentially represent idea plus function plus sound. To illustrate, it might be worthwhile to work with simple words in Cherokee in order to ferret out literal meanings.

Beginning Cherokee by Holmes and Smith (1976) provides literal translations of verbs in ways that illustrate how phonemes work in this language. A literal translation of each of the glyphs of the verb phrase ᎤᏒᏁᎳ, /wiganela/ 'she is living away from the speaker' demonstrates how the syllabary is linked to the semantic and grammatical meanings of each syllable uttered. For instance, working from the verb base /ne/, meaning 'to inhabit or live within,' they show how the verb phrase ᎤᏒᏁᎳ /wiganela/ is built with subsequent affixes:

ᎤᏒᏁᎳ	Ꭴ /wi/ the action of the verb points away from the speaker
	Ꮢ /ga/ 's/he/it' as subject
	Ꮑ /ne/ 'to live'
	Ꮃ /la/ 'is happening now'

This word in total means that a singular third-person subject ('s/he/it') is living away from the place where the speaker currently is: for example, a speaker who lives in Michigan speaking of her sister in California (see Holmes and Smith 1976: 188–91 for more examples). In this way the syllabary codifies eighty-six meaningful units, grammatical markers, and phonemes, not just sounds.

Holmes and Smith offer a few literal translations based on the syllables for nouns that stem from verb phrases, such as ᏗᏥᎣᎯᎯ / ditiyohihi/, which literally means 's/he/it argues repeatedly with a purpose.' ᏗᏥᎣᎯᎯ /ditiyohihi/ refers to lawyers who are characterized by their actions of arguing frequently and with purpose (vi). Literal translations of Cherokee help to show the meaning behind each of the syllables, the syntax, and one facet of the cultural logic of the tribe that describes people in part by what they do.

Each Cherokee verb phrase is a complete sentence that has specific rules governing where syllables can be used. In their simplest form, verb phrases can include prefixes, verb roots, and suffixes in rule-governed order (the word's morphology). The order of characters within a word and the morphological information they carry in conjunction with each other activate specific meaning potentials in each syllable and in the word. To decode Sequoyan, we must move beyond the sound-character correspondence and understand meaning created between syllables, ordered correctly within the word, arranged correctly with other words, and all related to the physical and conceptual context of the whole written statement. Thus the verb phrases carry tremendous informational weight in Cherokee.

Each part of the Cherokee verb phrase provides information that helps listeners and readers picture who is doing what action with whom in what contexts and when. The information is sequenced in a predictable order:

1. three-part verbs showing who, what, and when.
2. four-part verbs showing
   a. where, who, what, and when
   b. who, what, how, and when
3. five-part verbs showing
   a. where, who, what, how, and when
   b. who, to or with whom, what, how, and when
4. six-part verbs showing
   a. where, who, to or with whom, what, how, and when.

Not all verbs paint detailed pictures, so it's best to start with the simplest of these verb phrases, which show who is doing what and when. These verbs can be thought of as taking no objects and showing no reflexivity and have the components shown in table 2.7.

The simplest Cherokee verbs have ten ways to count person, an infinite numbers of actions, and at least ten commonly used tenses. Two sets of prefixes are commonly used to count person (Feeling 1975 refers to them as set A and B pronoun prefixes). These prefixes use slightly different pronouns depending upon the beginning sound of the verb root. Table 2.8 shows paradigm-A pronouns with verb roots that begin with consonants, while table 2.9 shows paradigm-A pronouns with verb roots that begin with vowels.[6] Note that no transliterations are included in these tables. The reason for this will become more apparent in the next chapter; suffice it to say here that

Table 2.7. Cherokee Verb Phrases and Their Names

	Who	*What*	*When*
Common Name	Person/People	Action	Time
Grammatical Name	Subject Pronoun	Verb	Tense Marker
Linguistic Name	Pronoun Prefix	Verb Stem	Suffix

Note: These intransitive verbs typically have no objects and are not reflexive.

Table 2.8. Cherokee Verb Phrases Showing Set-A Prefixes with Roots That Begin with Consonants

| | | | *Cherokee Verb Phrases Showing Who + What + When* | | | | |
| | | | Person + Roots Beginning with Consonants + **Present Time** | | | | |

Person (Set A)		B()T 'enter'	ᏧᎯ 'speak'	ᎪᎿᏴ 'read'	ᏍᏬ 'bake'	ᎬᏬ 'fall off'	ᏪᏃ 'appeal'
ᏣᎳᎩ	ᎰᎾᏍ						
Ꮮ	I	ᏆᏴᏯᏪ	ᏆᏬᎮᏪ	ᏆᎪᎿᏴ	ᏆᏍᏬᏃᏍ		ᏆᏪᎿᎲᏪ
Ꭿ	You	ᎭᏴᏯᏪ	ᎭᏬᎮᏪ	ᎭᎪᎿᏴ			ᎭᏪᎿᎲᏪ
S or D	S/he/it	ᎠᏴᏯᏪ	ᏍᏬᎮᏪ	ᎠᎪᎿᏴ			ᎠᏪᎿᎲᏪ
Th	You & I	ᎢᏂᎡᏴᏯᏪ	ᎢᏂᎡᏬᎮᏪ				ᎢᏂᎡᏪᎿᎲᏪ
ᎣᏍᎫ	S/he & I	ᎣᏍᎫᏴᎠᏴᏯᏪ	ᎣᏍᎫᎡᏬᎮᏪ		ᎣᏍᎫᏍᏬᏃᏍ	ᎣᏍᎫᎬᏃᏍ	ᎣᏍᎫᏪᏪᎿᎲᏪ
ᏙᎫᎫ	You, 2	ᏙᎫᎫᏴᎠᏴᏯᏪ	ᏙᎫᎫᎡᏬᎮᏪ			ᎢᏙᎫᏍᏬᏃᎫ	ᏙᎫᎫᏪᎿᎲᏪ
ᏔᎫ	We, 3+	ᏔᎫᏴᏯᏪ	ᏔᎫᏬᎮᏪ				ᏔᎫᏪᎿᎲᏪ
ᎣᏙᎫ	Others & I	ᎣᏙᎫᏴᎠᏴᏯᏪ	ᎣᏙᎫᎡᏬᎮᏪ				ᎣᏙᎫᏪᏪᎿᎲᏪ
ᏘᎫ	You, 3+	ᏘᎫᏴᏯᏪ	ᏘᎫᏬᎮᏪ				ᏘᎫᏪᎿᎲᏪ
Dh	They	ᏓᎭᏴᏯᏪ	ᏓᎭᏬᎮᏪ	ᏓᎭᎪᎿᏴᎦ			ᏓᎭᏪᎿᎲᏪ

(continued)

Table 2.8.—*continued*

Cherokee Verb Phrases Showing Who + What + When

Person (Set A)		BᎤᎢ 'enter'	Ꭴh 'speak'	AᏁB 'read'	SᎥ 'bake'	GᎥ 'fall off'	WᎥ 'appeal'
				Person + Roots Beginning with Consonants + Future Time			
GWY	ᎭᎠS						
Ꮢ	I	ᏂᎢBᏫ	ᏂᎢᏬhᏫ	ᏂᎢAᏢᏰᏗ	ᏂᎢTSh	ᏂᎢGᏫ	ᏂᎢWᏫᏫ
Ꭿ	You	ᏓBᏫ	ᏝᏬhᏫ	ᏣAᏢᏰᏗ	ᏣSh		ᏓWᏫᏫ
Ꮝ or Ꮫ	S/he/it	ᎤBᏫ	ᎤᏚᏬhᏫ	ᎢᎠᏢᏰᏗ	ᎤSSh		ᎤWᏫᏫ
Th	You & I	ᎤᏂBᏫ	ᎤᏂᏬhᏫ		ᎤᏂSh		ᎤhWᏫᏫ
OᏬᎷ	S/he & I	ᎤᏂᏬᏈBᏫ	ᎤᏂᏬᏗᏬhᏫ				ᎤᏂᏬᏗWᏫᏫ
TᏬᎷ	You, 2	ᎶᏗᏈBᏫ	ᎶᏗᏬhᏫ				ᎶᏗWᏫᏫ
TᎷ	We, 3+	ᎢᏗBᏫ	ᎢᏗᏬhᏫ				ᎢᏗWᏫᏫ
ᏬᎵᎢ	Others & I	ᎤᏂᏘBᏫ	ᎤᏂᏘᏬhᏫ				ᎤᏂᏘWᏫᏫ
ThᎢ	You, 3+	ᎤᏂBᏫ	ᎤᏂᏬhᏫ				ᎤᏂWᏫᏫ
Dh	They	ᏓᎯBᏫ	ᏓᎯᏬhᏫ	ᎤᏂAᏢᏰᏗ	ᏓᎯSh	ᏓᎯGᏫ	ᏓᎯWᏫᏫ

Note: This table shows the consistent pattern of pronouns used in these verb phrases. All of the verb roots shown here are intransitive (they don't have objects).

All future tenses begin with /da/ Ꮣ and end with T, showing that the action is approaching the speaker in time. When Ꮣ is used alone as a verb prefix, it indicates that the action is starting at a distance from the speaker and approaching.

Use the blank columns to practice with similar verb roots, such as ᏬᏚᎵ 'open' (use the verb endings for 'go'), ᎬᏙᏬ 'paint' (which adds Ꮝ to root in present tense and Ꮰ in future tense), or ᏨᏯ 'bail' (use the verb endings for 'go').

Table 2.9. Cherokee Verb Phrases Showing Set-A Prefixes with Roots That Begin with Vowels

			Cherokee Verb Phrases Showing Who + What + When					
			Set-A Personal Pronouns + Roots Beginning with Vowels + Present Time					
GWY ᎠᎾᏍ	ᎠᎾᏍ	()DhY 'leave'	GWY Ꭱ	ᎠᎾᏍ	RS 'go'	GWY Ꭳ	ᎠᎾᏍ	()ᏍᎪᏗᎬᏗ 'approve'
GWY Ꭰ	I	ᏍᎭᏯᎢ	Ꭾ	I	ᎯᏍ	Ꭰ	I	ᎠᏒᎬᏗᎢ
Ꭴ	You	ᎤᎭᏯᎢ	Ꭲ	You	ᎢᏍ	Ꭲ	You	ᎢᏒᎬᏗᎢ
D or Ꮝ	S/he/it	DhᏯᎢ	R or Ꭽ	S/he/it	R.Ꮝ	A or Ꭳ	S/he/it	A ᎦᏒᎬᎬᎢ
ᎥᎶ	You & I	ᎢᎣᎭᏯᎢ	ᎢᏞ	You & I	ᎢᎥᏍ	ᎢᏃ	You & I	ᎢᏃᎬᏗᎢ
ᎰᎣᏡ	S/he & I	ᎥᎣᏢᎭᏯᎢ	ᎣᎣᏞᏢ	S/he & I	ᎥᎣᎥᏍ	ᎥᎣᎥ	S/he & I	ᎥᎣᎥᎬᏗᎢ
ᏙᎣᏡ	You, 2	ᏙᎣᏢᎭᏯᎢ	ᏙᎣᏞ	You, 2	ᏙᎣᎥᏍ	ᏙᎣᎥ	You, 2	ᏙᎣᎥᎬᏗᎢ
ᏫᏞ	We, 3+	ᏔᎭᏯᎢ	ᏔᏍ	We, 3+	ᏔᏍᏍ	ᏔᎠ	We, 3+	ᏔᏞᎬᏗᎢ
ᎥᏣ	Others & I	ᎥᎦᎭᏯᎢ	ᎥᏤ	Others & I	ᎥᎥᏍ	ᎥᎬ	Others & I	ᎥᎬᎬᏗᎢ
ᏔᏣ	You, 3+	ᏔᎦᎭᏯᎢ	ᏔᏫ	You, 3+	ᏔᎥᏍ	ᏔᎬ	You, 3+	ᏔᎬᎬᏗᎢ
ᎠᎣ	They	ᎠᎣᎭᏯᎢ	ᏛᏞ	They	ᎠᎭᏍ	ᎠᎭ	They	ᎠᎭᎬᏗᎢ

Note: This table shows the consistent pattern of pronouns used in these verb phrases. All of the verb roots shown here are intransitive (they don't have objects).

In Cherokee the vowel sounds of the roots are bridged with consonant sounds from the subjects, showing who is doing what action when. The subjects are the same as the subject pronouns from table 2.8 except that they combine with the sounds from the verb roots, D, R, Ꭳ (/a/, /e/, and /o/).

using only the syllabary clarifies how the visual information of each character becomes reinforced through repetition.

Just as character order within a word activates meaning potentials of a syllable, the word order (syntax) activates the meaning of a sentence. For example, both ᎠᎫ /s/ and Ꮆ /ge/ are verb suffixes that indicate questions, but the word order of the sentence dictates which suffix is used when asking a person to identify this or that. In the sentence ᏫᏗᏎᎦ ᎤᏬᏗᎨᎮ /yonegas uwodigeke/ 'is it white or brown?' the ᎠᎫ /s/ at the end of the first word indicates a "this" question, while the Ꮆ /ke/ at the end of the second word indicates a "that" question. A character's meaning potential is activated by its location both within a word (the interrogative markers ᎠᎫ /s/ and Ꮆ /ge/ predictably come at the end of the word) and within a sentence (the ᎠᎫ /s/ character predictably comes in the first word of the sentence, while the Ꮆ /ke/ comes on the second word).

THE IMPLICATIONS OF USING A MORPHOGRAPHIC AND SYLLABIC WRITING SYSTEM

Why might it matter that Sequoyah ended up choosing this particular form of representation over others that he systematically tested? Choosing the syllable-character correspondence the way he did increased the representation potential of each character. More than simply representing sounds, this system has the potential to represent deep levels of meaning. Henry Rogers (2005) provides a useful view of the relationships of writing, sound, and meaning. Linguists identify five levels of meaning in a language:

1. semantics (the structure of meaning),
2. syntax (the word order of sentences),
3. morphology (the structure of words),
4. phonology (the structure of the sound system), and
5. phonetics (the detailed representation of sounds). (280–84)

Semantics, syntax, and morphology involve the deeper levels of language, rich in meaning, while phonology and phonetics impart less meaning, dealing with the sound systems of the language. Analysis of the Cherokee syllabary—even the categorization of it as a syllabary—presumes that it is only necessary to analyze it at the shallowest linguistic levels. Characters represent sounds: end of story.

But the Cherokee writing system can actually represent four out of five of these levels of meaning outlined by linguists. While most writing systems relate to the words and sounds of their languages, each Cherokee glyph potentially communicates sounds as well as semantic, morphological, and syntactic meaning. This depth of linguistic information is unusual. Rogers (2005: 281) notes that "units of writing are commonly related to both morphology and phonology, but not generally to semantics, syntax or phonetics." A native speaker of Cherokee knows what meaning a written or spoken syllable can carry, given its position in a verb or noun phrase.

Linguists have studied the segmentation of Cherokee syllables into their morphemic functions by looking at verb structures (Reyburn 1953a, 1953b, 1954; Pulte 1985; Scancarelli 1992) and exploring their linguistic acculturation (King and King n.d.); curiously, though, linguists have not made the connection between the meaningful potentials of each syllable and the writing system. Often linguists simply refer to the writing system as a syllabary, or in some cases an alphabet, but never acknowledge its morphographic qualities. This may be because they have focused on parts of speech, phonetics, and speech in general as opposed to writing systems.

Defining this writing system based upon the common notion that the glyphs represent only the syllables provides a limited view of the syllabary, influenced by its possible similarity to alphabetic literacy. Holmes and Smith (1976: 8), for instance, incorrectly define a syllabary as a type of alphabet: "A syllabary is a variety of alphabet in which each letter in a word stands for a whole syllable . . . instead of a brief sound." To be fair, they were probably trying to compare this writing system to the one they presumed their audiences were most familiar with, as Worcester did with his "systematic arrangement" of the characters.

Incorrectly grouping the Cherokee syllabary into a category of alphabets reduces the instrumentality of this system and obscures understanding of the language. More recently linguists have begun to appreciate the ways in which this writing system communicates linguistic information. As Brad Montgomery Anderson (2007: 18) notes,

"While the syllabary does not express some crucial distinctions, it does often provide information as to the underlying structures of words before the application of phonological changes." He goes on to describe some of the linguistic benefits of the syllabary, but only at the phonological level of meaning. Most of his discussion of the syllabary rests on pronunciation rules and tonal distinctions not represented by the writing system (93–98). Focusing solely on the sound systems, linguists have presumed that the instrumental workings of writing systems must be similar to those of an alphabet and that the writing systems can only work through letter-sound correspondence.[7]

Ultimately, it is not simply glyph-to-sound correspondence that may have contributed to the widespread dissemination and transference of the Cherokee writing system. When the syllabary was first introduced, Cherokee native speakers could have learned the sounds of the writing system simultaneously with meaning, syntax, and rules for syllable orders within verb and noun phrases. For many Cherokees, as Bender (2002: 129) notes, "the syllabary is treated with such respect and seen as such a bearer of linguistic accuracy and knowledge, then, not because as in English, writing is seen as the *representation* of a standard pronunciation, but rather because it is seen as *being* a standard—itself a source of semantic and historical encoded information" (emphasis in original). The analysis presented here confirms Bender's observation and was confirmed by the language teachers and users with whom I spoke: reading and writing in Sequoyan codifies linguistic information in ways that may not be transparent to users and learners who only think of it as a syllabary. The first learners of Sequoyan would have linked the meaning, logic, perspective, location, and time to the sound and character of each syllable. In other words, the syllabary is useful for Cherokee perseverance because it presents meaningful linguistic, historical, and cultural information each time it is used.

USE OF A MORPHOGRAPHIC SYSTEM
AND LANGUAGE PERSEVERANCE

Thus the analysis of Daniels and Bender, the Cherokees in Oklahoma with whom I've worked to learn the language, and the linguistic study of Cherokee all confirm that reading and writing with the syllabary is a process of gathering meaning, not just sound, from each syllable. When Sequoyah finally chose to have a character represent a sound unit, he captured the inherent structure of this polysynthetic language. Polysynthetic languages carry meaning potentials in most syllables, while isolating languages, like English, have comparatively fewer morphemes. With a structure that predictably occurs in consonant-vowel/consonant-vowel combinations, Cherokee morphemes can be as short as one sound unit; thus any character paired with these bounded sound units will correspond to one- or two-unit morphemes. The letters of the alphabet do not match morphemes, requiring one letter for each consonant and each vowel. Therefore it takes more letters to write in English than it takes characters to write in Cherokee.[8]

Given the historical context in which the Cherokee writing system was created and the amazingly deep ways in which it works to represent language, it's safe to say that it is not just a syllabary after all. Sequoyan represents the workings of the Cherokee language in many ways, having the qualities of syllabic and morphographic systems. The eighty-six individual symbols can potentially represent both syllables and morphemes, the smallest units of meaning.[9] Calling the writing system a syllabary comes close to explaining its mechanics: the glyphs do in fact represent many of the sound units in Cherokee. As this analysis reveals, however, each glyph can also represent a meaningful unit and/or grammatical function in addition to sound alone.

The Cherokee syllabary works much more like a logographic system, such as Chinese, than was previously understood, even though it has a finite number of sound units. In some respects, the Cherokee writing system took advantage of the instrumental force of two representational systems at once, combining the economy of a syllabary with the informational weight of a logographic system.[10]

The standardized arrangement of characters forced Sequoyah's original order (fig. I.1) into an alphabetic one that limits the Cherokee writing system. It was primarily seen as working solely on the level of a character-sound correspondence because the standardized arrangement reinforces that alphabetic bias (fig. 2.1). Viewing the Cherokee writing system in this way obscures much of its meaning potential.

The mistaken belief that the Cherokee writing system is an alphabet or simply a syllabary has implications not only for the teaching and learning of the syllabary but also for understanding the ways in which the original syllabary worked instrumentally. Those outside of the tribe have been inclined to see the Cherokee writing system through an alphabetic lens since its inception. While Worcester was not alone in developing the print version of the syllabary, he did arrange it based on the English language's vowel-plus-consonant pairing, thus forcing it into an alphabetic order. Print versions of the syllabary chart often have the incorrect title "Cherokee Alphabet" (as seen in fig. 2.1). Even the most comprehensive Cherokee language instruction (Holmes and Smith 1976) refers to the syllabary throughout as an alphabet and to each of the characters as a letter. Yet the historical and linguistic evidence suggests that the Cherokee writing system developed separately from the instrumental logics of the alphabet for important reasons.

Granted, this analysis is preliminary and depends upon a great deal of follow-up research that could verify my findings. Research that explores the linguistic weight of characters in verb phrases would reveal the ways in which meaning potential is activated in various morphologies. Such research would include further examples of writing in Sequoyan (especially manuscripts that have yet to be translated), which can show how particular types of knowledge were codified with the script. Finally, translations and analyses of sections of the New Testament in relation to the intersection of the Cherokee worldview and Western religion could prove particularly powerful in revealing how the syllabary codifies a worldview that endures after colonization.

W. A. Phillips was absolutely correct when he said that Sequoyah had disdain for the alphabet (as noted at the beginning of this chapter). This disdain may have come not only from Sequoyah's awareness of the increasing and negative impact of alphabetic literacy on those around him but also from the demonstrated power of developing a system that so closely matches the working of the language. Transliterations of the Cherokee language and reordering of the syllabary into an alphabetic orthography may seem to provide English language users with a useful crutch. But language learners, historians, and theorists of writing systems would do better to understand its profound limits and avoid it, keeping in mind Phillips's (1870: 544) observation that "it is almost impossible to write Indian words and names correctly in English. The English alphabet has not capacity for its expression." The linguistic evidence presented here demonstrates why the Roman alphabet fails the Cherokee language and, more importantly, why Sequoyan so brilliantly represents it.

At the first stage of its development, the syllabary's instrumental logic not only proved useful for codifying linguistic information but might also have contributed to the ease with which it was taught and learned. Given that most people in the tribe learned to read and write Sequoyan within the span of a few years after its introduction, the instrumental logics that took a decade to perfect proved invaluable in linking the characters to the most important units of the language. It is indeed a pity that Worcester's arrangement obscures this map because its primary goal was to make this writing system accessible to English speakers. The instrumental logics of the syllabary helped to ensure its continued use within the tribe: even as its material forms changed, its instrumental logics were retained.

These instrumental logics (noted but never substantiated in previous scholarship on the syllabary) help to explain the systematic ways in which the syllabary worked. They offer at least an initial answer to the mystery of how the tribe might have become literate within a short time without mass education or print. At the beginning stages of its development, Sequoyah's choice not to rely on the orthography of the alphabet had profound consequences for the representational power of the system he invented. The sheer ease of use of the Cherokee syllabary provided language users with an effective, economical, and readily learned means of codifying their language, history, laws, and religions, as subsequent stages of the syllabary's history reveal.

Though Sequoyah's original arrangement reveals no apparent connections to meaning, he surely had a reason for this order. It was taught and used by so many other Cherokees even after print developed that it must have had some logic behind it. So questions still remain: Why did Sequoyah arrange the characters in the order he did? And how might have this arrangement facilitated the learning of a totally new representational technology? The answers to these questions provide evidence of key design features. When coupled with the historic and linguistic evidence presented here and in chapter 1 they paint a picture of why and how Sequoyah chose to eschew the influence of the Roman alphabet when inventing this writing system.

CHAPTER 3

The Syllabary's Design

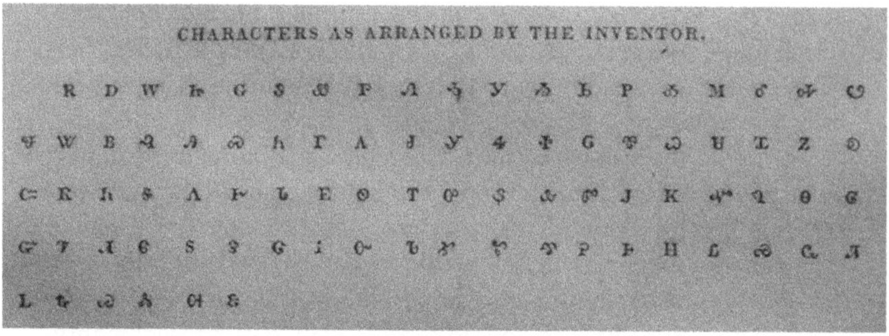

Figure 3.1. Excerpt from the "Cherokee Alphabet" printed in the *Cherokee Messenger* in 1844. This arrangement does follow the order of individual glyphs but fails to follow the precise line breaks used repeatedly by Sequoyah (see fig. I.1).

As an anthropologist who worked fairly closely with Cherokee language and culture at the end of the nineteenth century, James Mooney (1892: 63) had difficulty reading and using the Cherokee writing system, noting that in script the characters "require several strokes in the making." Certainly at first glance the script's design seems arbitrary and complex as Sequoyah originally arranged it. We know that Mooney had help from both Swimmer and Will West Long's mother, Ayasta, in transliterating and translating the approximately six hundred manuscripts he had collected. According to George Ellison (1992: 21), "Every day he worked for up to eight hours with

Long, transliterating all of the formulas, and translating in full the difficult ones that baffled him back home in Washington." Despite working tirelessly for years to understand the language and being immersed in it, Mooney never felt comfortable learning the syllabary.

To those who learn the English alphabet first, the Cherokee writing system can seem far more complex on the face of it, with its eighty-six characters and seemingly arbitrary relation to sound. Even when the syllabary is recognized as a morphographic system, it is still complicated to learn because the design of the characters has no apparent pattern, especially in the longhand form shown on the left side of each cell in figure I.1. In its first evolutionary stage, the Cherokee syllabary in script appears devilishly tricky to those accustomed to the alphabet.

Yet the Cherokee writing system was initially developed, learned, introduced, accepted, and disseminated through the tribe in manuscript form, not print. Historians Willard Walker and James Sarbaugh debunk the myth that the syllabary was introduced in print form in their essay "The Early History of the Cherokee Syllabary" (1993). Using the two important documents attributed to Sequoyah from the John Howard Payne papers (see chapter 1), they confirm that the arrangement of the syllabary as originally produced in manuscript form bears little resemblance to the syllabary in print. According to Walker and Sarbaugh (1993: 79), "It is worth noting that these two manuscripts, attributed to Sequoyah, both present eighty-six characters in the same order. This sequence of characters is confirmed by a third document" (excerpted here in figure 3.1). Though no apparent logic emerged from an examination of the linguistic values of each of the glyphs as arranged in the original, it still stands to reason that Sequoyah's original arrangement may have been logical, for three reasons.

First, the ease with which Cherokees initially learned the system suggests that it must have been logical. We have examined the systematic process by which Sequoyah created this system. In addition, his goal in developing this writing system and his choice to represent himself as a monolingual Cherokee speaker even though he probably had knowledge of English literacy indicate that he was politically motivated to create a system that would be easy to learn and would immediately be useful to the tribe.

Second, the system was consistently arranged in this manner in two different drafts of the writing system that Sequoyah himself produced for John Howard Payne. This arrangement appears again in the version of the syllabary reproduced in the *Cherokee Messenger* (see fig. 3.1), though the newspaper did not follow the line breaks that Sequoyah used. The same arrangement is found in two documents. It occurs in the letters and fiscal papers of ᎢᎾᎵ /Inali/ Black Fox from 1848 to 1881 on a small piece of folded notebook paper that serves as a useful key to his handwriting (Inali [ᎢᎾᎵ] 1848–81). This arrangement also appears in a copy of the syllabary produced by Will West Long, a tribal council member, historian, and linguist of the North Carolina Cherokees who served as primary cultural liaison and translator for Mooney, Frans Olbrechts, and a host of other anthropologists (Witthoft 1948). The copy of the syllabary written by Long in 1947 included the printed characters in the order first arranged by Sequoyah. These reproductions of the syllabary suggest that Sequoyah's original arrangement was still in use as late as 1881 and had been handed down to Long by an elder who taught it to him in Big Cove, North Carolina.

Finally, since the discovery of the handwritten syllabary (fig. I.1), scholars have considered the possibility that some mnemonic or perhaps acrostic may have helped Cherokees learn this system in the more visually complex manuscript form. As Bender (2002: 124) writes, "Sequoyah always wrote the characters out in the same order. . . . It stands to reason that there is a mnemonic pattern structuring this ordered list, but I have not been able to ascertain what it is." Though chapter 2 shows that no specific meaning or set of meanings helped Cherokees learn the syllabary, it makes sense that some sort of logic to the arrangement would have aided learners. Cherokee anthropologist Anna Gritts Kilpatrick and her husband, Jack Kilpatrick, suspected that "Sequoyah's original arrangement of the symbols in his syllabary formed an acrostic which served as a mnemonic aid to the inventor" (Kirkpatrick and Kirkpatrick 1968: 9).[1] While acrostics typically are keyed to semantic content, it is possible that some additional logic was at work in the original arrangement.

If the syllabary had a logic that did not lie in the semantic relation of syllable to glyph, then what system might have influenced its arrangement? Might the manuscript characters (the first form in which the syllabary was learned) provide evidence of a systematic arrangement? Tonia Williams, the Cherokee Nation's webmaster, and I talked about this one day as we were working on a project for the website. We sat in her office (decorated with dozens of drawings, feather fans, cards, photos, and Tasmanian devils of all sizes, neatly arranged). She pulled from her bookshelf a bound notebook that contained every copy of the syllabary she could find, which she had studied in order to create the computer font that the Cherokee Nation had standardized before moving to Unicode (more on this in chapter 8). Turning to the page that contained a copy of the syllabary housed at the Gilcrease Museum (reproduced here in fig. I.1), she mentioned that the original arrangement made some sense to her. At some point in the process of developing the original computer font for the syllabary, she had scripted each of these original glyphs by hand to see if she might be able to use any part of the design in the font. Pointing to the first column of glyphs, she noted: "They all build on these first ones. Well, maybe not all of them. But the patterns begin to repeat as you draw these."

Following her lead, I analyzed each of these glyphs using image-editing software in order to see if they perhaps had an overarching design. First, I created a separate file for each glyph from the high-definition digital reproduction purchased from the Gilcrease Museum. Each glyph was scaled up then traced onto a new layer, using an electronic pen set to draw like a quill. Each digital representation of Sequoyah's original glyphs was layered into one file according to the row in which it appears. This revealed that the angle of stress and stem lines seemed to be consistent for almost all of the glyphs. While that makes some sense given the nature of script, it says nothing about the logic of the arrangement. I considered Tonia's statement again. What if each glyph evolved from the one at the first of each line (shown in figure 3.2)? Could these glyphs have formed an acrostic of sorts, as the Kilpatrick and Kilpatrick (1968) suspected?

While many of the glyphs did resemble each other in angle of stress and length of stem lines, the pattern was inconsistent and incomplete. Encouraged by the modest promise of this finding, though, I analyzed the first row of glyphs from Sequoyah's script (the characters that today are R, ♂, Ɫ, E, Ⱬ, and Ɫ) to see if any pattern emerged.

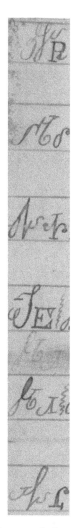

Figure 3.2. The first column of characters in Sequoyah's original arrangement. Courtesy of Gilcrease Museum, Tulsa, Okla.

THE DESIGN OF THE SYLLABARY

Mooney (1900) thought that the Cherokee writing system took too many strokes to create, making writing in script a painstakingly slow process. This is the perspective of someone approaching the script as though it was akin to a set of letters. Sequoyah did not approach the design of these glyphs from this perspective, however, because he disdained English. Though he did know something of the design of letters, he purposely chose other forms of representation to create a uniquely Cherokee writing system. Sequoyah was widely esteemed for his abilities to draw, create portraits, and do silver work even before he created the syllabary. It's possible that his abilities to represent with line and form and in multiple media influenced the invention of the scripted characters. When it is viewed from the perspective of a person drawing shapes rather than as individual letters, the materiality of the syllabary becomes more apparent.

The materiality of alphabetic literacy has been explored in some detail (Havelock 1986; Finnegan 1988; McLuhan and McLuhan 1988; DeFrancis 1989; McLuhan 1994; Faigley, 1999; Christin 2002). Following Marshall McLuhan and Eric McLuhan (1988), Johanna Drucker (1997: 5) finds that "the importance of letters or other written marks is not just that they are material in form but that they bear meaning through their form." This materiality of letters figures prominently in the making of history: "it is obvious that the construction of history depends upon the record retained in both material artifacts and documents—castles and their record books, desks and their papers, objects and their accounts. The meaning of any particular written record is not merely linguistic" (4). Exploring the materiality of a writing system may illuminate ways in which it can aid in the perseverance of language and worldviews. Sequoyah's drawing of the characters of the syllabary could have influenced the learning, rapid dissemination, and retention of the script.

Too often, the scripted syllabary is approached from the perspective of alphabetic systems or seen as a collection of eighty-six arbitrary characters, with no logic to their presentation. When the glyphs are viewed as drawn characters, however, repetitions between shapes emerge throughout the syllabary. The work of perceptual psychologist Rudolph Arnheim is helpful in demonstrating the logics of this visual design, because he understands how shapes become conceptual categories. To begin with, "the shape of an object is depicted by the spatial features that are considered essential" (Arnheim 1954: 48). If Sequoyah was drawing shapes, he would have included clues as to which spatial features of these characters are essential to all the rest; these clues might be found in the six characters that begin each line of his arrangement. Since "we recognize these shapes within the context of other shapes" (49), we cannot recognize these confluences if we view the syllabary as a collection of eighty-six separate characters. These characters need to be recognized within the context of the whole and in relationship to each other (Deloria and Wildcat 2001). Seeing these characters in isolation from each other, like letters, would make the system extremely difficult to learn, especially for those whose first language is English. Each of the characters would seem completely new, without any relationship from one glyph to the next.

Analysis of the visual structure of the syllabary in script (fig. I.1) reveals an internal system in its original arrangement. The design of the syllabary in script—without exception—is keyed to the first character of every row, as seen in figure 3.2. Because the syllabary groups into seven primary forms of characters, memorization of the remaining characters might be much easier.[2] If a native speaker learned these glyphs first, the remaining glyphs would make much more sense because they are repetitions of the root forms, with variations, transpositions, and flourishes to differentiate each shape. Once learned, these shapes would have reinforced the forms, incorporating them into the concepts behind all the other characters. As Arnheim (1954: 97) notes, "Whenever we perceive shape, consciously or unconsciously, we take it to represent something, and thereby to be the form of a content." For example, these individual shapes (❋ ❋ ✳ ✳) share the form or concept of a "snowflake," and these shapes (❋ ✳ ✿ ❀) share the form or concept of a "flower." The seven shapes that begin the six rows of Sequoyah's original arrangement of the syllabary become the forms behind the other glyphs; the similarities and differences between the shapes emerge from these forms.

SEVEN FORMS FOR SEVENTY-NINE SUBSEQUENT SHAPES

The features found in the scripted characters R, ♂, ♄, E, ⅃, Ⴑ (/e/, /le/, /so/, /gv/, /di/, /tla/; see also fig. 3.2) become the concepts behind the remaining glyphs. A brief demonstration of the analysis that led to this conclusion is in order. I hand-traced each of Sequoyah's scripted characters with a digital drawing pad set to quill point (the ink and pen strokes on the page suggest that Sequoyah was using a quill). Each character was then saved as a separate file with layers. Using the transparency function set to 50 percent, each form that might suit the shape was imported then overlaid to establish a structural comparison of the form and shapes. Table 3.1 shows the form Ᏻ /so/ and the shapes that are informed by it. The overlays of these two characters in the third column show the form of Ᏻ /so/ under the shapes of the subsequent characters.

A similar visual analysis was created for each of the eighty-six characters, with the overall results presented in table 3.2. Whenever rotations of characters were made, these were documented in the initial stages of visual analysis. Once similar analytics had been created for all the shapes and their forms, the results were tabulated (table 3.2). The left side of this table shows Sequoyah's arrangement of glyphs in their scripted version alongside a description of each shape's features. The specific glyphs in which these forms appear are shown in the third column. In sum, all subsequent characters use the forms shown in the first column of Sequoyah's arrangement.

These seven base forms could have been understood as roots, with different flourishes indicating each particular shape. Repeated drawing of these forms throughout the learning of the script might have reinforced the learning of the general forms and individual shapes. Seeing these initial characters as drawn shapes that become forms for a whole range of other shapes might have facilitated the quick uptake of the entire syllabary. In effect, the shapes work visually just as the language does morphologically. As Cherokee is a polysynthetic language, words build meaning from roots with the addition of prefixes and affixes to indicate the precise content of the message with an economy of words. Visually, the script uses root forms around which flourishes are affixed to mark difference (table 3.2).

In figure 3.3 each of the base forms is shown on the right next to one similarly shaped glyph on the left. As these images demonstrate, the roots of the forms can be so closely aligned to the subsequent shapes that only small differences in flourishes would be noticed by Cherokee learners, readers, and writers, perhaps adding to the frustration expressed by Mooney (1892: 63): "A number of the characters are so nearly alike that they can scarcely be distinguished even in the most carefully written manuscript."

The seemingly small differences in flourishes might have been sufficient for Cherokee speakers and writers, given the way the

Table 3.1. A Comparison of One Cherokee Character Form and Corresponding Shapes Derived from It

Form	Shape	Shape-Form Overlay	Remarks
/so/ Ꮼ	/lv/		No transformations were needed to show the influence of the overall form on this shape. Note the vertical central upstroke with ornamentations on either side that key the shape of Ꭹ /lv/ to the form Ꮼ /so/.
/so/ Ꮼ	/ni/		No transformations were needed to show the influence of the overall form on this shape. Note the vertical central upstroke with ornamentations on either side that key the shape of Ꮒ /ni/ to the form Ꮼ /so/.
/so/ Ꮼ	/tso/		Tilted 15 degrees counterclockwise to effect the overlay on the form Ꮼ /so/. Fundamentals of the shape and form remain: a vertical upstroke with ornamentations on either side.
/so/ Ꮼ	/yu/		No transformations were needed to show the influence of the overall form on this shape. Note the vertical central upstroke with ornamentations on either side that key the shape of Ᏻ /yu/ to the form Ꮼ /so/.
/so/ Ꮼ	/me/		Flipped horizontally, tilted to account for angle of stress (fig. 3.4). Note the vertical central upstroke with ornamentations on either side that key the shape of Ᏽ /me/ to the form Ꮼ /so/.
/so/ Ꮼ	/quv/		No transformations were needed to show the influence of the overall form on this shape. Note the vertical central upstroke with straight-line serifs on either side that key the shape of Ɛ /quv/ to the form Ꮼ /so/.
/so/ Ꮼ	/ha/		While no transformations were applied, this shape did seem to match the form of Ꮧ /di/. But its manuscript shorthand Ꭽ and the overlay here suggest that it fits at least as well with the form Ꮼ /so/.

Form and shape figures courtesy of Gilcrease Museum, Tulsa, Okla.

Table 3.2. The Visual Mnemonic of Seven Root Forms in the Eighty-six Characters in the Original Arrangement of the Syllabary

Glyph Form	Description of Shape	Characters Using This Form
/e¹/ R. (glyph) **Total: 10**	Central to all glyphs that use circles, half-circles, or curls as stand-alone characters, this shape is the first stem of R. /e/.	G, Ꮾ, Ꮃ, Ꮧ, Ꮻ, Ꮎ, i, Ꮯ, Ꮬ /nah/, /wol/, /ta/, /hv/, /tlu/, /quu/, /que/, /v/, /tsa/, /s/
/e²/ R. (glyph) **Total: 20**	Small loops at the top and bottom of the main stem. An entry tail or flourish leads to the top loop, while the bottom loop exits low on the stem to the flourish.	D, Ꮒ, Ꮽ, Ꮷ, M, Ᏼ, ꭲ, C, Ꮗ, Ꮖ, Z /a/, /wu/, /we/, /si/, /lu/, /yv/, /yo/, /tli/, /qui/, /qua/, /no/ Ꮳ, Ꮝ, Ꮖ, Ꮟ, Ꮒ, Ꮶ, Ꮝ, Λ /tsv/, /ga/, /da/, /i/, /ye/, /na/, /yi/, /o/, /do/
/le/ (glyph) **Total: 11**	Parallel stem strokes, often containing a needle-eye flourish in one stem and connected by a flourish or bridge in the middle.	ꮅ, Ꮽ, Ꭺ, Ꮍ, Ꭼ, G, Ꭶ, ꭹ, Ꮆ, Ꮙ, Ꮏ /li/, /tlo/, /go/, /tsu/, /nu/, /lo/, /ma/, /wa/, /ge/, /mu/, /hna/
/so/ ꮞ **Total: 8**	Flourishes around a central unadorned stem.	Ꮉ, ᏂᏢ, K, G, Ꮝ, Ꮿ, Ꮞ, G /v/, /ni/, /tso/, /yu/, /me/, /quv/, /se/, /mv/

Table 3.2.—*continued*

Glyph Form	Description of Shape	Characters Using This Form
/gv/ E **⟨glyph⟩** Total: 6	Left flourishes lead to a main stem that falls back upon itself.	Ᏼ, Ꭼ, Ᏻ, Ꮩ, Ꮋ, Ꮧ /tsi/, /hu/, /sa/, /tse/, /mi/, /ti/
/di/ Ꭰ **⟨glyph⟩** Total: 15	Larger upper and lower loop around the main stem. The upper loop has no apparent entry point. The lower loop or half-loop exits to a flourish on the right.	Ꮃ, Ꮲ, Ꮂ, Ꮉ, Ꮙ, Ꮥ, Ꮻ, Ꮳ, Ꮎ, Ꮁ, Ꮆ, Ꮀ, Ꮁ /la/, /tlv/, /ha/, /mo/, /dv/, /de/, /nv/, /su/, /u/, /ho/, /ka/, /tle/ Ꮥ, Ꮎ, Ꭺ /hi/, /wi/, /ne/
/tla/ Ꮈ **⟨glyph⟩** Total: 10	The flourish leads to a single upper loop on a straight stem that exits to another flourish.	Ᏹ, Ꭱ, Ꭻ, Ꮺ, Ꮪ, Ꮾ, Ꮛ, Ꭾ, Ꮧ, Ꮞ, Ꮳ /gi/, /sv/, /gu/, /quo/, /du/, /te/, /he/, /ya/, /wv/, /dla/
Grand Total: 86		

Form figures courtesy of Gilcrease Museum, Tulsa, Okla.

The script for /wo/ Ʊ on the left with the form /e¹/ R next to it.

The script for /we/ Ꮺ on the left with the form /e²/ R next to it.

The script for /go/ A on the left with the form /le/ Ꮄ next to it.

The script for /ni/ ꮐ on the left with the form /so/ Ᏺ next to it.

The script for /tsi/ Ᏺ on the left with the form /gv/ E next to it.

The script for /dv/ Ꮫ on the left with the form /di/ Ꮣ next to it.

The script for /he/ Ᏸ on the left with the form /tla/ Ꮈ next to it.

Figure 3.3. A comparison of character shapes with their root forms. Form figures courtesy of Gilcrease Museum, Tulsa, Okla.

language works: one syllable can mean the difference between 'your sister' and 'the sister of the opposite sex to the speaker.' For instance, in figure 3.3 the difference between the root forms of the shape of Ꮫ /dv/ on the left and Ꮣ /di/ on the right would leap out to an eye trained to see minute differences and express these differences with economy. The form Ꮫ /dv/ does not have the lower loop on the stem but is very nearly the same shape as the form Ꮣ /di/.

Again, only when seen in the context of other shapes do the root forms themselves make sense as roots and the shapes make sense as instances of the root. The visual shades of difference between individual characters would parallel the shades of meaning potentials brought forward when each glyph is placed alongside the other. Each character makes sense visually and semantically when placed in relation to the others. This aspect of the scripted syllabary remains the same even when the roots are transposed, transformed in scale, and inverted, as the next set of examples demonstrates.

The script form R /e²/ on the left with the script for ꝺ /di/ on the right.

The script form B /yv/ on the left with the script for ꝺ /ha/ on the right.

The script for Oʃ /me/ on the left with the form Ф /so/ on the right. This side-by-side comparison suggests that Oʃ /me/ mirrors Ф /so/.

This transformation becomes more evident when the characters are flipped horizontally and tilted to account for the angle of stress, with the script for Oʃ /me/ on the left and the form Ф /so/ on the right.

The script for ꝺ /tlu/ on the left with the form R /e¹/ reversed and tilted for the angle of stress on the right.

The influence of the form E /gv/ becomes more evident in the script for ꝺ /ti/ when it is flipped horizontally and tilted to account for the angle of stress.

Figure 3.4. Comparisons of characters showing subtle differences and transformations. Form figures courtesy of Gilcrease Museum, Tulsa, Okla.

Small but important differences in the root forms R /e/ and ꝺ /di/ exemplify the difficulty in viewing this syllabary as a constellation of eighty-six separate and separable characters. The structures of R /e²/ and ꝺ /di/ seen here in the first row and column of figure 3.4 seem similar, especially since both have loops at the tops and bottoms and flourishes to the right of the main stems. Their differences emerge when viewed in the context of additional shapes within the syllabary. The loops at the top and bottom enter and exit the stem in different places. The loops are smaller for the form /e²/, so that more of the main stem is exposed when the bottom loop exits than in the form for ꝺ /di/.

While these shapes are largely similar, the overlaps between them are distinguishable when seen in the context of the other glyph shapes. The script shapes for B /yv/ and Ꮂ /ha/ are shown in the second column of the first row of figure 3.4. While the loops of B /yv/ are similar to those of Ꮂ /ha/, they fill less of the central stem. The loop at the top of B /yv/ begins to the left of the main stem, while the loop at the top of Ꮂ /ha/ begins on the stem, about half-way down. The flourish on the right of B /yv/ includes a loop, while Ꮂ /ha/ has a vertical line in its flourish to the right of the stem. Once they are seen in the light of their subsequent shapes, the other-wise overlooked differences between the forms and shapes of the glyphs will become apparent to a trained eye. It is likely that the Cherokees who learned this script were also learning the visual thinking that Sequoyah demonstrated from a young age. As Arn-heim (1954: 79) suggests: "Comparisons, connections, and separa-tions will not be made between unrelated things, but only when the setup as a whole suggests a sufficient basis. Similarity is a prerequi-site for the noticing of differences." The setup of the syllabary as a whole offers a sufficient basis for noticing the differences between what otherwise appear to be similar shapes. By viewing these glyphs as drawn shapes, Cherokees learning this writing system would have been poised to compare, associate, and differentiate between the forms and shapes. Sequoyah's arrangement of the syllabary sug-gests that the first six glyphs can be seen as seven forms that are the heart of the rest of the shapes.

ROOT FORMS IN UNLIKELY SHAPES

These forms can also be transformed in order to create various shapes. These transformations include tilting the angle, flipping along a vertical or horizontal axis, scaling to different proportions, and rotating the character. For example, the glyph for Ꭳ /me/ seems to mirror the form for Ꮞ /so/, as seen in the second row of figure 3.4. This mirror image was achieved by flipping the character along a horizontal axis and tilting it to adjust for the angle of stress; the mir-ror image of Ꭳ /me/ makes the inherent structure of the form more visible.

Two other examples suggest the kinds of transformations at play in the shapes of the syllabary. As seen in the third row of figure 3.4, the glyph for Ꮏ /tlu/ seems to be a mirror of the looping form found in Form R /e^1/, while Ꭲ /ti/ seems to mirror the horizontal flip of E /gv/. Transformations in scale, angle of stress, vertical and horizontal direction, and rotation do not make a difference in the structural elements underpinning the characters, which are linked to conceptual categories of form more than to specific instances of shape. We can recognize wrens, cardinals, jays, owls, and hawks as all being instances belonging to the conceptual category of birds. They all have wings, beaks, tails, and often featherless legs—structural elements that show they're in the same category. Regardless of whether we see them from the front (standing on the ground), from underneath (in flight), or from the side (perched on a tree limb), their shapes indicate that they belong to the category of bird. Similarly, once they are understood as the structural skeleton of the subsequent glyphs, these seven forms can be found in the remaining shapes, even when transformed.

Arnheim (1954: 90–95) discusses transformations of shape in some detail, referring to art and cognitive psychology to support his main definition of shape and offering the example of a triangle that remains a triangle despite changes in axes. "The structural skeleton of each triangle derives from its contours through the law of simplicity: the resulting skeleton is the simplest structure obtainable within the given shape" (94). No matter what kinds of transformations take place to the shape (such as rotating, inverting, resizing, or altering its angle of stress), the "same structural skeleton can be embodied by a great variety of shapes" (95). Arnheim analyzes the simplest of drawings in order to come to these conclusions about shapes and how they become concepts behind entire categories of objects. The seven glyphs that open each line of Sequoyah's syllabary are forms precisely because they represent the simplest structural elements of the remaining glyphs, "and thereby [are] the form of a content" (96). Transformations of particular shapes do not alter the inherent structure provided by the form: form is a concept, while shape is a particular instance of that concept.

The forms of the glyphs can be found in all of the shapes, so Cherokees would really only be learning seven shapes that then became the forms for constellations of glyphs. In this respect, the materiality of the scripted syllabary had an economy of form that rivals the alphabet. Seven shapes form the basis of the other seventy-nine glyphs.[3] This might help explain one reason why the tribe became fluent in Sequoyan within the span of a few short years with no formal education, mass communication, or print.

VISUAL AND LINGUISTIC INFORMATION: THE FIRST STAGE OF DEVELOPMENT

The very design of the glyphs suggests that Sequoyah was concerned not only with the ways in which Cherokees might learn this writing system but also with the ways in which it could be understood as uniquely Cherokee. Cherokees may well have been able to learn the system, use it, and teach it to others with some ease because seven forms governed the creation of subsequent shapes. Rapid dissemination of this writing system could have been made possible through this visual mnemonic that organized all the glyphs into seven root forms. It would have had a heuristic value if the syllabary was first taught and learned in manuscript form. Cherokee speakers would have been tapping into their already existing visual and linguistic intelligence.

Writing systems scholars have begun to understand the ways in which writing moves beyond the mere recording of sound to include important semantic content (Coulmas 2003) and linguistic elements (Rogers 2005) and to serve as a visual representation that also conveys meaning (DeFrancis 1989) and has materiality (Drucker 1997). Chapters 1 and 2 extend these understandings by establishing the instrumental workings of this writing system in its first iteration, as a script, and suggest possible reasons for the ease with which Cherokees learned it. First, like a morphographic system, Sequoyah's characters can potentially impart linguistic knowledge coupled with the sounds of each syllable. In the Cherokee writing system, the sound and meaning can be attendant upon each other, with neither taking precedence over the other. Further, each glyph is similar to a root form, so that the shapes of seventy-nine characters in the script stem from seven forms. The root forms govern the basic elements of the resulting shapes in the syllabary, so it would only have been necessary to learn a basic set of stems and flourishes to be able to write in longhand with the syllabary.

At its initial phase of development, the Cherokee syllabary conveys much more linguistic and visual information than previously understood. From the first moment of its invention, the writing system mapped onto the workings of key facets of Cherokees' linguistic and visual intelligence. As discussed in chapter 2, verb phrases in Cherokee build pictures with each syllable uttered, offering information about who is doing what and when in the simplest of verb phrases. Each verb phrase is a complete thought that can potentially illustrate action, actors, place, time, motion, and abstractions such as habitual behavior across time. Six-part verbs, for instance, depict information with each syllable in the order of where, who, to or with whom, what, how, and when. Every Cherokee language teacher and expert with whom I've spoken confirms the close relationship between spoken and written verb phrases and the ways in which they involve illustrating and visualizing the scene. Given the economical relationship between visual and linguistic information in spoken verb phrases, it makes sense that Sequoyah sought to create a writing system that also incorporates visual information to cue learners. Linguistic intelligence and visual intelligence are closely coupled in the Cherokee language.

As the historical, linguistic, and visual evidence presented in chapters 1 to 3 indicates, the original longhand form of the Cherokee writing system shows no influence from the Roman alphabet in its instrumentality and design. Importantly, none of the longhand forms and shapes bear any resemblance to alphabetic letters. The internal consistency of the longhand glyphs and their coherence as a system marked the syllabary as an invention without an alphabetic influence. As the next chapter shows, these longhand characters influenced the shape and design of the majority of the shorthand characters that would be used for print.

If Sequoyah had even modest facility with the Roman alphabet (and evidence suggests that he had more than a modest facility), then he deliberately eschewed it in favor of a writing system unique to the Cherokee people and language. He chose to create a completely exclusive system. As the process of its creation, its linguistic features, and its design illustrate, his invention of the syllabary was a political statement of Cherokee self-reliance as much as it was a tool for his people. Sequoyah could have included designs or instrumental features of the Roman alphabet at any point along the way but chose not to. The lack of Western influence represented practical and political choices.

The quick spread and wide use of the syllabary by the tribe played a key role in signaling to outsiders the intellectual ability of Cherokees, who now had a marker of their civilization that equaled the alphabet. Within the tribe, Sequoyan facilitated communication and connections among Cherokees despite massive land loss, increasing encroachment of whites and their culture, internal fractionalization, and voluntary westward migrations. Because Sequoyan was learned and used so quickly, Cherokees developed an increased sense of peoplehood and a growing sense of nationalism, as the next chapter demonstrates. Its logics presented Cherokees with a powerful invented tradition through which change could be made on their own terms because it was in their own terms. To help define these terms and disseminate them widely, Cherokees went on to create the designs for typefaces and control a printing press. The second evolutionary phase of the Cherokee syllabary sheds light upon historic events in ways not previously understood and reveals how Sequoyan in print came to mediate cultural change.

CHAPTER 4

The Syllabary from Script to Print

The version of the syllabary in figure 4.1 is ubiquitous: it's sold in gift shops, reproduced on posters, and included in countless books as an illustration of the Cherokee writing system. This arrangement and style of the syllabary is often credited to Samuel Worcester, a missionary who worked tirelessly with the Cherokees in the early 1800s.[1] His peaceful resistance to a Georgia law that forbade whites from entering Cherokee territory without state permission led to a landmark Supreme Court case, *Worcester v. The State of Georgia*. Worcester remains an important historical figure in the Cherokee story. His version of the "Cherokee Alphabet" is the one most commonly seen in Cherokee stores, language resources, and books (Bender 2002). "It is important to note," Bender (2002: 129; emphasis in the original) writes, "that it is largely the *printed* syllabary as codified by Worcester in the *Phoenix* . . . that is seen" by the North Carolinian Cherokees as the standard for linguistic accuracy and historical knowledge. While the print version of the syllabary is commonly credited to Worcester, the scholarly record suggests that it should not be. This inconsistency and the apparent design features of the printed Cherokee syllabary have led some to conclude that the Cherokee writing system was largely based on the alphabet. A closer examination of the evolution of the Cherokee syllabary from its initial manuscript to print forms is needed to clarify the extent to which it may have been

A version of this chapter was published in *Ethnohistory* (Fall 2010).

Cherokee Alphabet.

D*a*	R*e*	T*i*	Ꮨ*o*	O*u*	i*v*
S*ga* Ꮎ*ka*	℉*ge*	Ꭹ*gi*	A*go*	J*gu*	E*gv*
ᕼ*ha*	Ꭾ*he*	Ꭿ*hi*	Ᏺ*ho*	Γ*hu*	Ꮻ*hv*
W*la*	Ꮳ*le*	Ꮅ*li*	G*lo*	M*lu*	Ꭹ*lv*
Ꮣ*ma*	Ꮚ*me*	H*mi*	Ꮽ*mo*	Ꮑ*mu*	
Ꮎ*na* Ꮤ*hna* G*nah*	Ꮕ*ne*	Ꮁ*ni*	Z*no*	Ꮓ*nu*	Ꮕ*nv*
Ꮖ*qua*	Ꮗ*que*	Ꮙ*qui*	Ꮚ*quo*	Ꮖ*quu*	Ꮛ*quv*
Ꮜ*sa* Ꮝ*s*	4*se*	Ꮂ*si*	Ꮠ*so*	Ꮢ*su*	R*sv*
Ꮪ*da* W*ta*	Ꮞ*de* Ꮏ*te*	Ꮧ*di* Ꮨ*ti*	Ꮩ*do*	S*du*	Ꮫ*dv*
Ꮬ*dla* Ꮃ*tla*	L*tle*	C*tli*	Ꮰ*tlo*	Ꮱ*tlu*	P*tlv*
Ꮳ*tsa*	V*tse*	Ir*tsi*	K*tso*	Ꮶ*tsu*	Ꮳ*tsv*
Ꮹ*wa*	Ꮺ*we*	Ꮻ*wi*	Ꮼ*wo*	Ꮽ*wu*	6*wv*
Ꮿ*ya*	Ᏸ*ye*	Ᏹ*yi*	Ᏺ*yo*	Ᏻ*yu*	B*yv*

Sounds represented by Vowels

a, as *a* in *father*, or short as a in *rival*
e, as *a* in *hate*, or short as *e* in *met*
i, as *i* in *pique*, or short as i in *pit*

o, as *aw* in *law*, or short as o in *not*.
u, as *oo* in *fool*, or short as u in *pull*.
v, as *u* in *but*, nasalized.

Consonant Sounds

g nearly as in English, but approaching to k. d nearly as in English but approaching to t. h.k.l.m.n.q.s.t.w.y. as in English. Syllables beginning with g. except Ᏽ have sometimes the power of k.t.s.o. are sometimes sounded to, tu, tv, and Syllables written with tl except Ꮃ sometimes vary to dl.

Figure 4.1. Samuel Worcester's arrangement of the Cherokee syllabary (Mooney 1900: 113).

influenced by the alphabet, by white missionaries, and by the larger sociocultural milieu as it developed into a widely disseminated material form.

A detailed and thoroughly researched essay on the history of the Cherokee syllabary by Walker and Sarbaugh (1993: 70) addresses this very topic, arguing that "the Cherokees alone developed the syllabary and adapted it to the requirements of printing." While their essay should have set to rest any claims to the contrary, recent histories of writing systems and print still erroneously attribute this development to Samuel Worcester. Joseph Thomas of Cornell University credits the creation of the print version of the Cherokee writing system to Worcester and the American Board of Commissioners of Foreign Missionaries (ABCFM). Thomas (2008: 14) claims that Worcester's arrangement of the characters and other changes in the selection of the glyphs point to his authority over the development of the Cherokee syllabary into print: "Samuel Worcester's influence on the standardization of the syllabic characters and the potential for appropriation of native means of expression certainly represent an addition to the scholarly record of American Indian publishing history." This chapter explores the extent of Worcester's influence.

If Thomas (2008: 6) is correct in his description of Worcester's role, then it appears that "the first Cherokee types . . . were not made to correspond to manuscript characters, but rather to conform to some degree with the appearance of already respected typefaces used for English." Yet it is unclear why Cherokees would be motivated to make Sequoyan conform to Roman alphabet typefaces. And if, as Thomas concludes, "the appearance of the Cherokee types was not designed specifically with Cherokees in mind" (6), then for whom were they designed and why? The extent to which the Cherokee writing system in print corresponds to manuscript characters or to the "already respected typefaces" merits further consideration—not only to maintain accuracy in the historical record but, more importantly, to understand the ideological intricacies at play when peoples innovate and alter their writing systems.

At first glance the print version of the Cherokee syllabary certainly appears to be quite distinct from the manuscript version developed by Sequoyah (fig. I.1). To an untrained eye and hand, the script and print characters bear little resemblance to each other. As Walker and

Figure 4.2. Detail of the syllabary that Sequoyah is believed to have produced for Payne in 1839. Courtesy of Gilcrease Museum, Tulsa, Okla.

Sarbaugh (1993: 82) describe it, the "right-hand characters undeniably contrast with those on the left. It is not clear, however, that the right-hand forms can be attributed to Worcester." It does indeed appear that the right-hand glyphs in each of the pairs shown in figure 4.2 and in figure I.1 retain little of the visual information from the characters on the left written in longhand.

Based only on initial observations, then, the Cherokee writing system in print appears to be (1) completely different from the longhand characters originally learned by Cherokees, (2) deeply influenced by the Roman alphabet, and (3) designed with audiences other than Cherokees in mind. With these apparent differences between Cherokee script and print, "how, then," Thomas (2008: 6) rightly asks, "might Cherokees familiar with handwritten versions of the syllabary adjust to the changes necessitated by casting it in type?" If indeed the Cherokee type sets were created to resemble the alphabet, and thus were markedly different from the original manuscript version of the writing system, we might expect a decrease in reading and writing indicators after print arrived on the scene. Such was not the case.[2] These inconsistencies call for a closer examination of the historical evidence. To what extent do the script and print versions of each character of the Cherokee writing system differ? To what extent might the Roman alphabet have inspired the design of the print version of this writing system? And, finally, what was at stake for the tribe as its newly invented writing system made its way from script to print?

These questions matter a great deal, because writing systems are not simply neutral tools used to facilitate day-to-day communication but point to the social processes that influence the formation of group identities. Choices of which scripts to use and when, how to develop and disseminate a new script, and what scripts are to be mandated are all fraught with issues of power, identity, and culture. Research in cross-cultural approaches to literacies explores how literacy artifacts, events, and practices come to be valued by those who use them (Street 1993, 1995; Cushman et al. 2001; Collins 2003; Coiro et al. 2008). In a seminal study of the cognitive and social consequences of Vai script, Sylvia Scribner and Michael Cole (1991) analyze the ideological import of the invention, selection, and continued use of writing systems other than the alphabet.

Sociolinguistic research on writing systems by Mark Sebba (2009: 42) explores the ways in which orthographies are situated in social processes that shape cultures and identities: "The establishment of a script . . . can be a powerful symbol of group membership, identifying the users as belonging to or differing from other groups using the same or different scripts." The alphabetic influence on the development of scripts, Sebba finds, "is not coincidental, nor is it because of some inherent superiority"; it is, rather, a consequence of the script mediators who first introduce the writing system (41). The story of the development of the Cherokee syllabary from manuscript to print is also the story of identity formation and political maneuvering. A closer examination of the evolution of the Cherokee syllabary clarifies the roles that Cherokees played in moving the syllabary from script to print and qualifies claims about the extent to which it may have been influenced by the alphabet, by white missionaries, and by the larger sociocultural milieu.

THE NATURE OF THE CHARACTERS

All of the eighty-six glyphs created in the original syllabary were developed into a shorthand version, though only eighty-five were cast into type. On the changes made from Sequoyah's original syllabary, Worcester (1828a: 162) writes: "The present number is 85; the necessity of one of the characters not having been found sufficient to require that it should be retained. The arrangement of the characters, as made by the inventor, like that of other alphabets, is entirely without system." Thus Worcester describes what were to him negligible changes in the overall number and arrangement of characters from the original manuscript version to the final version in print, except for the deletion of one glyph, which was G /mv/. This would seem to contradict the visual evidence presented in the document that Sequoyah created for Payne (fig. I.1) in which, on the face of it, the manuscript and print versions of the characters seem to be distinct.

To determine the ways in which the design features of the Chero-kee characters might have changed from script to print, I completed a systematic analysis of each glyph pair in the writing system as Sequoyah had demonstrated it to Payne. First, using digital imaging software, each pair of glyphs was copied from a high-resolution im-age of the document provided by the Gilcrease Museum in Tulsa. Sequoyah indicated the boundaries of glyph pairs with vertical zigzag lines and consistently included the script version of the char-acter on the left and the print version on the right. The print version of each glyph pair was compared to the syllabary in Hicks (1825: fig. 4.3) and a conventionalized syllabary chart (fig. 4.1) (Mooney 1900: 113).

Glyphs were then grouped according to visible levels of corre-spondence between the script and printed elements. These levels of resemblance were:

1. direct correspondence, showing clear relationship between the script and print glyphs;
2. some correspondence, showing one or two transformations of visible elements;
3. little correspondence to former scripted glyphs, showing deeply revised or newly invented glyphs created for print;
4. no correspondence to former scripted glyphs and borrowing from an alphabetic glyph.

Table 4.1 includes an overview of the results, showing a compari-son between Sequoyah's script and print designs for each selected glyph. The level of correspondence indicates the number and type of visual elements retained from script to print versions for each glyph. Sixty-seven of the characters retained some visual relation-ship between the print and the original scripted glyph: forty-four of these glyphs had either a direct or some correspondence to the vi-sual elements from original scripted forms, while twenty-three re-tained little visual information. When the glyph showed no corre-spondence, its design features seemed to have been borrowed from the Roman alphabet. Three glyphs, ℎ /ni/, ℱ /yo/, and Ᏺ /tsi/, did not fit conclusively into any of the categories, which is why the total number of glyphs fitting any of categories is eighty-three. Because

Table 4.1. Levels of Correspondence between Glyphs in Script and Print

Level of Correspondence	Characters	Sample Glyph in Script and Print	Analysis
Direct (Total 21)	Ꭶ, Ᏸ, Ꭿ, Ꮝ, Ꮳ, Ꮼ, Ꮯ, Ꭹ, Ꮣ, Ꮖ, Ꮚ, Ꭱ, Ꮟ, Ꮂ, Ꮳ, Ꮧ, Ꮒ, Ꮬ, Ꮩ, Ꭲ, Ꮃ		The top right flourish was retained to create the final print glyph for Ꭴ /ka/ to the left. Other glyphs in this category retained key elements of the original to create the print.
Some (Total 23)	Ꮟ, Ꭷ, Ꮺ, Ꮤ, Ꮃ, Ꮢ, Ꮪ, Ꮴ, Ꮩ, Ꮝ, Ꮵ, Ꮀ, Ꮎ, Ꮞ, Ꮟ, Ꮷ, Ꭾ, Ꮃ, ꭵ, Ꮧ, Ꮯ, Ꮓ, Ꭼ		In the glyph Ꮟ /si/ the flourishes were reduced and replaced by line serifs with circular sweeps made into half-circles. The transformations of the scripted glyphs in this category might have included a selection and amplification of elements (e.g., Ꮪ /ga/ selects the top and bottom ornamentations and adds a horizontal line to replace the middle filigree), an inversion of the script (as Ꮢ /se/ has flipped horizontally), or straightening of lines that were once curved (e.g., Ꭾ /hu/, Ꭲ /qua/, and Ꮓ /no/).
Little (Total 23)	Ꭿ, Ᏼ, Ꮣ, Ꮵ, Ᏹ, Ꮧ, Ꮜ, Ꮤ, Ꮞ, Ꮳ, Ꮣ, Ꮯ, Ꭲ, Ꮽ, Ꮿ, Ꮝ, Ꮣ, Ꮄ, Ꮬ, Ꮦ, Ꮨ, Ᏺ, Ꮙ, ꭼ		The script for Ꮕ /nu/ seems to retain an element from the middle of the first upstroke: a circle that nearly closes upon itself. The transformations of the scripted glyphs in this category may have little correspondence with the original script and instead may represent altogether new shapes.
None (Total 16)	R, Ꮢ, D, W, G /nah/, Ꮅ, Ꮲ, M, B, A, E, T, J, K, H, L		The print version for Ꮭ /lu/ has no correspondence with its original script. All the glyphs in this category seem to have been borrowed from the alphabet.

Glyph figures courtesy of Gilcrease Museum, Tulsa, Okla.

one glyph, G /mv/, was dropped from the entire system when it moved to print, it was also deleted from this comparison.

A total of sixty-seven characters corresponded to the scripted original in some fashion or showed little correspondence to the print version. This would seem to indicate that the print version took its cues largely from the original script forms of the glyphs, making it potentially recognizable to the Cherokee readers and writers who would be the audience for materials printed in the Cherokee language. These sixty-seven glyphs showed no correspondence to the Roman alphabet. Thus 79 percent of the print characters corresponded to visual elements present in the manuscript characters, as opposed to conforming "to some degree with the appearance of already respected typefaces" (Thomas 2008: 6). The majority of the scripted and print characters in Sequoyah's original alphabet were more alike than different, undermining claims that the print versions of these characters were developed in order to appeal to the eye of outsiders.

Historical evidence bears out the results of this visual analysis. In a letter that Worcester wrote to the American Board of Commissioners of Foreign Missions (ABCFM 1827a), he considers which letters might be modeled after the alphabet. Sixteen of the characters could easily be represented with capital letters from the Roman alphabet. In a letter to Jeremiah Evarts, Worcester (1827) specifies that "there will be no occasion for new matrices for sixteen of the characters, viz. R, D, W, G, P, M, B, A, Z, E, T, J, K, S, H, L, as the small capitals of the English fount will answer every purpose." Sixty-nine of the eighty-five glyphs that he sent to the typesetters (81 percent) needed completely new matrices to be developed because they had no counterpart in the existing alphabetic typefaces. The majority of the glyphs used a design drawn from their predecessors in longhand and needed to have new matrices developed for them.

Thus it seems likely that visual cues from the scripted version of the characters might still inform the shape of most of the print versions.

THE INFLUENCE OF THE ALPHABET

But what of those sixteen characters that Worcester suggested would need no new type cast because capital letters of the Roman alphabet might suffice? Does this number of characters that could be replaced

Table 4.2. The Script and Print Versions of S /du/, Λ /do/, and Z /no/

/du/	
/do/	
/no/	

Crops of figure I.1 courtesy of Gilcrease Museum, Tulsa, Okla.

by capital letters suggest a noteworthy influence of the alphabet on the Cherokee writing system? To begin, three of those sixteen glyphs that Worcester mentioned were incorrectly changed by the typesetters: the glyphs for S /du/, Λ /do/, and Z /no/ (see table 4.2).

To an alphabetic eye, the shape of S /du/ was similar to the capital letter "S"; but in Sequoyah's hand it was oriented horizontally, with a stronger emphasis on the serifs, which nearly formed half-circles (as seen in table 4.2). In the print developed by the typesetters, the glyph was oriented vertically, making it appear to be more like the alphabetic letter "S" than originally designed. Likewise, the print version of Λ /do/ was originally developed with longer serifs and was flipped vertically to look more like a pyramid (as it does in table 4.2). In 1834 Worcester himself changed the orientation of that glyph, informing the Missionary Board that he would start using a capital letter "V" for this character (Thomas 2008: 5). Finally, the scripted and print versions of the glyph Z /no/ had little relation to the type cast for this glyph, which was replaced with a capital letter "Z." The original script had an almost vertical line connecting the two serifs at top and bottom, which balanced each other as they extended in opposite directions. The resemblance of these three glyphs to letters of the alphabet seems more imagined than real: the type casters and Worcester necessarily used the forms of letters in the alphabet as their baseline for design judgment.

Examination of the remaining thirteen glyphs that were thought to have been influenced by the alphabet reveals that nine of them actually have elements in common with the original scripted versions, suggesting a logic behind the borrowings. If an element of the capital letter in English could be mapped onto the design elements of the script, it seems to have been borrowed. The first scripted version of the syllables R /e/, D /a/, G /wa/, P /li/, P /tlv/, R /sv/, E /gv/, K /tso/, and L /tle/ have visual elements that carry over to the corresponding print glyphs borrowed from the English alphabet. These visual cues can include the shapes of the glyphs when taken as a whole (as in R /e/, D /a/, and P /li/).

When Sequoyah was inspired by the design elements of alphabetic letters, he apparently borrowed elements that resemble those he developed in the script. These borrowings were difficult for Worcester to illustrate to the type casters, who had to revise several of their original punches to match his illustrations and descriptions of differences. Worcester remarks that "the foundry had to cut 18–20 [punches] anew, and have nearly as many more altered" (quoted in Thomas 2008: 6). The punchcutters had to modify nearly forty punches significantly to create the type set for the Cherokee syllabary. While they were relying upon a small number of punches already at hand for printing done in English, they were also trying to be true to the designs sent to them.

Analysis of the glyphs suggests a modest connection between the Cherokee writing system and the Roman alphabet, with only seven of the glyphs being outright borrowings from the design of capital letters and bearing no resemblance to the original scripted characters. Three Cherokee print glyphs not mentioned by Worcester might have been modeled after the lowercase letter "h" (Ir /tsi/, h /ni/, and ft /yo/); as Thomas (2008: 6) points out, Worcester had taken pains to explain differences in these glyphs to the type casters. Visual analysis and historical records do not clarify the visual heritage of these glyphs.

It seems that Sequoyah might have borrowed the designs for these seven glyphs from the Roman alphabet. Walker and Sarbaugh (1993) quote contemporaries of Sequoyah, most notably John Howard Payne, who had interviewed Sequoyah in 1841 and for whom Sequoyah apparently had written each of the eighty-six original characters in script with its corresponding print character next to it (fig. I.1).[3] According to Payne, "The first characters which he invented resembled German text. Few or none of them were retained. At the house of Mike Waters, he was struck with the 'bible Book' as Waters called it, of Sally Waters, his wife. He was then studying for characters to make use of in print. He copied out some of the letters and said those would do for print & the old ones for writing" (quoted in Walker and Sarbaugh 1993: 84).

Sequoyah was visiting the house of his brother-in-law, Mike Waters, at that time, searching for design ideas for the characters to use in print. Prompted by the shape of the letters in the Bible on the shelf, he seems to have modeled some of his glyphs for print. But he did not choose all of the letters; in fact, he said that the new glyphs "would do for print & the old ones for writing." According to Payne, then, Sequoyah was the most influential person, if not completely responsible for the creation of the syllabary in print. Sequoyah eschewed the English language even though he seems to have been literate in English (see chapter 1), so he chose letters for their shape and their appearance and not their sound correspondence to Cherokee.[4]

The results of the visual analysis of the Sequoyah manuscript (see fig. I.1) suggest the possibility that the printed glyphs may have been modeled after a manuscript shorthand already in use by the tribe before the print was developed. In a letter dated January 14, 1825 (Hicks 1825) addressed to Thomas McKenney, the head of the Bureau of Indian Affairs, Charles Hicks (second chief of the Cherokees) provides a description of all the ways in which the Cherokees "may be considered as a civilized people," with the chief indicator being their development and use of this writing system. At the end of this letter Hicks includes a reproduction of this "alphabet" together with a sample of the transliterations of each of the characters into English phonetics (fig. 4.3). The Hicks syllabary, created before the advent of the print syllabary and arranged in Sequoyah's original order, reveals that the shorthand of the script appeared prior to the creation of the printed characters.

Hicks's shorthand syllabary nearly matches the glyphs that were produced on the right side of each pairing in the syllabary that Sequoyah produced for John Howard Payne, with perhaps one exception: the glyphs for Ꮪ /da/ and Ꮥ /te/ seem to be the same. This letter was penned two years before the Cherokee Nation commissioned the foundry to create a typeface and nine months before Worcester arrived at Brainerd. Walker and Sarbaugh (1993: 91) believe that the Hicks syllabary was an engraver's copy, though Thomas (2008: 6)

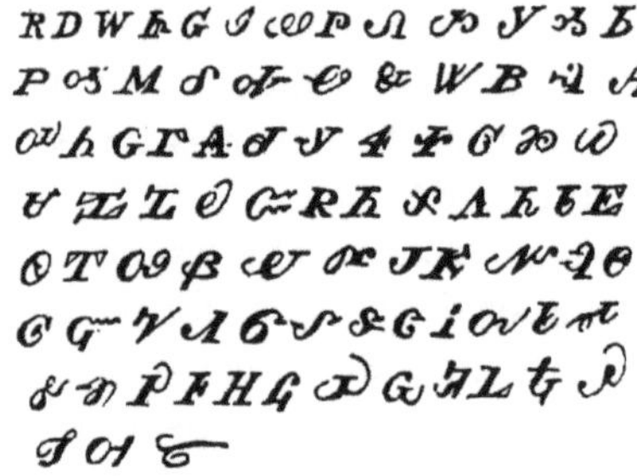

Figure 4.3. A handwritten syllabary produced by Chief Charles Hicks in a letter to Thomas McKenney of the Bureau of Indian Affairs in 1825, two years before type sets were cast for the Cherokee syllabary, suggesting that the typecasts were modeled after a manuscript shorthand already in use (Hicks 1825).

argues that "Barbour had this syllabary engraved and printed to support his report to Congress." In any case, if this shorthand of the Cherokee cursive was in use before the models for these characters were sent to the foundry, then the print version of the syllabary would have been immediately recognizable to Cherokees.

While manuscript forms of Cherokee handwriting dating before 1827 are rare, the Inali manuscripts collected by James Mooney and housed in the Smithsonian Institution's National Anthropological Archives (Inali [ᎢᎾᎵ] 1848–81) provide evidence of the existence of a shorthand manuscript form in use after Cherokee became available in print. Kilpatrick and Kilpatrick (1966) first suggested this possibility in "Chronicles of Wolftown," in which they describe the handwriting in the Inoli/Inali (Black Fox) manuscripts that had been gathered in North Carolina from the Eastern Cherokees. The manuscripts in this collection were produced roughly from 1849 to 1884 and reveal a handwriting style that appears to have been little influenced by printed Cherokee. According to Kilpatrick and Kilpatrick (1966: 8), "In general, the calligraphy is inferior to that of Western Cherokee manuscripts of the same period. We suggest that this is due to less familiarity with printed Cherokee. The presses were in the Cherokee Nation, not Qualla." The Inali manuscripts (Inali [ᎢᎾᎵ] 1848–81) seem to have been penned with little influence from the print forms, suggesting to the Kilpatricks that "Eastern Cherokee calligraphy of Inoli's day more closely resembled the original concepts of

Sequoyah than did the Western which was patterned upon the type faces" (8, also quoted in Walker and Sarbaugh 1993: 82).

These manuscripts contain a total of three syllabary charts in Inali's hand, arranged according to Sequoyah's original order. All the characters are indeed less influenced by the standardized print version of the Cherokee syllabary, except Λ, which matches Worcester's changed orientation. The shape and style of the characters more closely match the shorthand model demonstrated by Sequoyah on the right side of each cell in figure I.1, with the following exceptions: Ɫ /tla/ is inverted, Ꙃ /de/ approximates Sequoyah's longhand version, and V /tse/ and Ꙗ /qui/ resemble neither version and appear to be self-styled. This suggests that a shorthand more closely related to Sequoyah's original designs of the characters had developed from reductions to the longhand version and was still in use even after print had been developed.

Given this visual analysis and historical evidence, a number of points can be made regarding the process by which this writing system developed from script to print. First, the design of the print version of the syllabary seems more closely related to the original longhand manuscript version of the syllabary than was previously understood. This makes sense: the creator of the writing system was interested in facilitating ease of learning and use of the writing system, so major changes between the two forms of script and print would have been inconsistent with this goal. Given the number of glyphs that carry forward from script to print, Cherokee readers might easily have recognized the syllabary in print as a shorthand of the Cherokee cursive. This continuity between longhand and shorthand suggests that Cherokees had already become accustomed to using a shorthand manuscript form developed from the longhand.

Second, Sequoyah himself had a considerable role to play in ensuring that the designs for type were based on his original. Importantly, these designs had little relation to alphabetic ones, with the majority of the glyphs resembling some aspect of the original longhand characters. When any letters were borrowed from the alphabet, they seem to have been chosen because they showed some correspondence to the original longhand. Although the characters look alike to some scholars and current language learners and may seem to have relied on the Roman alphabet, that was not the case. The designs of these characters owe their visual heritage to the original longhand and shorthand already in use.

This means that the role that Samuel Worcester played in developing the print version of the Cherokee writing system has been largely overstated. Worcester's contributions to the Cherokee Nation's maintenance and formation of a political identity are undeniable. He was central in bringing the Cherokee removal and the Georgia state militia's infringement into the national limelight. Moreover, his research on the Cherokee language to be used in missionary materials has had lasting impact for English speakers and Cherokees who use the Cherokee Bible as a staple for language instruction (Bender 2002). However, Worcester's role in the linguistic and political perseverance of the tribe should not be conflated with the development of models for the type casters or standardization of the print version of the syllabary. The arrangement of the glyphs that he proposed did indeed provide English speakers with a recognizable organization of the characters, but it may have obscured the visual and linguistic logic behind Sequoyah's original arrangement and therefore made the print version of syllabary charts less useful to Cherokee speakers and language learners.

Sequoyah's research into models of type designs and the continuity in characters between manuscript and shorthand point to the political importance of Sequoyan and raise a few questions. Why go to such lengths to ensure that something of the visual heritage of these characters would remain intact as it moved from script to print? Why and to whom did the designs of Sequoyan characters matter so much?

NATIONAL IDENTITY IN PRINT

The development of the Cherokee syllabary from script to print happened at a time when Cherokees were fending off the unwanted introduction of a foreign writing system. Worcester's role in the development of standardized print for the Cherokee writing system again deserves attention. It illustrates precisely what was at stake and for whom in controlling the writing system that the Cherokee Nation would use for printed materials. When Worcester arrived at Brainerd Mission, the Cherokees were already a reading and writing tribe. He described for readers of the *Missionary Herald* in 1828 (Worcester 1828b: 330) the ways in which the Cherokees' writing and reading developed:

> Probably no people in the world can learn to read their own language, when written, so easily as the Cherokee; and of course, among no other people, probably, could knowledge be disseminated so rapidly, and with so great facility. . . . This is evident from the fact, that so large a portion of the people could read before the language was printed. The press and types arrived in the nation in February last. Previous to that time the people had no other means of language to read, than such scraps of the language as were found, written, or painted, or cut.

Worcester observed that Cherokees could easily learn this writing system and seemed to have developed many means to reproduce this script. Given the ease with which Cherokees could read and write with their own system, it would have made little sense for the tribe to develop type that departed dramatically from the original script. Their practice with the Cherokee writing system in longhand suggests that the status of the syllabary was already established within the tribe before their type set even arrived in New Echota.

Despite the use-value that the syllabary had for Cherokees even before print, Worcester had to convince the ABCFM to support the creation of a Cherokee font and to abandon its efforts to print religious materials for the Cherokees in an alphabet-based orthography developed by philologist John Pickering in 1819. First and foremost, he argues in a letter cited by the editors of the *Missionary Herald*, Cherokees pride themselves on the superiority of their own writing system: "If books are printed in Guess's character, they will be read; if in any other, they will lie useless. . . . Whether or not the impression of the Cherokees is correct, in regard to the superiority of their own alphabet for their own use, that impression they have, and it is not easy to be eradicated" (ABCFM 1827a: 212). Second, he reports on the ubiquity of handwritten Cherokee, a writing practice that an introduction of alphabetic printed materials would be unlikely to change. "Their enthusiasm is kindled; great numbers have learned to read: they are circulating hymns and portions of Scripture, and writing letters every day" (ABCFM 1827a: 212). Finally, it simply would not have been pragmatic to print scriptural materials in English because the creation of Cherokee type was currently underway: "As a fount of types, *on the model proposed by Guess and approved by the principal men among the Cherokees,* is in a course of preparation, it may be expected that the Cherokees will soon have the means, as many of them certainly now have disposition, to become a reading people" (ABCFM 1827a: 212; emphasis added).

By Worcester's own admission, the model for the font was proposed by Sequoyah himself, not created by Worcester. The font was in the course of preparation before Worcester arrived at Brainerd through funding and initiative taken by the Cherokee Nation's principal people. Worcester helped to put this model into place with the support of two Cherokees who were also influential with the press, George Lowrey and John Ross. Walker and Sarbaugh (1993: 84) conclude that "Worcester's concern was not to design types to suit his own fancy, but to adhere to standards set by politically powerful Cherokees, specifically John Ross and George Lowrey." In these respects, Worcester was working at the behest of Cherokees, helping with an initiative that they had already undertaken. Worcester's letter reveals allegiance to the value that Cherokees placed on their own script. This was noteworthy because he was undermining work that the ABCFM had already undertaken to standardize and adopt an alphabetic orthography of Native languages.

The ABCFM had planned to develop printed religious materials using the orthography and grammar created by Pickering (fig. 4.4). Indeed, the editors of the *Missionary Herald* expressed their reluctance to have the Cherokees develop their own system of print in an essay (ABCFM 1826). Worcester seems to have been responding indirectly to this essay in his 1827 report. Speculating on the ease of use of Sequoyah's syllabary when compared to Pickering's, the editors argue: "One would think it must take longer to express the sounds by means of Guyst's alphabet, than by means of the alphabet, which has been recommended by Mr. Pickering for the Indian languages" (ABCFM 1826: 47). After questioning the instrumentality of the writing system, the editors reveal their ideological position on learning English and using it in daily writing. "It should, also, be remembered, that, by the use of this alphabet, to the exclusion of the English, the Cherokees will be deprived, in great measure, of an

A a	*A a*	long, as in *ah;* short (ă) as in the first, or unaccented syllable of *aha'*.
Ā a	*Ā a*	long, as in *all;* short (ä) as in *although*. See *Remarks; p. 13.*
D d	*D d*	*as in English, nearly. See Remarks, p.* 13.
E e	*E e*	long, as the first *e* in *where,* or like *a* in *made;* short (ĕ) as in *when, met.*
G g	*G g*	always hard, as in *gate, get, give,* &c.
H h	*H h*	*as in English. See Remarks, p.* 13.
I i	*I i*	long, as in *antique,* or like *ee;* short (ĭ) as in *antick.*
K k	*K k*	*as in English. See Remarks, p.* 13.
L l	*L l*	*as in English.*
M m	*M m*	*as in English.*
N n	*N n*	*as in English.*
O o	*O o*	long, as in *tone, mole;* short (ŏ) as in *intonate, immolate.*
S s	*S s*	*as in English at the beginning of words.*
T t	*T t*	*as in English. See Remarks, p.* 14.
U u	*U u*	long, as *u* in *rule,* or *oo* in *pool;* short (ŭ) as *u* in *bull,* or *oo* in *wool.*
U u	*U ʋ*	as in *dumb;* short (ŭ) as in *undo. See Remarks, p.* 14.
Ų ų	*Ų ų*	nasal, as in pronouncing the first part of the words *uncle, hunger,*&c. *See Remarks, p.*14.
W w	*W w*	*as in English.*
Y y	*Y y*	*as in English.*

Figure 4.4. Pickering's orthography for the Cherokee language based on the Roman alphabet (Pickering 1830: 10).

acquaintance with the many excellent works, in the English language, on religion and general science." In one final argument in favor of Pickering's alphabetic orthography for the Cherokee language, the editors cite the bottom line of having to print editions of the Bible solely for Cherokee use when "there could not be sufficient prospect of a sale, to authorize, in many instances, the publication of any but works of small magnitude." For these three reasons, the ABCFM understood that the Cherokees' move to develop a font for printing their language represented a practical, financial, and ideological problem.

Though Pickering's work had been underway since 1819, the ABCFM decided not to use this system for printing its materials. At the urging of Worcester, it chose to support printing in the Cherokee syllabary, for instrumental and political reasons. As Worcester notes, "As it is, the difference in the time of writing, between his [Sequoyah's] and Mr. Pickering's alphabet, is found by experience to be small, and the variation to which practice in writing will naturally lead, will probably soon make the difference in favor of Guess, on count of the fewness of the characters required" (ABCFM 1827a: 212). Worcester considers the syllabary to be just as economical in time, number of characters, and space needed to create printed materials as Pickering's orthography. In his estimation, the letter-sound correspondence in Pickering's alphabetically based system seemed less likely to account for variation in the pronunciation of Cherokee words.

Worcester also goes on to list a number of political reasons for aiding the Cherokees in their development of their writing system into print: "It would be a vain attempt to persuade them to relinquish their own method of writing. . . . At their national council they have listened to a proposal to substitute an alphabet like Mr. Pickering's, and have rejected it: they have talked much of printing in the new and famous character. . . . Tell them now of printing in another character, and you throw water upon the fire which you are wishing to kindle" (ABCFM 1827a: 212).

According to Worcester's account, the Cherokees had already attached a national pride to their own writing system and desired to see it in print; the tribal council had considered replacing it with a system of writing similar to Pickering's and rejected the proposal outright. They had been eagerly anticipating a printing press and a Cherokee type set based on the shorthand version that Sequoyah had developed. By 1827, six years after its introduction at tribal council, the Cherokee syllabary had become a symbol of the nation and had accrued considerable cultural value.[5] Cherokees understood that Sequoyan was valuable in its own right and eschewed the alphabetic orthography that Pickering developed.

Yet, even as the tribe was coalescing in support and developing a national identity around this writing system, missionaries had already begun to use Pickering's orthography in their materials to try to convert Native peoples to Christianity (Pickering [1887] 2009: 352). John Pickering's linguistic materials bent the Cherokee language to the rules of spelling for the Roman alphabet, and he was unaware at the time when he was laboring to develop this orthography that the Cherokees had developed and were extensively using their own writing system. None too happy with the Cherokee script being used for print, Pickering criticized the writing system in a letter to Baron Humboldt in 1827:

> A gazette or newspaper in the Cherokee and English languages is about to be published in the Cherokee nation. The types are now making in this city [Boston] for a new set of characters, made by a native Cherokee. I should inform you that this native, whose name is Guest, and who is called by his countrymen "The Philosopher," was not satisfied with the alphabet of letters or single sounds which we white people had prepared for him in the sheets of Cherokee Grammar formerly sent to you, but he thought it fit to devise a new syllabic alphabet, which is quite contrary to our notion of a useful alphabetic system. (quoted in Pickering [1887] 2009: 353)

Though Pickering did not explain the basis for these claims about Sequoyah's motives for developing the syllabary, he certainly believed that the development of the print version of Cherokee would steal the thunder from his own system for representing spoken Cherokee.

Feeling spurned by the ABCFM's choice to print in the Cherokee type, Pickering incorrectly says that Sequoyah has "taken Roman letters as the basis, and has added to them some little mark, or has distorted their shapes, in order to suit his purpose. This is much to be regretted as respects the facility of communication between these Indians and the white people" (quoted in Pickering [1887] 2009: 353). Pickering's motives for developing an orthography for the Cherokee ran contrary to Sequoyah's and illustrate the important symbolic and functional weight of writing systems circulated in print. Pickering favors a spelling and printing convention based upon the alphabetically encoded sounds of the Cherokee language because it will facilitate communication "between these Indians and the white people." He is not simply objecting to what he perceives to be a distortion of the alphabet in print. Whites perhaps could more readily have mediated the Cherokee language by using the rules and letters of the alphabet; however, Cherokees surely would have been at a loss in this arrangement, because the Cherokee language and its logics do not bend easily to alphabetic convention. This unique writing system designed for and by Cherokees, apart from the alphabet and as a close match to this polysynthetic language, was not easily understood by people accustomed to the alphabet. The syllabary works well to unite Cherokees through the language, marking a boundary for outsiders who learned the alphabet as part of their first language. The syllabary deliberately does not facilitate communication with whites.

Pickering was not only begrudging Sequoyah's invention and its adoption into print; his efforts were linked to larger paternalistic ideologies at play in the federal government. In 1825 Pickering had been corresponding with Thomas Jefferson regarding progress on developing the orthography of the Cherokee language. In these letters Pickering writes that he has been "obliged to form an alphabet, as well as reduce the language to grammatical order. . . . I might flatter myself that you would find in this particular dialect some matter of no little novelty, as well as interest to a philosophical inquirer" (quoted in Pickering [1887] 2009: 335). In his reply, Jefferson responds favorably, commenting upon the ways in which Pickering's work coincides with his own ongoing mission to understand Native languages: "We generally learn languages for the benefit of reading the books written in them; but here our reward must be the addition made to the philosophy of language" (335), referring to the ways in which words related to state systems might carry universal meanings for all governed.

The Jeffersonian philosophy of language relates to the politics and governance of the "children" of the republic. Peter Thompson (2003: 191) notes that "Jefferson's statecraft was predicated on the assumption that certain words, for example, 'father' or 'republic,' indicated ideas bundled together in a particular and, from his point of view, commendable and instructive fashion. Jefferson sought through his study of languages a confirmation of this position." As patriarch to the country, Jefferson relied upon all of his "children," such as Indians, to agree upon the manner in which he used words, particularly in English, as organizing concepts of governance. Thus he undertook a study of languages to facilitate the communication of his paternalistic concepts. "Jefferson's willingness to present himself as a father figure to the Cherokee, . . . even at the risk of rejection or opposition, suggests the attraction to him of a political understanding of paternalism that his study of languages could have challenged but ultimately confirmed" (223). Jefferson's philosophy of language was helpful to him in developing a paternalistic role vis-à-vis his Cherokee "children"; Pickering supported this philosophy and hoped that Jefferson would see the value of the Cherokee system he had developed.

John Pickering's development of an orthography for the Cherokee language was connected to national political ideologies of the time, in which Native languages were considered obstacles that hindered communication between Indians and white people (Pickering [1887] 2009: 335). While Worcester and others lauded the accomplishment of the Cherokees in developing a writing system and font, Pickering found it strange: "So strong is their partiality for this national alphabet that our missionaries have been obliged to yield to the impulse, and consent to print their books in future in the new characters" (353). Understanding the Cherokee syllabary in print as a symbol of national pride and identity for the Cherokees, Pickering reveals the political significance of developing this writing system into print. The ABCFM was obliged to use the Cherokee syllabary in print if it hoped to reach Cherokee readers and writers. The commission and creation of a Cherokee type set and press undermined the articulation of an English-based philosophy of language that Pickering shared with Jefferson. For Cherokees, the revision of the writing system from script to print secured a right to mediate and distribute knowledge in the Cherokee language, using a writing system foreign to outsiders.

IMPLICATIONS OF THE
SYLLABARY IN PRINT

While Cherokees had practical reasons for facilitating the development of the syllabary from script to print, the political reasons were just as compelling and were supported by Samuel Worcester. Those who first learned the syllabary in script easily learned the print version. It is possible that the visual elements coupled with the linguistic qualities of the writing system facilitated the ease of transference from the script to the print versions, as described in earlier chapters. Though some scholars presume that the Cherokee syllabary was influenced by the alphabet and claim that Worcester developed it for print, the evidence presented here corrects these misunderstandings. The print version of the syllabary was successfully integrated into everyday life with minimal effort because a Cherokee developed it by and for Cherokees as a matter of peoplehood and pride.

The second evolutionary moment of the development of this writing system sheds light on the social pressures that Cherokees faced in adopting an alphabetic font and orthography. Their tenacity in retaining Cherokee designs for print maintained the visual and much of the instrumental integrity of Sequoyah's creation. This insistence on Cherokee designs was a seminal moment in Cherokee resistance to the groundswell of cultural change imposed upon them by outsiders. Their development of a typeface using uniquely Cherokee designs presented a Cherokee counterpart to Western civilization's letters. Sequoyan would be available to outsiders to marvel at but accessible only to insiders familiar with its design and instrumentality.

Though Sequoyan had only been in widespread use by the tribe for six years, its shorthand designs had been imbued with pride and use-value and would appear in print, despite subtle national pressures to adopt an alphabetic orthography developed by an outsider. Indicating their continued disdain for alphabetic literacy and orthographies, John Ross, Sequoyah, and George Lowrey insisted on retaining the visual designs of the characters. Because of their efforts, and with Worcester as their proxy, Cherokees experienced continuity between manuscript and print forms as they developed histories, laws, a Constitution, and religious material that codify Cherokee identity and perseverance.

Nothing less than the symbolic creation of a national identity for a tribe and people was at stake in this moment of history when a writing system developed from one material form to another. This era in the evolution of the Cherokee syllabary marks a time when the Cherokees developed an identity separate and separable from the paternalistic one that the federal government had fashioned for them (see also Cushman 2010 for further elaboration of these points). The commissioning of a Cherokee type set proved to be a political move ensuring that printed materials would reflect the Cherokee writing system with its design integrity, instrumentality, and transparency left intact for Cherokee readers and writers. It also made it possible to continue to write the central tenets of Cherokee peoplehood in Sequoyan.

Print developed a means for codifying Cherokee sovereignty as a nation with a political face distinct from and intricately connected to tribal ways. The second evolutionary moment of the Cherokee writing system ushered into national consciousness the understanding of Cherokees as a "civilized tribe." Because Sequoyan in print excluded outsiders even as it catered to their ideology, print mediated (to the extent possible) the terms in which Cherokee would govern themselves. The development of Cherokee writing from its initial manuscript form to print indicated and facilitated Cherokees' cultural change at a time of sweeping social upheaval. As the next chapter reveals, the distinction between Cherokee national and tribal identities was further facilitated by the evolution of the Cherokee manuscript form into print by the work of Elias Boudinot on the *Cherokee Phoenix*.

CHAPTER 5

ELIAS BOUDINOT AND
THE *CHEROKEE PHOENIX*

Figure 5.1. Newspaper masthead from issue 6, no. 5, of the *Cherokee Phoenix*, March 20, 1828.

As chapter 4 demonstrates, Sequoyan in print developed in close relation to the original manuscript designs to preserve the integrity of the tradition that Sequoyah had invented and to indicate to outsiders that the Cherokees had developed a symbol of civilization. Sequoyah and his representatives ensured minimal alphabetic influence in the designs of the types, and the tribe altogether rejected the introduction of an alphabetic orthography. The second stage of development of Sequoyan from script to print marked a key moment in Cherokee history in which a national identity came to be associated with this writing system. The creation and use of Cherokee type sets had practical and ideological importance. It helped to articulate a distinction between the Cherokee tribe and nation and between Cherokee and white societies.

This chapter explores the ways in which Elias Boudinot, editor of the first American Indian newspaper, the *Cherokee Phoenix*, and the newspaper itself were agents of perseverance for the tribe.[1] This newspaper afforded Cherokees and, just as importantly, white reformer audiences information regarding the language, land negotiations, and political strife of the time. The *Phoenix* was published from 1828 to 1834 and included communications between the Cherokee government and people, especially in regard to the impending removal. Situated in a time of competing ideologies and difficult social challenges, this newspaper provides a glimpse into a historical moment wherein a tribe defined itself for its citizens and for wider society.

Through an exploration of Boudinot's role as editor as well as an analysis of the content of the *Phoenix*, this chapter shows how the newspaper became a vehicle for a nationalist agenda: it elicited sympathy from white reformers in the North as it provoked hostility from the Georgia militia. For Cherokees themselves, the paper did less to preserve cultural information and language use than it did to set the nation's agenda, inform and identify a citizenry, and sanction the syllabary as an emblem of the Cherokee Nation. The *Cherokee Phoenix* marks the first time that the Cherokee Nation became recognizably distinct from the Cherokee tribe. This was an irreversible historical moment of identity formation for the Cherokees.[2]

THE BUCK AND THE *PHOENIX*

One of the key problems of understanding Elias Boudinot and the *Phoenix* has been that historians have hoped to see in them indicators of traditional Cherokee identity, presuming that such an identity is static and unchanging. Boudinot's complicated role in bringing a message of salvation and "civilized" ways to the Cherokees has been the subject of the writings of William McLoughlin (1984, 1986) and Theda Perdue (1983, 1994). His case has been cast in terms of Cherokees' acquiescence and resistance to becoming assimilated through religious and government-sponsored institutions (McLoughlin 1984; Thornton 1985, 1993; Young 1981). This focus has led Perdue (1977: 217) to question the very validity of the *Phoenix* as an ethnohistorical source: "the newspaper probably reveals more about what philanthropic Whites in the early 19th century expected of Indians than it does about how most Cherokee actually lived, what they believed, and how they viewed themselves." But Perdue misses the point here. The newspaper is so interesting precisely because it reveals less than promised about "traditional Cherokee culture."

The question is not the extent to which Boudinot believed that the "newspaper would be an agent for continuing progress by the Cherokees and an advocate for the cause of Indian civilization" (Perdue 1977: 207). The question is, rather, how did this paper function as an invented tradition in ways that reveal Cherokee perseverance and peoplehood? This newspaper can best be understood through a framework that admits the possibility that a people can form an identity on their own terms.

Elias Boudinot, known as Buck Watie or the Buck to the Cherokees in Spring Place, where he attended the Moravian Mission School (near what is today Chatsworth, Georgia), was the eldest of nine children born to Oowatie and Susanna Reese. On his way to the American Board School in Cornwall, Connecticut, Buck Watie met American Bible Study president Elias Boudinot. Buck Watie was so impressed with President Boudinot that he changed his name and enrolled in the American Board school as Elias Boudinot (Perdue 1983: 5–8). According to Adelaide L. Fries (quoted in Perdue 1983: 7), as a student Boudinot learned the missionary purpose of the American Board school: to train students as "physicians, teachers, interpreters, and ministers so that they could 'communicate to the heathen nations, such knowledge in agriculture and the arts as may prove the means of promoting Christianity and civilization.'" Boudinot benefited from the American Board School because it enabled his contact with powerful northeasterners, educated him in privileged language conventions, and, upon graduation, ostensibly sanctioned his role as an agent on behalf of its system for bringing the word to the "savages."

ESTABLISHING THE PRESS

Even before the arrival of the printing press, James Mooney (1900: 110) notes, "No schoolhouses were built and no teachers hired, but the whole nation became an academy for the study of the system." Samuel Worcester describes this national movement sans schools in somewhat more detail in a letter excerpted by the editors of the *Missionary Herald*: "I suppose there has been no such thing as a school in which it [the syllabary] has been taught, and it is not more than two or three years since it was invented. A few hours of instruction are sufficient for a Cherokee to learn to read his own language intelligibly . . . there is no part of the nation, where the new alphabet is not understood" (ABCFM 1826: 47). Widespread use of the writing system in a variety of genres was made possible, perhaps because it was so easy to learn. Cherokees taught each other the writing system: some traveled for days to sit by the side of another tribe member to learn the syllabary, return home, and teach it to kin there. Once they had learned it, the Cherokees' use of the writing system in manuscript form proliferated: "great numbers have learned to read: they are circulating hymns and portions of Scripture, and writing letters everyday" (ABCFM 1827a: 212). Cherokees became agents of their own mass education movement designed to teach each other to read and write their shared writing system.

To facilitate the widespread use of the system, Sequoyah himself acted as a postal carrier cum teacher, delivering letters from the Cherokees in Arkansas to the Eastern Cherokees. He would there remain long enough to teach other Cherokees to use the system in order to read the letters and then would deliver their new attempts at letter writing to relatives living in Arkansas. Thus, concludes Grant Foreman (1938: 7), "he bound together the widely separated divisions of his tribe by ties that were novel to them, demonstrated the great utility of his work, and awakened a general interest in and appreciation of it." The Cherokee syllabary in handwritten form had been circulating for some time, written and read by many and taught in part by Sequoyah, whose students would in turn teach other family, clan, and town members to learn the system. By 1825 Cherokees David Brown and John Arch had composed manuscript versions of the New Testament and St. John's gospel, respectively, which were then copied by hand and distributed (Mooney 1900: 110–11; Foreman 1938: 7). So Cherokee reading and writing spread, without schools and print and across a number of genres, among the Eastern and Arkansas Cherokees.

The establishment of the Cherokee press occurred at a time of high reading and writing rates among Cherokees, who had been using the manuscript form of the writing system for a variety of purposes after its introduction to the tribe in 1821. Samuel Worcester marveled at the representational economy of the Cherokee syllabary and suggested that its ease of use was nothing short of "a wonder." Worcester (1828a: 162) notes that the Cherokee language has fewer consonants and each syllable ends in a vowel so that the syllabary has only 96 possible consonant-vowel combinations for syllables, compared to "1536 possible syllables in the letter."

The economy and precision of this writing system continued to enable quick progress in learning to read and write and long-distance communication as the writing system moved from script to print. It was precisely because the Cherokee writing system was already in such widespread use that the ABCFM (1826: 47) hesitated to support establishment of the Cherokees' own press for fear that they would be denied access to the knowledge of English if they remained reliant upon their own writing system (see chapter 4). But the values attached to the writing system both inside and outside of the Cherokee tribe multiplied as it moved into print. Indeed, the writing system worked so well as an instrument for encoding speech that the Cherokees were eager to see their language in print, as a matter of convenience, continuity, and pride. Significant demand for print prompted the tribal leaders to request that a type set be cast for them. The newspaper was understood as a logical stage in the cultivation of this newfound reading and writing ability, which had already become an identity marker for the tribe (even if few outsiders actually saw or understood how this writing system worked). The press would provide ample opportunity to demonstrate this writing system, solidify its value for Cherokee language speakers, and create an articulated boundary between English and Cherokee speakers.

Commissioned by the tribe in 1826, the type and press were finally ready by 1827. The punches and matrices for the type took some time to cast, so the Cherokees set about building a log house for the press and staff in their capital, New Echota, in what is today Georgia. The commissioning of the type and press reflected Cherokee prosperity and national pride. Between 1824 and 1828 Cherokees had developed considerable economic means to support themselves, among other achievements. They had a new capital, New Echota, which included the building for the press as well as several other new buildings. "They had staved off two federal attempts to remove them totally from their homeland," McLoughlin (1986: 366) notes, and "rejected several federal attempts to obtain more land cessions." The Cherokees were in the process of creating a national presence for the tribe and did this through the syllabary, which "evoked a new sense of their identity, history, and potential" (367).

In January 1828 the press, type, and other materials necessary for printing arrived in New Echota. The first issue of the *Cherokee Phoenix* was published in February of that year. Two years earlier Elias Boudinot had been charged by the Cherokee Nation to secure funding from outside sponsors to procure both English and Cherokee fonts and to establish an office in New Echota. In anticipation of the arrival of the press, Boudinot issued a prospectus for the newspaper and sent it to potential subscribers around the United States and internationally. Samuel Worcester readied religious materials for the press as well, completing five verses of the Book of Genesis to be published in the December 1827 issue of the *Missionary Herald: Containing the Proceedings of the American Board of Commissioners of Foreign Commissioners.* These five verses were the first printed materials produced in the Cherokee writing system (see fig. 5.2).

John Pickering, the philologist who had developed an alphabetic orthography of the Cherokee language that was rejected by the tribal council (see chapter 4 and fig. 4.4), received a copy of the

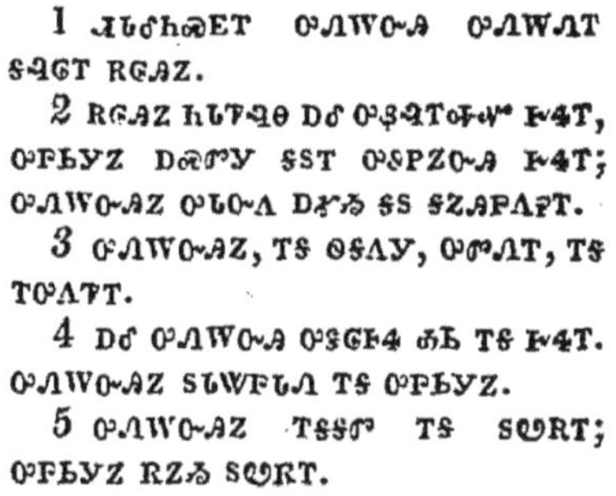
1 ᏗᏓᎴᏂᏍᎬᎢ ᎤᏁᏔᏅᎯ ᎤᏁᎳᏁᎢ
ᎦᎸᎶᎢ ᎡᎶᎯᏃ.
2 ᎡᎶᎯᏃ ᏂᏓᏈᎸᎾ ᎠᎴ ᎤᏇᎸᎢᏬᎨᏧ ᎨᏎᎢ,
ᎤᎵᏏᎩᏃ ᎠᏍᏛᎩ ᎦᏚᎢ ᎤᏑᎵᏃᏅᎯ ᎨᏎᎢ;
ᎤᏁᎳᏅᎯᏃ ᎤᏓᏅᏙ ᎠᏰᎸ ᎦᏕ ᎦᏃᎯᎵᏙᎲᎢ.
3 ᎤᏁᎳᏅᎯᏃ, ᎢᎦ ᎾᎦᏙᎩ, ᎤᏛᏁᎢ, ᎢᎦ
ᎢᎤᏙᏢᎢ.
4 ᎠᎴ ᎤᏁᎳᏅᎯ ᎤᎦᎶᎨᏎ ᎣᏏ ᎢᎦ ᎨᏎᎢ.
ᎤᏁᎳᏅᎯᏃ ᏚᏓᏔᎸᏓᏁ ᎢᎦ ᎤᎵᏏᎩᏃ.
5 ᎤᏁᎳᏅᎯᏃ ᎢᎦᎦᏛ ᎢᎦ ᏚᏬᎡᎢ;
ᎤᎵᏏᎩᏃ ᎡᏃᏍ ᏚᏬᎡᎢ.

Figure 5.2. Five verses of the Book of Genesis in the *Missionary Herald,* the first text to appear in Cherokee print (ABCFM 1827b: 382).

prospectus for the *Phoenix* with a letter from Elias Boudinot sent from Echota, Cherokee Nation, dated December 17, 1827: "In this undertaking of the Cherokees I would not wish to promise much. I hope, however, that our Northern friends will not turn off with disdain. I will try to make the paper as respectable as my limited means will allow" (quoted in Pickering [1887] 2009: 357). After receiving the prospectus and letter from Elias Boudinot, Pickering wrote a letter to Baron Humboldt dated January 14, 1828, enclosing the Boudinot letter and prospectus and a sample of the Cherokee writing system. Pickering notes that Humboldt "will perceive that his [Boudinot's] English style is perfectly correct" (357). At the same time, Pickering frames these artifacts as a "great curiosity in Europe" (357), suggesting that their exotic nature would serve to generate interest in the newspaper if not support for it. The addition of a baron to the list of subscribers to the newspaper and suggestion that Boudinot's writing in English was stylistically correct lent respectability to the Cherokee efforts to introduce the paper and tribe on the national and international scene.

Boudinot recruited readers whose subscriptions would bring prestige and financial support. Sometimes these efforts included pandering to white readers' privileged sensibilities by qualifying the Cherokees' efforts as modest and cautioning readers not to expect too much from a humble newspaper that was only as good as Boudinot's "limited means will allow" (quoted in Pickering [1887] 2009: 357). The newspaper would be a topic of discussion for Pickering and Baron Humboldt in terms of both its linguistic information and its political information. Boudinot secured a network of readers and gathered support for the Cherokees. These supporters would later turn into potential allies of the Cherokee Nation as it attempted to retain its land rights.

Boudinot (1828c: 1) published the entire prospectus for the *Phoenix* in the second issue. He opens with the goals that outsiders have proposed to the Cherokee Nation in publishing this paper:

> It has long been the opinion of judicious friends to the civilization of Aborigines of America, that a paper published exclusively for their benefit and under their direction, would add great force to the charitable means employed by the public for their melioration. . . . There

are many true friends to the Indians in different parts of the Union. . . . On such friends must principally depend the support of our paper.

Acknowledging the larger ideological project of the "civilization of Aborigines of America," Boudinot frames the publication of this newspaper as an effort to provide information to the Cherokees' "judicious friends" who seek the "melioration" of the tribe. In the same breath, Boudinot also acknowledges that friends of the tribe would like the paper to be by and for the Cherokees. The development of the newspaper coincided with a historical exigency: on the one hand, sympathetic and curious whites wanted to know more about the Cherokee language, culture, and traditions; on the other hand, Cherokees wanted a paper that would deliver their news and information in their own prized writing system.

Boudinot's prospectus for the newspaper promised to serve Cherokees' interests by sanctioning a space for the print version of the language, laws, stories, letters, and Bible translations (many of which were gathered by Samuel Worcester):[3]

> For it must be known that the great and sole motive in establishing this paper, is the benefit of the Cherokees. This will be the great aim of the Editor, which he intends to pursue. . . . The alphabet lately invented by a native Cherokee . . . forms an interesting medium of information to those Cherokees who are unacquainted with the English language. For their benefit Cherokee types have been procured. The columns . . . will be filled, partly with English, and partly with Cherokee print; and all matter which is of common interest will be given in both languages in parallel columns. (Boudinot 1828c: 2)

Printing the first American Indian newspaper in the first American Indian writing system developed with the first set of type created for a Native writing system marked a boundary for the Cherokees. The language, type set, and writing system were not intended for outsiders to understand, even if they were appreciated as curiosities. The creation of this writing system in script and print ensured that outsiders would not easily find their ways into the logics of the language, as we have seen, while Cherokees who knew the language and understood the internal structure of the syllabary's design would have no problems reading the paper in print. In other words, the paper and Boudinot intentionally provided different and differential access to the paper's content. In the initial stages of the paper, the Cherokee language would be for the benefit of the many Cherokees fluent in and proud of the writing system, and its content would be presented equally in both languages. As time progressed, however, printing the paper in a completely bilingual way became impossible for many reasons.

The prospectus outlines four ways in which the paper's content would be tailored to its goal of benefiting Cherokees, by including:

1. The laws and public documents of the nation.
2. Account of the manners and customs of the Cherokees, and their progress in Education, Religion, and the arts of civilized life. . . .
3. The principal interesting news of the day.
4. Miscellaneous articles, calculated to promote Literature, Civilization, and Religion among the Cherokees. (Boudinot 1828c: 3)

Each issue was fairly consistently organized into these four categorizes of content, with greater or lesser portions of the paper devoted to the first two as needed. The first issue, printed on February 21, 1828, includes the Cherokee Nation's Constitution printed in side-by-side columns in both languages. Because Cherokee needs far fewer glyphs to express meaning, large white spaces appear after each section of the Cherokee version (fig. 5.3).

Cherokee written in script does not have punctuation. Word borders are indicated by space: one Cherokee word can be equivalent to an entire compound sentence in English, so spacing between words sufficed to show sentence boundaries. But punctuation was added to the Cherokee published in the *Phoenix* and the verses of the Psalms. These conventions would have indicated more to English-speaking audiences than to Cherokee readers, allowing them to match the Cherokee to the English. This side-by-side layout of columns does more than simply present information in a systematic way for the two audiences; white readers might have perceived themselves as being privy to insider access to the Cherokee language through this system. This was the first appearance of the Cherokee syllabary in

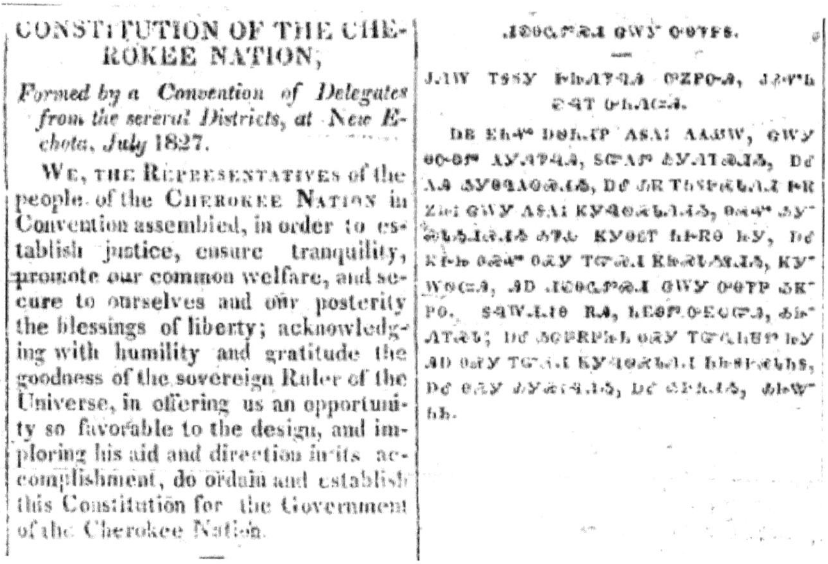

CONSTITUTION OF THE CHE-
ROKEE NATION;

*Formed by a Convention of Delegates
from the several Districts, at New E-
chota, July 1827.*

WE, THE REPRESENTATIVES of the
people of the CHEROKEE NATION in
Convention assembled, in order to establish justice, ensure tranquility,
promote our common welfare, and secure to ourselves and our posterity
the blessings of liberty; acknowledging with humility and gratitude the
goodness of the sovereign Ruler of the
Universe, in offering us an opportunity so favorable to the design, and im-
ploring his aid and direction in its accomplishment, do ordain and establish
this Constitution for the Government
of the Cherokee Nation.

Figure 5.3. Preamble to the Constitution of the Cherokee Nation, published on the first page of the first issue of the *Cherokee Phoenix* in 1828 (Boudinot 1828a).

print in a newspaper; it would have been a novelty to outsiders simply on the face of it.

But this design choice also served as visual reinforcement of the parallel structure of the Cherokees' government and the United States Federal government. As Perdue (1983: 16) notes, "By publishing official correspondence and documents, legislation passed by the National Council, and notices . . . Boudinot not only informed Cherokee readers of events in the Nation but also demonstrated to white readers the remarkable accomplishments of his people." Boudinot's choice to include these two languages side-by-side, despite the large amounts of white space in the Cherokee version, presented the two systems of government as visually equal, as did the content of the documents. Note that the Cherokee Constitution's preamble models its language closely on the preamble of the U.S. Constitution: "We the People of the United States, in Order to form a more perfect Union, establish Justice, insure domestic Tranquillity, provide for the common defence, promote the general Welfare, and secure the Blessings of Liberty to ourselves and our Posterity, do ordain and establish this Constitution for the United States of America." This first issue of the *Phoenix* draws upon conventions and models of language, content, and design presented in the mainstream, catering to the white audience's desire to see Cherokees becoming "civilized" and, at the same time, allowing Cherokees their own means to maintain the exclusivity of their language.

The Cherokee Constitution in and of itself marked an important turning point for Cherokees: this was the first manifestation of a sovereign, self-supporting, equal Cherokee Nation vis-à-vis the federal government codified in both English and Cherokee. Though treaty signing certainly played a role in legal recognitions of the Cherokee Nation as a sovereign state, the constitutional meeting and sanctioned government symbolized and established sovereignty in ways not previously respected by citizens and settlers at large. As McLoughlin (1986: 396) notes, this draft "of the constitution was obviously designed as a capstone of Cherokee Nationalism. . . . The drafters wished to demonstrate to the world that politically—as a nation—the Cherokees were now fully civilized and republicanized." For Cherokees not used to seeing government documents written in the syllabary, the printing of the Constitution was a moment when the Cherokee Nation identified for itself its citizens, territory, rights, and privileges. This Constitution printed in the syllabary shows perseverance on Cherokee terms and through Cherokee means.[4] These terms included, first and foremost, a definition of territorial boundaries, identification of citizens, and the jurisdiction of the Cherokee government.

THE PRESS AND PRINT: PERSEVERING AS A NATION AND A TRIBE

In his annual message to the Cherokee Nation, Chief John Ross ("Annual Message," October 13, 1828, in Moulton 1985: 1:141) encouraged funding support for the press. "The public press deserves the patronage of the people, and should be cherished as an important vehicle in the diffusion of general information, and as a no less powerful auxiliary in asserting and supporting our political rights." Having duly emphasized the value of the press, Chief Ross was able to marshal support for its continued finance. Thus when Boudinot declined to serve as editor of the *Cherokee Phoenix* until he received compensation comparable to that of the missionaries with whom he worked to produce the paper, Ross penned a letter to the National Committee and National Council requesting that it increase Boudinot's pay by one hundred dollars a year (November 4, 1829, in Moulton 1985: 1:176–77). Hence the press itself required monetary resources and maintenance for its continued use as a delivery mechanism for Cherokee views. This plea for support came at a time when the Cherokees were facing hostility from the Georgia militia, further incursions on their lands, and hostility from white settlers.

Though suffering economic instability, the paper had become important in keeping the nation informed, publishing all stakeholders' perspectives on the impending removal of Cherokees from their tribal lands. A letter signed by John Ross and George Lowrey asked the Cherokee people to have faith in the law of the U.S. federal government and not to be afraid of the words of Andrew Jackson. "The Treatys [*sic*] entered into between us and the General Govt. are very strong and will protect us in our right of soil. The Govt. have agreed to keep our lines clear [referring to the borders with the Creeks] and keep all intruders off our lands. If Georgia was to extend her laws over us it would be a violation of our treaties with the Genl. Govt. and the laws of the United States. We dont [*sic*] believe they will extend their laws over us" ("To the Cherokee People," July 1, 1829, in Moulton 1985: 1:166).[5]

The newspaper became a primary avenue for the chief's communications to Cherokees. Chief Ross was using the paper to ask Cherokees to trust in the treaties made with the U.S. government, to understand that the state of Georgia had no legal right to extend its laws over the tribe, and to know that Andrew Jackson's posturing should not scare them. The newspaper was a resource that helped Ross provide correct legal information in his letter, which was published in Cherokee. This letter, printed in the same issue in which the topic of land rights was being discussed in English, was meant to calm growing uncertainty among the Cherokees about their impending removal. The press acted as an agent of information and reassurance for Cherokee citizens, even as it worked to rally white sympathizers to the Cherokee cause. This same issue of the *Phoenix* explained to English-speaking audiences the causes and troubles behind the increasing strife involving Cherokees, Creeks, and the state of Georgia.

Just as the press enabled communications from the nation to whites and Cherokees, it also published the perspectives of northern sympathizers on the situation of the Cherokees. The November 4, 1829, issue of the *Phoenix* reprinted William Penn's essay "Present Crisis in the Condition of the American Indians," which chronicled the infractions of the state of Georgia against the Cherokees and was originally published in the *National Intelligencer*. Penn's essay outlines the articles of the Treaty of 1819 signed in Washington, D.C., by John C. Calhoun, then secretary of war, and Cherokee leaders. Penn goes on to demonstrate how the state of Georgia sent surveyors of the Cherokee/Creek boundary as its agents and in so doing violated article 5 of the Treaty of 1819. Penn questions the state's authority to survey the Creek boundaries and to attempt to take land from Creeks and Cherokees. He suggests that in legal terms the treaties are "enough for the perfect defense of the Cherokees, till they voluntarily surrender their country, this being the only way that their title can be *legitimately* extinguished" (Penn 1829: 1; emphasis in original). The press served as a vehicle for the Cherokee Nation to coalesce the support of white readers around the issues of Cherokee sovereignty, land rights, and the increasing problem of hostility from the Georgia militia, using both white views of the situation and Cherokee voices. Importantly, these voices all contributed to the distinctions between the nation and the tribe. The nation came to be recognized by its political and legal maneuvering to garner white support and define its legitimate sovereign rights. The social exigencies of the time demanded that the *Phoenix* follow a political path by printing information to help inform the tribe and whites of the serious problems with Andrew Jackson and the state of Georgia that the Cherokees faced.

THE POWER OF THE CHEROKEE PRESS

As the state of Georgia increasingly attempted to extend its legal authority over the Cherokees, the nation continued to argue its case for sovereignty. The press served as an important resource manager in English and in Cherokee to express and build alliances for the nation's positions. The problem of Georgia's encroachment on Cherokee lands was exacerbated by the 1830 passage of the Indian Removal Act, which authorized Andrew Jackson to send agents into Cherokee country to recruit emigrants to the West. Jackson directed Indian agent Colonel Hugh Montgomery to withhold the annual annuity owed to the tribe by the federal government for lands ceded in the 1819 treaty. With the national treasury strangulated, the funding for the press was jeopardized, requiring Boudinot to travel around the country to seek financial assistance from allies who had subscribed to the paper and other white sympathizers. He returned to the nation after a year of fund-raising and after the Supreme Court had ruled that Georgia's laws did not extend over Cherokee land. But Jackson and the Georgia militia refused to support the ruling, so Boudinot saw little hope for the Cherokees' continued presence on their ancestral lands and supported removal. When leaders of the Cherokee Nation learned of his decision, they asked him as editor of the *Phoenix* not to publish his views. In protest against censorship and the Cherokee Nation's fight to remain on ancestral lands, Boudinot stepped down as editor. Ultimately, the ways in which the press served as a voice and a face for the nation spelled the demise of Boudinot as its editor. His role as editor ended because he was seen as working against the tribe and nation with his support for removal. When he signed the Treaty of New Echota as one of a handful of Cherokees who advocated for the removal of the tribe, his fate was sealed: he was assassinated in 1839.

The type and the press, so valued among the Cherokees, continued to produce printed materials concerning their removal, their legal battles, and especially their ill treatment at the hands of the Georgia Guard. In a letter to Lewis Cass from Washington, John Ross (April 22, 1836, in Moulton 1985: 1:417–18) tells the story of the press's demise:

> The Cherokee Council, held in the spring of 1835 resolved to remove the nation's Printing Press to Red Clay, and to issue a paper at that place, in as much as the Cherokees were prohibited from holding their councils at New Echota within the limits of Georgia. . . . The Press, and materials were at New Echota and he [the new

editor, Richard Fields] sent a wagon for them. The messenger returned with information, that before he arrived at that place, the whole had been seized by the Georgia Guard. . . . Thus the public Press of the Cherokee Nation has been lawlessly taken, is yet retained, and has been recently used by the agents of the United States, in the publication of slanderous communications against the constituted authorities of the nation, &c.

The very gesture of the Georgia Guard in stealing the Cherokees' press suggests its value, threat, and import in developing a face for the Cherokee Nation, which sympathizers around the country would recognize as wronged. The press itself served as a material vehicle that conveyed the Cherokee language, its tradition, and some tribal ways. Equally importantly, however, it marked a distinction between the "civilized" face of the nation and the people of this nation who used it as an interface, protector, and liaison for their continued survival.

Though results were surely mixed, the press facilitated the Cherokees' efforts to resist removal and make a place for themselves as a nation standing parallel to the U.S. federal government. Print culture is central to the development of any notion of nationhood because it allows for the simultaneous experience of the world and history. It creates a sense of kinship and unity through the ritual of reading the news. Print culture, as Benedict Anderson argues, fosters the development of a national identity because readers of newspapers and novels build a shared sense of communion and simultaneous experience that traces to historically important cultural expressions. "Nationalism has to be understood by aligning it, not with self-consciously held political ideologies, but with the large cultural systems that preceded it, out of which—as well as against which—it came into being" (Anderson 2006: 12). But the imagined community produced by reading the *Phoenix* seems to have differed for Cherokees and English readers, a negotiation of shared experience not altogether captured by Anderson's idea of imagined communities.

The Cherokee language appearing in print alongside English also helped to codify a Cherokee national identity during the height of federal pressures to "civilize" Indians and Georgia's pressure to extend its jurisdiction over a sovereign nation. The paper exploited two languages to deliver its various messages to tribal members and outside readers. For Cherokees, the *Phoenix* served as a vehicle for sovereignty, printing its governmental structure and laws, informing and unifying the tribe against outsider intrusion, and documenting the nation's extensive legal battles to secure Cherokees' peace and land. For outsiders, the paper consolidated support from sympathizers, symbolized Cherokees' "civilized" nature, and offered a crafted image of the Cherokee people.

The *Cherokee Phoenix* may have been less reliable as an ethnohistorical source for Cherokee tradition and language in the period leading up to removal and more an indicator of the ways in which the tribe managed its public face. But Boudinot and the newspaper both served as vehicles for Cherokee meaning-making and nation-building. Perdue (1977) points out all the ways in which the paper masked and downplayed traditional Cherokee ways and catered to its white readership. Thus her essay provides a useful check for those ethnohistorians who deem the *Phoenix* a valuable source of insider information about the tribe.

Yet it is precisely this boundary between a Westernized face and traditional culture and language that is of interest here. It is indicative of two very important political and cultural acts. First, the boundary indicates to outsiders all the ways in which the tribe had progressed, become a nation unto itself, and become "civilized," using a technology central to the formation of national identity (Hardt and Negri 2000; Anderson 2006). In doing so, it carried out the important rhetorical work of advancing the interests of the political arm of the nation that sought to use the language of being civilized to elicit white sympathies and cultivate outrage. Second, the boundary indicates the ways in which the nation became the political face of the cultural and tribal practices that it protected. This distinction between nation and tribe still obtains (Cushman 2010), and the publication of the *Cherokee Phoenix* became an agent through which Cherokee identity came to mean both. The *Cherokee Phoenix* might disappoint historians as an ethnohistorical source. But when viewed as the vehicle for key formative moments of a national identity, the paper (and Boudinot's work on it) might be rescued from critiques of what it did not accomplish and instead be seen in a light of what it did.

The Cherokee syllabary in print not only allowed for a codification of the governmental and legal institutions that indicated a nationalistic spirit but also grew to symbolize one facet of the ways in which the tribe was a nation. Historian William McLoughlin offers some credit to the newspaper and the Cherokee Constitution printed in the Cherokee font as key indicators of the manifestation of a national identity in the tribe. McLoughlin (1975: 551) notes that the Cherokees were a large, wealthy tribe that occupied 15 million acres in the early 1800s, cutting across the borders of Georgia, Tennessee, Alabama, and North Carolina. The tribe had "adopted a written constitution in 1827 . . . , published a national newspaper in their own language (utilizing the unique Sequoyan syllabary)," and developed a governmental structure that, while modeled after the U.S. federal government, retained traditional aspects of Cherokee government such as a tribal council (547).

Historians are quick to point to indicators of Cherokee national identity such as institutions, laws, and organized drives toward self-governance (Denson 2004). But few have noted that a completely innovative writing system developed from script to print is an indicator of a national identity, despite the evidence that "the only items consistently translated into Cherokee were the laws of the Nation, letters and articles about Cherokees' struggle against removal, and biblical passages" (Perdue 1977: 213). While Perdue found it regrettable that the newspaper did not have more bilingual content, what it did publish represented an important moment in Cherokee history. The Cherokee Nation developed a face for outsiders and a language of government and shared responsibility and rights for insiders. In fact, the newspaper consistently included the content areas central to Cherokee peoplehood—religious materials, historical rationales against removal, and legal battles over land—and thus served the interests of peoplehood and the nation. This writing system helped Cherokees to codify laws, develop a national newspaper, and present a face of the tribe to readers around the country. These achievements should also be included as indicators of the ways in which linguistic tools enable the formation of a national identity.

Even if the *Cherokee Phoenix* did not use Sequoyan to the extent that historians might wish, the struggle to develop Cherokee typefaces and get Sequoyan into print suggests the ways in which the tribe persevered to represent itself in its own language and on its own terms. The second stage of evolution of the syllabary, as it moved from script to print, tells the story of a people keen on seeing Cherokee knowledge, perspectives, and governmental structures written in their own language. The choice to maintain dual languages in the newspaper points to the strategy of establishing a government parallel and equal to the federal government, outside of Georgia's jurisdiction. Print in Sequoyan symbolized sovereignty as it codified it.

Printed Sequoyan demarcated boundaries, protecting and serving central facets of the Cherokee tribe as it created the public face and legal mechanisms of the nation. This evolutionary stage of Sequoyan responded to social pressures on multiple levels and helped to ensure that Cherokee tribal government would exist into the next centuries. As the following chapters demonstrate, Sequoyan survived through two of the most disruptive eras in Cherokee history; after these great challenges, Sequoyan proliferated and ushered in cultural renewal, creating the literary legacy inherited by today's Cherokees.

CHAPTER 6

THE BREADTH OF THE CHEROKEE WRITING SYSTEM, 1840–1920

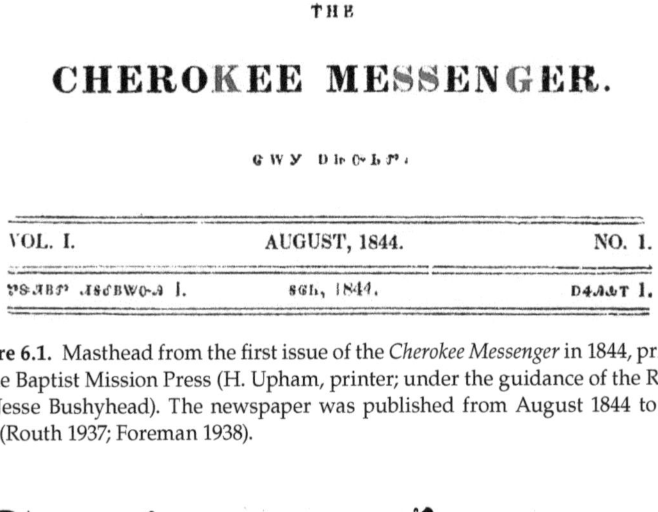

THE

CHEROKEE MESSENGER.

G W Y D Ꮢ �ꭹ.

VOL. I.	AUGUST, 1844.	NO. 1.
ᎤᏚᏝᏗ ᎠᏎᏆᏦ Ꮎ 1.	8Ꭶh, 1844.	Ꭰ4ᎠᎬᎢ 1.

Figure 6.1. Masthead from the first issue of the *Cherokee Messenger* in 1844, printed by the Baptist Mission Press (H. Upham, printer; under the guidance of the Reverend Jesse Bushyhead). The newspaper was published from August 1844 to May 1846 (Routh 1937; Foreman 1938).

THE CHEROKEE ADVOCATE.

PUBLISHED BY THE CHEROKEE NATION AT $1.50 PER ANNUM IN ADVANCE—TO THOSE WHO READ CHEROKEE ONLY—FREE.

VOL. 18.	TAHLEQUAH, CHEROKEE NATION, I. T., JANUARY 10, 1894.	NO. 19.

Figure 6.2. Masthead from the *Cherokee Advocate* newspaper in 1894. The paper was published weekly until 1877, when it moved to a triweekly schedule; publication was suspended three times, with the longest suspension during the Civil War period: June 23–October 27, 1852; September 28, 1853–April 26, 1870; January 30, 1875–March 1, 1876.

Because key figures in Cherokee history had insisted on developing Sequoyan type that maintained the visual and linguistic integrity of the writing system, its place in the everyday life and production of a Cherokee written legacy was secured. Presses were intermittently run between 1840 and 1920, challenged by the Civil War and ongoing outside pressures to adopt an alphabetic orthography. The impressive range of available (though not often seen) documents from this period indicates how Sequoyan in both script and print imbued every corner of Cherokee life. Because Sequoyan had been flexible enough to evolve in its material forms and had maintained central features of its visual and instrumental designs, it continued to be a central tool for expressing Cherokee peoplehood in a wide array of documents.

The trend toward using Sequoyan as both a symbolic means of differentiating the tribe from outsiders and unifying the tribe through massive social change continued after the Trail of Tears (1838–39). Many Cherokees entered lands assigned to them in Indian Territory (today Oklahoma), while a number remained in Georgia and other states. From 1840 to 1920 Cherokees entered into two eras of prosperity: the first was interrupted by political strife over allegiances during the Civil War, and the second lasted until the allotment era in the 1900s. During this time Sequoyan in print and script reflected the social advancement of Cherokees even as it threatened outsiders. The Cherokee syllabary also worked as a stabilizing tool for the tribe and became an instructional resource as well as an institutional and national resource for peoplehood. Both script and printed Cherokee enabled a codification of Cherokee language, culture, religious tracts, and governmental documents on a widespread scale. This chapter demonstrates the wide range of texts produced in manuscript and print, revealing the ways in which Cherokees maintained the language and social fabric through communications as well as the sacred and secular forms of institutionalized reading and writing.

Materials in Sequoyan were certainly important in recording, communicating, and archiving the troubling news of the day. Cherokee-run newspapers, such as the *Messenger* and *Advocate* (pictured in figs. 6.1 and 6.2), chronicled the failed attempts to stem the tide of white settlers in Cherokee country. They also provided ease of communication between members of a tribe living long distances from each other. The nature, content, and purpose of printed artifacts in Sequoyan contrast with the breadth of manuscript documents produced by everyday Cherokees. These forms and genres provide further evidence of differences between tribal members and the nation, differences that at times were exacerbated by outsiders and bridged by Cherokee leaders and teachers. During this time Sequoyah again emerges as a key player who facilitated peaceful unification of the tribe through a shared language and writing system.

INVENTOR CUM DIPLOMAT

The treaty of 1817 had the effect of convincing 3,000 Cherokees voluntarily to move west to Arkansas; these Cherokees then became known as "old settlers" (Mooney 1900: 133–36). Mooney (1900: 136) estimates that Sequoyah had been living in Arkansas since visiting the old settlers in 1822 to introduce his syllabary to them. Foreman (1938: 45) estimates that Sequoyah had been there since 1818, when he emigrated west with John Jolly. In any case, Sequoyah had established himself as a noteworthy person among the old-settler Cherokees because of his invention. His social standing would be important in helping to unify the tribe and bring about a renaissance for the people after the Trail of Tears.

By 1832 Sequoyah had become a national hero both in the United States and in the Cherokee Nation for his invention. General Ethan Allen Hitchcock, who visited the nation before removal, noted that Sequoyah's invention furnished Cherokees "with considerable reading in their native language, including translations of portions of scripture. The entire gospel of Matthew and John and several of Paul's Epistles; and they have a neat little volume of hymns in Cherokee" (quoted in Foreman 1938: 47). The popularity and widespread use of the syllabary increased after the Trail of Tears, when the tribe had time, resources, and help to create numerous print artifacts in Cherokee. Chief Ross wrote a letter to Sequoyah (January 12, 1832, in Moulton 1985: 1:234) in recognition of his accomplishment: "The present generation has already experienced the great benefits of your incomparable system." Because Sequoyah's accomplishment had helped the tribe in so many ways, he was awarded a medal that he wore every day.

Sequoyan alone would not save the Cherokees from a forced removal from their homes and capital in New Echota, as pressures mounted to cede more land and move west. A small group of Cherokees, led by Major John Ridge and Elias Boudinot, signed an illegal treaty in 1835 that ceded the Cherokee Nation's entire remaining lands for the sum of $5 million (Mooney 1900: 121–25). Having done this against the will of the majority of the tribe's representatives as well as Cherokee Nation law that prohibited the sale of any additional lands by individual Cherokees, the Treaty Party effectively signed their own death warrants. Though John Ross and the majority of the Cherokees resisted removal, the Treaty of New Echota ultimately took effect, leading to the Cherokee Trail of Tears (1838–39). Thousands of Cherokees were removed to what is today Park Hill, Oklahoma, and its surroundings. The Treaty Party leaders (Major John Ridge, his son, and Elias Boudinot) were all killed on the same night in 1839 for what most considered their treasonous act (Mooney 1900: 134).

With the arrival of some 14,000 Cherokee emigrants from the East in 1839, Sequoyah worked with John Ross and John Drew to help unify the newly arrived Eastern Cherokees and old settlers under one Constitution, a process that took considerable negotiating (Mooney 1900; Starr 1921; Strickland 1980). One month after the deaths of the Treaty Party leaders, on July 12, 1839, the old settlers, remaining Treaty Party members, and newly arrived easterners passed an act of union under the leadership of John Ross and with the help of Sequoyah. Sequoyah signed it as president of the council for the old-settler Cherokees (Mooney 1900: 135). Another Constitution, which created a governmental structure similar to the one created in the East, was ratified in September 1839.

Dedicated to bringing together all Cherokees in their new home, Sequoyah (now perhaps in his late fifties) set forth from Park Hill with several men to find the lost band of Cherokees. These Cherokees were rumored to be living in Texas and Mexico after having chosen to break from the old-settler Cherokees in Arkansas. Sequoyah died en route (Mooney 1900: 147–49; Foreman 1934: 374–75,

1938: 48–66). Two years later, on December 24, 1844, not knowing whether Sequoyah was still alive, the Cherokee Nation voted to give him and his family a pension for the creation of the Cherokee writing system. When no word of Sequoyah's whereabouts was heard, the commissioner of Indian Affairs approved a small stipend to be used by a search team to find out what had happened to the man whose technology and diplomacy had helped unify the tribe. Grant Foreman (1938) includes a translation of the report written in Cherokee from a member of the search party, ᎤᏃᎵ /unoli/, delivered to agent P. M. Butler on May 15, 1845. ᎤᏃᎵ /unoli/ had met members of the party that had accompanied Sequoyah and had spoken to Standing Rock, who had attended to Sequoyah during his sickness and eventual death (Foreman 1938: 374–77). Having dedicated his life to unification of the tribe, Sequoyah died during his continuing quest to bring together the diasporic groups of Cherokees, before he could see the blossoming of texts published and written in the script he had created.

(RE)UNITED THROUGH SCRIPT
AND PRINT, 1840–1870

The ubiquity of manuscript and print coupled with the ease of use of the syllabary made it a powerful tool in persevering in the Cherokee language for everyday life as well as documenting traditional ways and histories. "In addition to numerous Bible translations, hymn books, and other religious works," writes Mooney (1900: 112), "there have been printed in the Cherokee language and syllabary the *Cherokee Phoenix* (journal), *Cherokee Advocate* (journal), *Cherokee Messenger* (periodical), *Cherokee Almanac* (annual), Cherokee spelling books, arithmetic's, and other schoolbooks for those unable to read English, several editions of the laws of the Nation, and a large body of tracts and minor publications." Public uses of the syllabary were equally diverse and widespread: handwritten Cherokee was found in "letter writing, council records, personal memoranda, etc.," as well as extensive recording and documentation of medicines and prayers "for the purpose of preserving to their successors the ancient rituals and secret knowledge of the tribe" (112). Three presses contributed to the flourishing of literature published for Cherokees during this time: the Park Hill Press, Cherokee Nation Press, and Baptist Mission Press. Numerous manuscript items also remain as part of a legacy of social documents that Cherokees wrote in their everyday lives.

Between 1835 and 1860 the Park Hill Press run by Samuel Worcester took partial responsibility for the proliferation of printed materials available in Cherokee and English. "This press printed 13,980,000 pages of books, tracts, pamphlets, and passages from the Bible in both the Cherokee writing system and alphabet" (White 1962: 511). For Worcester, securing a new press was the first order of business upon his arrival at Park Hill, because the press in New Echota was badly damaged and remained in the hands of the Georgia militia, which had confiscated it.

Worcester had left Georgia knowing that the removal was impending. Getting to the West early to set up the press and his family would provide a better opportunity to help those who were to arrive after being forcibly removed. Worcester had requested a larger press with another set of types cast from the previous matrices used to establish the New Echota press. From the Dwight Mission, Worcester wrote to his friend and fellow missionary David Greene, on August 26, 1835, that the type sent West had been received at Fort Gibson. "I think the artist who made the alterations in the Cherokee type, which I requested last year, cannot be the same with the one who formed the original matrices, nor equally skillful in imitation. One letter, representing the syllable *mo*, will not answer at all. . . . We reject the new letter, and for the present supply the deficiency by altering another type" (quoted in Bass [1936] 1996: 187). Securing the correct type, additional irons for the press, and requisite paper (destroyed when the steamboat carrying it had sunk) consumed much of Worcester's time in reestablishing printed materials.

Questions still lingered as to whether or not the Cherokee writing system itself should be used or whether it should be replaced by John Pickering's alphabetic orthography. Worcester again put to rest any notion that an alphabetic orthography was suited for Cherokee or other Indian languages. "I do not know what is to be gained by the experiment of printing Cherokee in Pickering's alphabet with the syllables divided. . . . So much do I regard the syllabic method of writing, where it is practicable, as superior to the other, that I have often thought very seriously of writing to some of the missionaries at the Sandwich Islands, recommending the adoption of the syllabic method for that and kindred languages" (Bass [1936] 1996: 189). It remains unclear why the ABCFM would still be considering adopting the Pickering orthography. Taking into consideration the lengths to which the ABCFM had to go to secure an accurate Cherokee type set for the first and second presses, it made little sense still to be considering Pickering's orthography.

Establishing a press among the old-settler Cherokees also demanded political moxie. Worcester had to convince the antimissionary movement of old-settler Cherokees of his intentions.[1] Two days after his arrival at Dwight Mission in 1835 in what is today Arkansas, Worcester wrote a status report to the ABCFM saying that he was "determined on setting the press up at Union for the time being" and that the tribal council had adopted a resolution that "no new missionary establishment should be erected, until the General Council should provide for it by law, and grant permission" (quoted in Bass [1936] 1996: 184). The old-settler Cherokees did not know Worcester and were uncertain of his intentions as well as those of other missionaries.

Viewing each missionary with suspicion, they resolved to review the cases individually and grant permission to those they deemed worthy. According to Bass ([1936] 1996: 184), "The establishment of a mission press was said to have been objected to by some of the Rogerses, and the new chief was supposed by some to be of the same mind. These things were considered by Capt. Vashon, the Cherokee Agent, as at least a temporary triumph of the anti missionary party." From this point Worcester labored to establish himself as a missionary who wanted to promote the Cherokee language and proceeded to print two hundred copies of a sample of the writing system for the council and tribal members to view. It was "merely a little book of eight pages, filled chiefly with pictures, but containing the alphabet and a little more" (186). This small printing was enlarged into what might have become the *Cherokee Primer* (see figure 6.3). The work itself pleased the Cherokees, who eventually allowed the press to be established, initially at Union then permanently at Park Hill in 1836 (Bass [1936] 1996: 206) or 1837 (Foreman 1934: 365).

Figure 6.3. Inside cover page of the 1840 edition of the *Cherokee Primer.*

The number and kinds of publications issued by the Park Hill Press were at first slowed by a continual turnover in help, which eventually stabilized as the mission developed into a school, with forty-five students who could help with the press. In 1843 Worcester reported to the Bureau of Indian Affairs that the Park Hill Press had published in Cherokee, Choctaw, and Creek since 1835. He noted that 841 pages of materials in Cherokee had been printed in thousands of copies, including educational items such as a Cherokee primer, a children's book, an almanac, and a "child's guide"; secular publications including laws, addresses from the chief, and tracts on marriage and temperance; and religious materials such as epistles, gospels, catechism, passages of scripture, and hymns (Foreman 1934: 365–66). Copies of religious materials far outnumbered the secular and educational materials, however, with no less than 35,500 copies printed. All of these were printed in Sequoyan. In 1845 alone the Park Hill Press produced a total of 1,065,400 pages of copy in Cherokee, Choctaw, and Creek (Bureau of Indian Affairs report quoted in Bass [1936] 1996: 303). The Cherokee primer was printed in its fifth edition that year, the hymns were in their seventh edition, and the *Cherokee Almanac* was in its ninth year (301–302). The Park Hill Press was not alone in its contribution to the printed literature of the Cherokees during this period, for the Cherokee Nation soon established a press.

After the removal of Cherokees from their ancestral homeland in Georgia and successful unification of the old-settler Cherokees and newly emigrated Cherokees, Principal Chief John Ross began the arduous task of obtaining the resources promised them by the U.S. government through a series of letters written to the secretary of war, John C. Spencer.[2] Ross (letter of August 12, 1842, in Moulton 1985: 2:145) rejects the terms of negotiations that Spencer had apparently sent to him for consideration: "They do not in spirit provide for the important objects we desire should be embraced in a new Treaty, and we should utterly fail to convince our people that we had not abandoned their rights by signing these Articles." To correct any misunderstanding about what objects the Cherokee people desired and were promised in former treaties, Ross sent a memo listing the "leading objects, which the Cherokee delegation wish provided for in a New Treaty with the Govt." ("Memo for Provisions for a New Treaty," August 24, 1842, in Moulton 1985: 2:146). These goals included political objections concerning white settlers and inter-marriage, land ownership and titles, and the provision of infrastructure, including a mill, blacksmith shop, council house, and "printing press restored to the Nation" (147). Spencer made good on the treaty's promises to the Cherokees, and Ross was soon negotiating for the purchase of a new press strictly for use of the Cherokee Nation.

Successful in gaining the resources needed to rebuild the Cherokee infrastructure, Ross turned to securing the type sets and worked through missionary David Greene to help negotiate the purchase of a press: "the quality of the Press and types . . . the same as those once possessed by the Cherokees East of the Mississippi. The object being to publish a paper similar to that which was published at New Echota both in English and Cherokee. A sufficient portion of the types therefore should be of Gists [sic] Cherokee characters" (letter to Greene, September 22, 1842, in Moulton: 2:149). By 1843 the new printing press, type, paper, and ink had arrived. Ross's political maneuvering ensured that the press would be established in a manner that represented the Cherokee Nation and its people. His annual message to the Cherokee People reported that the press had arrived and was ready to be officially established by the tribal council. The purpose of the press and the materials to be printed was to represent the national government:

> Deeming it expedient that a printing Press should be established for the dissemination of useful information Among [sic] our People, as well as to spread abroad a correct knowledge of the true state of our affairs and of passing events, in order that the rumors too often reported through the news Papers in the States by designing demagogues to the prejudice of the border Tribes of Indians, might be disabused. I have . . . purchased a Printing Press of superior quality, with Types, both of English and Cherokee. . . . In this event, it will in the first place require that a law be passed to establish such a Press—prescribing the principles upon which the paper shall be conducted, so as to exclude all personal and scurrilous matter of a political character from its columns—also, of the duties, for the Government of the Editor and others who may be employed in conducting the business of the office. ("Annual Message," October 3, 1843, in Moulton 1985: 2:180–81)

The mission, goals, and roles of the Cherokee Nation Press differed quite a bit from the Park Hill Press. The rebirth of the Cherokee newspaper was to be a mouthpiece for the nation, in no uncertain terms. It would not have any relation with missionary work or with those who might voice opinions distinct from those of the government that supported the press, and it was to be legally sanctioned. Having been forced to deal with the outcome of the perceived treasonous editorials published by former *Cherokee Phoenix* editor Elias Boudinot, Chief Ross sought tight control over the content of the press as well as the role of the editor. More than ever, the paper was to present the national face of the Cherokees in both Sequoyan and English. It would correct stereotypes, address misleading rumors printed in white newspapers, and disseminate useful knowledge. While the syllabary and this newspaper defended the Cherokee Nation from outside influence, it also clearly served as a mechanism of control over dissenting voices, which were not allowed to represent the nation to outsiders. The *Phoenix* and Sequoyan both enabled and regulated through constraint.

Once enacted in law by the tribal council, the Cherokee Nation Press was established in Tahlequah, just a few miles down the road from Park Hill. The Cherokee Nation published its first newspaper since the last issue of the *Cherokee Phoenix* in 1834. The first issue of the *Cherokee Advocate* was printed on September 26, 1844, with William P. Ross, nephew of John Ross, as its first editor (Bass [1936] 1996: 293; Foreman 1938: 368). Like its predecessor, the *Cherokee Advocate* was the only tribally owned and published newspaper in the country (fig. 6.2). The series had a number of editors, including William P. Ross and Daniel H. Ross, James Vann, William P. Boudinot, and David Carter. It ran until 1853, when it was suspended due to lack of funding. After the Civil War, the press was revived and was publishing until 1875, when the office burned. It opened again for printing in 1876 and continued publishing until 1906, when the national government of Cherokees was dissolved with allotment.

The third press that produced printed materials in the mid-1840s was located in what is today Westville, Oklahoma. This press was run by Baptist missionaries and Cherokee preacher Jesse Bushyhead, who was son of Nancy Foreman and Bushyhead, and grandson of John Stuart and Susannah Emory (Routh 1937: 450). Bushyhead was fluent in Cherokee and English. The newspaper he helped start, the *Cherokee Messenger*, produced only twelve issues before ceasing its print run in 1846 (fig. 6.4). Bushyhead served as a chief justice for the Cherokee Nation (457), signed the Act of Union in 1839 (458), and helped translate into Cherokee the treaty negotiations of the nation during this time as well as several verses of the Bible, stories, and news from the nation. The *Messenger* included some of the most detailed linguistic analyses of Cherokee verb structure available at this time and was published almost entirely in Cherokee.

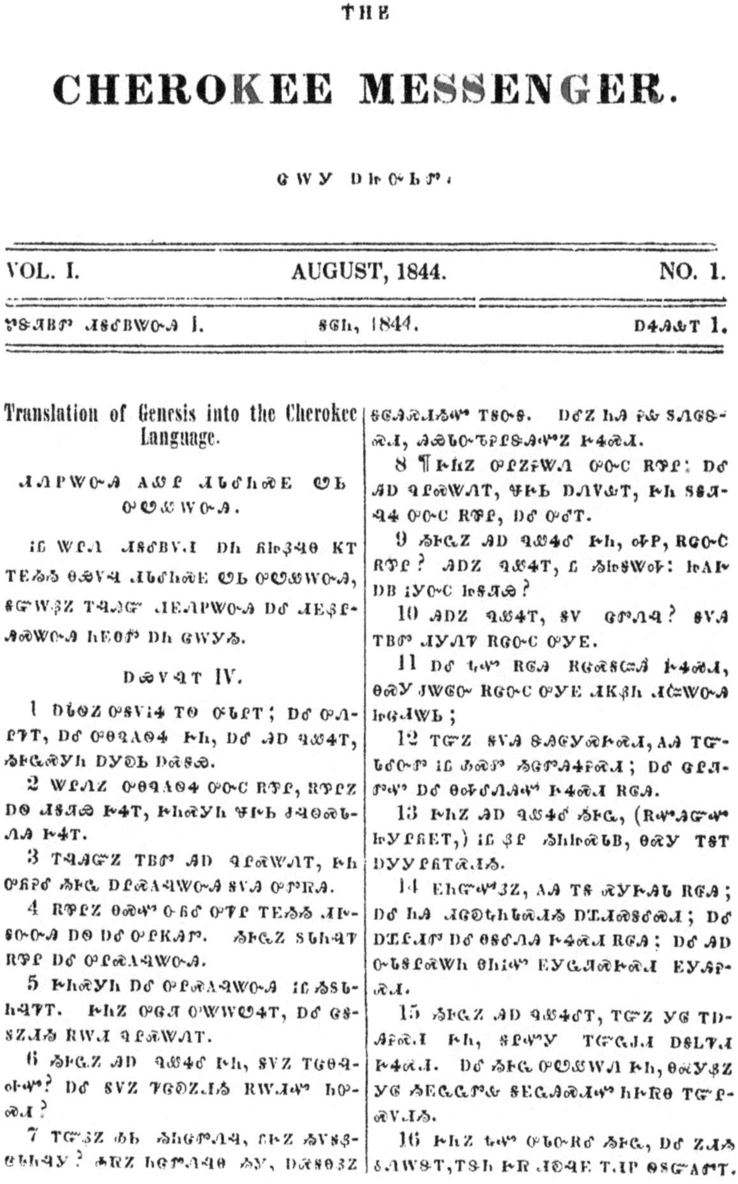

THE
CHEROKEE MESSENGER.

GWY DⱠO·᷄

VOL. I. AUGUST, 1844. NO. 1.

�̌ I.   1.

Translation of Genesis into the Cherokee Language.

 G.

D IV.

5 R.

6 ᷄ R?

8 ¶ R R.

9 , R R?

10 G R.

11 ᷄ R R᷄ R;

12 R.

13 , (R.

14 R R.

Figure 6.4. First page of issue 3 of the *Cherokee Messenger* (August 1844).

141

If the proliferation of texts produced by the Park Hill Press, Cherokee Nation Press, and Baptist Missionary Press is any indication, the mid-1840s to 1860s represent a time when the nation found some measure of social and intellectual stability in its printed materials. These presses all printed tracts against drinking, repudiations of whites and Cherokees who were acting criminally, educational materials, and tracts on marriage and the roles of women. Dr. William Butler, who was the U.S. Cherokee agent until 1851, describes the effects of these presses in an 1846 article published in the *Advocate,* saying that they were "instrumental in placing the Cherokees one half a century in advance of their late condition; providing an easy and cheap mode of diffusing instruction among the people, and stimulating them to further exertion and improvement" (quoted in Foreman 1934: 391). The presses helped Cherokees organize temperance meetings, publicize council meetings, develop a broad set of reading materials in Cherokee, provide studies of the Cherokee language, and keep the public posted on news of the country in an effort to mobilize the people.

In 1846 the Cherokee Nation funded the establishment of a male seminary and a female seminary, which opened in 1851. The nation also sponsored twenty-one primary schools. On the whole, the Cherokee educational system exceeded the common school systems for Arkansas and Missouri, in terms of both content and provision for advanced education (Foreman 1934: 410). The curriculum of these schools included geography, arithmetic, reading, spelling, English grammar, and writing. Much of the curriculum was in English, though the schools did employ a number of Cherokee teachers. The Female Seminary published *A Wreath of Cherokee Rose Buds,* a three-column, eight-page literary newspaper edited by students attending the school. Daniel Littlefield and James Parins (1984: 407) offer a description: "Devoted to the 'Good, the Beautiful and the True,' the paper contained original poems and prose by the students of the seminary, who signed the pieces with Cherokee names, initials or pen names." The paper contained articles on traditions, education, and experiences from the school, and a portion of it was printed in Cherokee.

In addition to these schools, missionaries also had established several schools. In 1854 Worcester reported having published at Park Hill over 756,000 pages for the *Cherokee Almanac* (half in English), the Book of Exodus, another edition of the *Cherokee Primer,* and the

ᏅᏙ ᏗᏎᏍᏗ

ᎤᏕᏘᏴᏌᏗᏒ

1861.

CHEROKEE ALMANAC

1861.

ᏂᎪᎯᎸ ᎡᎶᎯ ᎨᏒᎢ ᎥᏝ ᎤᏓᏅᏖᏗᏍᏗ ᏱᎩ ᎠᏫᏍᏛᏗ ᎠᎾᏍᏗᏱ ᎨᏒᎢ,
ᎠᎴ ᎦᏟᏏᏗᏱ ᎤᏍᏚᎩᏍᏗ, ᎤᏲᏃ ᎠᎴ ᎤᏗᏞᎩ, ᎪᎩᏃ ᎠᎴ ᎪᎳ,
ᎢᎦᏃ ᎠᎴ ᏒᏃᏱ. ᏙᏂᏏ 8: 22.

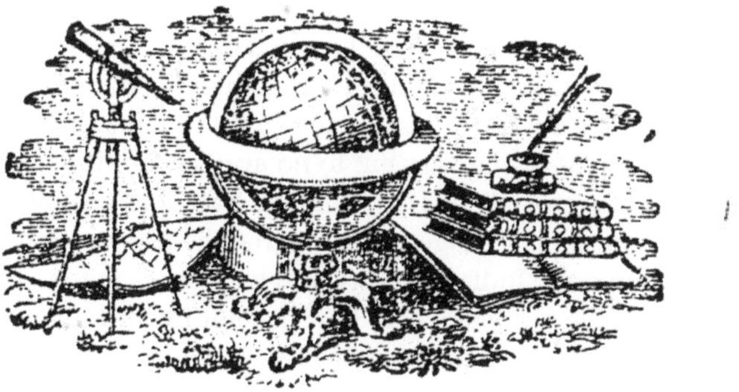

While the earth remaineth, seed time and harvest, and cold and heat, and summer and winter, and day and night shall not cease.—*Gen.* 8: 22.

Calculated by BENJAMIN GREENLEAF, A. M., Author of "National Arithmetic," "Practical Algebra," &c., for the Latitude and Longitude of Tahlequah, Cherokee Nation.

PARK HILL:

Mission Press: Edwin Archer, Printer.

ᎠᏍᏆᏂᎪᏗᏍᎩ: ᏗᏪᎳ ᏗᏟᏍᏆᏗᏍᎩ.

Figure 6.5. Cover page of the *Cherokee Almanac* for 1861 published by the Mission Press in Park Hill, Okla.

Gospel of John, all in Cherokee (Foreman 1934: 412; see fig. 6.5). The Cherokees had thirty schools attended by 1,500 students by 1858, and all but two had Cherokee teachers (419). The mix of printed materials for the education system and in Cherokee suggests that a growing number of Cherokees were becoming bilingual.

But the fortunes of the printed materials followed the fortunes of the tribe. The coming of the Civil War pitted pro-Confederate Cherokees against pro-Union Cherokees, with Indian Territory in the middle of the battles between the North and South. The Cherokee Nation was fractured politically: Confederate forces were fighting with Cherokee general Stand Watie, younger brother of Buck Watie (Elias Boudinot), and Union Cherokees stood with John Ross, who was driven from his home in Park Hill early in the war. The nation was geographically right in the middle, with pro-Union Kansas to the north, a divided Missouri to the east, and pro-Confederate states and Indians to the south (Gaines 1989: 6). John Ross hoped to mirror this middling geographic position and tried to remain neutral during the early part of the war, but to no avail. Ross ("Address to the Cherokees," August 21, 1861, in Moulton 1985: 2:481) acknowledged that neutrality was no longer possible, that the tribe must be united together with other Indian nations, and with states that had already aligned with the Confederates: "Our general interest is inseparable from theirs and it is not desirable that we should stand alone."

The nation's resources were plundered as soldiers pillaged stores and homes for food and supplies. Refugees of the war flooded into Tahlequah, only to starve when supply lines were cut. Stand Watie's men burned the council house and John Ross's home and took Union supply trains. Ross narrowly escaped and fled to Philadelphia, where his wife's family lived. Notwithstanding Watie's self-proclamation as leader of the Cherokees, Ross wrote to Abraham Lincoln to secure his understanding of the dire situation in which the Cherokees found themselves when they aligned with the Confederates. Cut off from help from the Union soldiers and undercut by Cherokees who harbored ill feelings over the assassinations of Treaty Party members, the Confederate Cherokees capitalized upon the initial wins of the Confederate troops and overran the Cherokee Nation headquarters. Stand Watie was "elected" as principal chief by a makeshift tribal council that represented only his side. The remainder of the

Cherokee Nation had little choice but to side with the Confederates, who had taken all the areas surrounding the nation.

When Samuel Worcester died in 1859, the Park Hill Press was packed and shut down. The remaining work in translating the Bible and other materials into Cherokee was left to the missionary Mr. Torrey, with the last part of Hebrews, Jude, and Revelation being entrusted to the translator Stephen Foreman (Bass [1936] 1996: 343–45). Chief Ross died in 1866, the same year the southern and northern Cherokees and the U.S. government signed a peace treaty that forced Cherokees to admit other tribes and freedmen as citizens of their nation, cede lands, and grant right-of-way to the railroads. The treaty was largely opposed by Cherokees, but they had little choice except to agree to its terms.

With the treaty of 1866 signed, Cherokees launched into another era of reconstruction, despite massive destruction of their resources, degradation of their unity, and erosion of control of land rights vis-à-vis the federal government and railroad companies. William P. Ross was elected to the office of principal chief of the Cherokee Nation and was immediately given the task of rebuilding a nation that now would face another influx of white settlers via the railroad who would illegally squat on Cherokee land.

THE STATE OF SEQUOYAH AND THE STANDING OF SEQUOYAN, 1870–1920

During this period Cherokee editors, particularly the descendants of Major Ridge and Boudinot, represented opinions and politics different from those of the Cherokee Nation and sponsored several newspapers. Independent journalism avoided the paternalistic control of the Office of Indian Affairs while responding to the rapid growth in the population and economy (Littlefield and Parins 1984: xiv–xv). The *Indian Sentinel* ran for eleven years between 1891 and 1902 alongside the *Tahlequah Courier, Vinita Globe,* and *Vinita Leader.* Elias C. Boudinot (son of the first editor of the *Cherokee Phoenix*), who was born in New Echota, edited two newspapers in Arkansas: the *Arkansian,* which had a circulation of 2,000, and the *Arkansas True Democrat.* Both newspapers took the South's position in the Civil War, running contrary to the Ross party position represented by the

Cherokee Nation's newspaper. Like his father, Elias C. Boudinot advocated rapid integration with the federal government and white culture, believing that acculturation would "accelerate that process and push the Indians toward political equality with whites" (Littlefield and Parins 1984: 32). No less than sixteen Cherokee-sponsored, non-national newspapers were published between 1859 and 1892, though the content in Cherokee was limited (Littlefield and Parins 1984: xv–xvi). Papers published in the 1880s and 1890s "were short-lived, but they were excellent sources for insights into the tribal factionalism that racked the Indian Territory in the last decade of the nineteenth century" (xvi).

Throughout Cherokee country in Indian Territory and North Carolina, where fewer than two thousand Cherokees had managed to escape removal and become a corporate body with a reserve in 1889 (Mooney 1900: 177–78; Bender 2002), the Cherokee writing system has been in use in manuscript form as well as print until the present day. The handwritten Cherokee served functions for the tribe's families and medicine people. Anna Gritts Kilpatrick and Jack Kilpatrick collected several manuscripts written in the Cherokee syllabary from the Eastern and Western bands. James Mooney gathered a number of manuscripts as well, placing them on reserve at what is now the National Anthropological Archives. The Kilpatricks compiled translations of several of these documents in *The Shadow of Sequoyah: Social Documents of the Cherokees, 1862–1964* (Kilpatrick and Kilpatrick 1965). Almost all of the original manuscripts that Mooney collected are available to view online through the Smithsonian Institution Research Information System (SIRIS: http://www.siris.si.edu).

Handwritten manuscripts include historic, cultural, and linguistic information, especially when kept by medicine people. Mooney collected hundreds of manuscript pages from Swimmer, Black Fox/Inali, and Gahuni, to name a few, in North Carolina and Oklahoma. In these manuscript pages Cherokees recorded love charms, uses of sacred plants, animal stories, understandings of colors, council meeting minutes, and letters (Mooney 1900). They were written in the syllabary, in the authors' own style. Kilpatrick and Kilpatrick (1965: 317) note that some of the papers were "written so long ago that the ink had almost faded from the paper; others were written with lead pencil so that in handling them, the characters soon became blurred and almost illegible; a great many were written on scraps of paper of all shapes and sizes." The Kilpatricks translated a small number of these manuscripts, as did Frans Olbrechts, Will West Long, and John Gillespie for reports to the Bureau of American Ethnology. The vast majority of these manuscripts have not yet been translated.

The archiving of Cherokee knowledge in manuscript form indicates the extent to which the syllabary had been integrated into the lives of everyday Cherokees. The manuscripts included in the collection of translations of social documents up to 1965 in Kilpatrick and Kilpatrick (1966) range from a "list of purchases of a Union Widow in 1867" (20) to public notices of revival meetings in 1878 (32) to a Charm for Assistance in War in 1894 (45) to temperance songs (35). A number of the manuscripts collected for this 1966 book were part of the Kilpatricks' own extensive collection, which has been passed on to East Carolina University by their children. Other manuscripts and rare books collected by Jack Kilpatrick, including a children's storybook from 1830, *Poor Sarah*, were given to the University of Tulsa. While the Cherokee Nation used printed materials to present a face to the country at large and correct misperceptions about Cherokees, manuscript forms of the syllabary, still widely used up until the early 1920s, provide a strong indication of Cherokee life, values, histories, and beliefs.

These manuscripts circulated at a time when the Cherokee Nation's sovereignty was quickly eroding and suggest a kind of normalcy in everyday life, despite larger social changes sweeping through Indian Territory. The land that had been ceded to Cherokees by treaty after the Civil War in 1866 soon became crisscrossed by railroads that brought hundreds of thousands of squatters onto the land. Cherokee rights to define who counts as a citizen were eroded with government mandates that former slaves and Indians from other nations be included in their census. The federal government broke with treaties and simply refused to enforce treaty provisions that provided federal protection from intruders. "Clearly, as since the days of Andrew Jackson," historian William McLoughlin (1993: 364) writes, "federal refusal to honor the requirement of removing intruders was to be the means of forcing the Indian nations to do what they did not want to do." In this case, the Cherokees were

forced to watch as illegal white squatters, freed slaves, homestead-
ers, and criminals flooded into Indian Territory between 1866 and
1887. Though Chief Oochalata wrote letters, talked with the commissioners of Indian Affairs, and appealed to presidents Ulysses S. Grant
and Rutherford B. Hayes, he found no relief from the onslaught of
squatters (McLoughlin 1993: 357–64). The federal government was
responding to public pressure to open Indian Territory freely to im-
migrants who were flooding the eastern and western seaboards. "The
fight to sustain Cherokee sovereignty and self-government was all
but over by 1880" (365), for in 1887 Congress had passed the Dawes
Severalty Act.

The federal government, following policies outlined by Charles
Dawes in the Dawes Severalty Act in 1887, demanded that tribal
governments cease to exist, that all collectively held lands be divided
among individuals, and that remaining acres be opened for white
settlement. While the five tribes who had removed to Indian Territory from the south (the Cherokees, Creeks, Seminoles, Choctaws,
and Chickasaws) had been exempt from the original act, the Curtis
Act of 1898 amended the Dawes Act and forced these tribes to allot
their lands and abolished tribal governments. Theodore Roosevelt
([1901] 1910: 594) described this policy toward the Indians in his
December 3, 1901, address to Congress as one that recognizes the
Indian as an individual as opposed to a tribal member and called
the allotment act "a mighty pulverizing engine to break up the
tribal mass." Perhaps no other policy in the history of a long series
of devastating government policies had so much impact among Native peoples.

Despite extensive peaceful and politically savvy resistance to the
allotment, lands in Indian Territory were assigned to individual
Indians from the Five Tribes, with the remaining lands opened to
white boomers. The first land was opened in the Iowa, Sac, and Fox
nations in 1891, and all of Indian Territory had been invaded by
boomers by 1906 (McLoughlin 1993: 770–73). So much surplus land
had been opened to boomers and squatters by 1905, when the rolls
for the Cherokees were finalized, that little surplus land remained
for those Cherokees who had enrolled after 1902 (376). Several tribes
banded together in 1905 to create a state constitution and petitioned
Congress to have a separate Indian state, named Sequoyah. Congress

declined, preferring instead to give white boomers and squatters representation through the state of Oklahoma, created in 1907 (376).

The Cherokee Nation had resumed printing the *Cherokee Advocate* in 1870 and continued publishing it until 1906. Wiley James Melton of Afton (in the Cherokee Nation) edited the last issues of the *Advocate*. According to Littlefield and Paris (1984: 72), his policy was to represent and defend the "fullblood Cherokees and their stand on dissolution of the tribe as he reported on the Final Settlement Bill, . . . [the] removal of restrictions on the sale of allotments, schools, the winding up of tribal affairs, and the approach of statehood." The paper supported and reproduced much of the material generated during the constitutional convention of tribes that met in Muskogee to develop the state of Sequoyah in 1905. The members of the convention created a Constitution, planned the organization of the state government, mapped the lands and tribes to be included in the state, and elected representatives to go to Washington to petition Congress on their behalf. The movement was popular enough to warrant the creation of political propaganda in the form of lapel pins to show support for the creation of an Indian state (figure 6.6). The inventor of the Cherokee writing system had become an icon of tribal unity, a symbol of revitalization (Perdue 1994), and an affirmation of Native peoples' desire to maintain self-governance in a state that would have been equal, alongside, and separate from the white intruders who had illegally gained lands rightfully belonging to all the Native peoples in Indian Territory.

With the dissolution of the tribal governments that this policy mandated, the Cherokee Nation press was no longer allowed to continue publishing the *Advocate* and ran its last issue on March 3, 1906. Though the national press was silenced, the American Baptist Society and the Dwight Mission School run by Presbyterian ministries and the Cherokee Orphan Training School both continued to publish texts in the Cherokee syllabary and in English (fig. 6.7). The Cherokee Nation managed the Dwight Mission after the Civil War had left the school and its buildings emptied. In 1866 the Cherokee National Council voted to reopen the school. For two years the school at Park Hill published a school newspaper, the *Interpreter*, which was one of the last periodicals to be published systematically and continually in both Cherokee and English (see figure 6.8 and Littlefield and Parins

Figure 6.6. Lapel pin circa 1905 showing support for the formation of the state of Sequoyah on display at the Sequoyah Cabin in Sallisaw, Okla. Courtesy of the Research Division of the Oklahoma Historical Society.

1984). The *Interpreter* issued a monthly eight-page newspaper, with two columns on each page (Littlefield and Parins 1984: 245). The editors of the newspapers ran stories on the war efforts, the debt that America owed to the Indians, and instructional pieces on American Indian history (246). Printer William Sevier was a Cherokee who had previously worked as a printer for the *Advocate*. Though the publication ran for only two years, "it was the last periodical to be published regularly in English and Cherokee" (246).

If Cherokee-sponsored printed materials in the syllabary were becoming increasingly rare in the early 1900s, manuscript versions

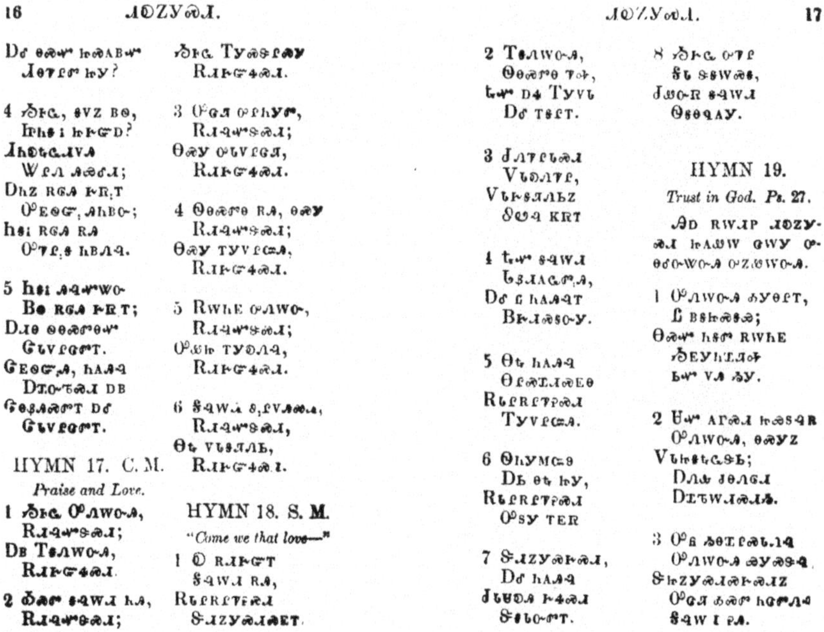

16   ᏠᏦᏴᎥᏗ.

D� bᎪABᏉᎢ
ᎯᎢᏝᎦ ᏏᏴᎧ?

4 ᎯᏛᎦ, ᏍᏴᏃ ᏴᏒ,
ᎢᏥᎯ Ꭲ ᏰᏍᎯᏗ?
ᎯᏂᏛᏣᎥᏗᏙ
ᎳᏝᎯ ᎪᏵᏗᎯ;
DᏂᏃ ᏒᏣ ᎭᏒ;Ꭲ
ᎤᏛᎬᏻᎢ, ᎭᏂᏴᎧ;
ᎯᏍ ᏒᏣ ᏒᎯ
ᎤᏛᏝᎦ ᎭᏔᏇᏇ.

5 ᎯᏍ ᎯᎦᏴᏯᎧ
Ᏼ ᏒᏣ ᏁᎢ;
DᏡ ᎨᏣᏳᎧᏴᏯ
ᎦᏴᏝᏱᎢ.
ᎦᏴᏛᎯᏝ, ᎭᏝᎯᏗ
DᎢᎧᏛᎦᏗ DᏚᏴ
ᎦᎤᏣᎦᎢ DᏛ
ᎦᏴᏝᏱᎢ.

HYMN 17. C. M.
Praise and Love.

1 ᎯᏛᎦ ᎤᏛᎠᏬᎧᏗ,
ᎡᎾᏴᏂᏴᏯᏗ;
DᏒ ᏣᎠᏬᎧᏗ,
ᎡᎾᏴᏈᏴᎰᏗ
2 ᏓᏍᏛ ᏍᏅᏔᎢ ᎳᏗ,
ᎡᎾᏴᏛᏴᏴᏗ;

ᎯᏛᎦ ᏏᏴᎾᏝᎧᏴ
ᎡᎾᏴᏛᏣᏴᏗ.

3 ᎤᏣᏗ ᎤᎢᎭᏴᎧᏛ,
ᎡᎾᏴᏴᏛᎣᏗ;
ᎡᎾᏴᎢ ᎤᏛᏝᎧᏗ,
ᎡᎾᏴᏛᏣᏴᏗ.

4 ᎡᎾᏴᎢᎧ ᏒᏗ, ᎡᎾᏴ
ᎡᎾᏴᏛᏴᎧᏗ;
ᎡᎾᏴᎢ ᏔᏳᏴᎢᎧᎯ,
ᎡᎾᏴᏴᏛᏣᏴᏗ.

5 ᏒᏬᎯᏎ ᎤᎠᏬᎧ,
ᎡᎾᏴᏴᏛᎠᏗ;
ᎤᎤᏰᏈᏴ ᏔᏳᎧᏝᎦ,
ᎡᎾᏴᏛᏣᏴᏗ.

6 ᏍᏆᏬ ᎤᏗᏝᎦᏥᎧᏴ,
ᎡᎾᏴᏴᏛᎦᏗ,
ᎡᎢ ᎥᏛᏝᎢᏝᏴ,
ᎡᎾᏴᎢᎧᏣᏴᏗ.

HYMN 18. S. M.
"*Come we that love—*"

1 ᎤᎤ ᎡᎾᎢᎧᎢᏛ
ᏍᏆᏬᎢ ᏒᏗ,
ᎡᎾᏴᏝᎢᏴᏴᏗ
ᏍᎢᏃᏴᏣᏗᎡᎢ.

---

17   ᏠᏦᏴᎥᏗ.   17

2 ᏔᎢᎠᏬᎧᏗ,
ᎡᎾᏴᏃᏴ ᏔᏉ,
ᏔᏴ DᏴ ᏔᏳᏳ
DᏓ ᏔᏝᎢᎢ.

3 ᏓᎳᏱᏞᏴᏗ
ᎥᏛᏝᏱᎢ,
ᎥᏛᏍᏝᎳᏴᏃ
ᏍᎤᏛᏛ ᎡᎢᎢ

4 ᎡᏴᎧ ᏍᏆᏬᏗ
ᏔᏝᎦᏟᏩᏗ,
DᏛ ᎡᎢ ᎳᎳᏘᏛ
ᏴᎢᏝᎧᏍᎧᏴ.

5 ᎡᎤ ᎳᎳᏱᏛ
ᎡᏝᏲᏝᏂᎧᏸᎡᎤ
ᎡᎤᏝᎦᏝᏱᏴᏗ
ᏔᏳᏴᏱᎢᏗ.

6 ᎡᎾᎤᎩᏃᏛ
DᏛ ᎡᎤ ᏒᏱ,
ᎡᎤᏝᎦᏝᏱᏴᏗ
ᎤᏍᏱ ᏔᎡᏒ

7 ᏍᎳᏱᎤᏴᎧᏛᎢ,
DᎢ ᎳᎳᏴ
ᏓᎤᏴᎳᏱ ᎢᎧᏗ
ᏍᎢᏓᎧᎲᎢᎢ.

---

8 ᎯᏛᎦ ᎤᏴᎢᏞ
ᏍᎤ ᏍᏍᏭᏴᎤ,
ᏓᏦᎤᎡ ᏍᎦᏩᏝ
ᎡᎾᏴᎤᎠᎤ.

HYMN 19.

Trust in God. Ps. 27.

ᎠᏛ ᎡᏬ.ᏝᏴ ᏠᏦᏴ-
ᏴᏗ ᏂᎠᏥᏬ ᎬᏫᎩ ᎤᏛ-
ᎡᎤᏴᎩᎧᏴ ᎤᏃᏑᏔᏴᏴᏗ.

1 ᎤᎠᏬᎧᏗ ᏍᏳᎡᎢᎢ,
Ꮆ ᎡᏁᎲᏣᏍ;
ᎡᎾᏴᎢ ᎭᏍᎦᎧ ᎡᏬᏂᎡ
ᎠᎡᏳᎲᎢᎠᎲᎢ
ᏔᏴ ᎸᏗ ᏍᏱ.

2 ᎡᎤᏴ ᎠᎠᏒᏗ ᎢᎠᏍ8Ꮢ
ᎤᎠᏬᎧᏗ, ᎡᎾᏴᏱᏃ
ᎡᎤᏴᎤᎠᎲᎦᏍᏅ;
ᏓᎳᎤ ᏓᏝᎡᎧᏗ
ᎡᏚᎳᏝᏣᎲᎤ.

3 ᎤᏒ ᎠᎡᏛᏝᏣᏳᎢᎤ
ᎡᎾᏴᎢᎧ ᎤᏯᏒᏣ
ᏍᎢᎤᏴᏱᏣᏛᎢᏣᎥᏃ
ᎤᏓᏣᎲ ᏍᎤ ᎭᎦᎢᎧᏔ
ᏍᏆᏬᎢ ᏡᎢ.

Figure 6.7. Hymns: part of 16, 17, 18, and part of 19 from the *Cherokee Hymn Book: Compiled by Several Authors, and Revised* (Philadelphia: American Baptist Publication Society, 1909). Courtesy of the Oklahoma Historical Society.

continued to use the language and enabled Cherokee tradition to persevere. The Nighthawk movement under the leadership of Red-bird Smith and his sons resisted the allotment and continued to practice traditional ways. Kilpatrick and Kilpatrick (1965: 53) include one document that they describe as being on rough brown tablet paper in Cherokee script, found "in the effects of a Keetoowah Society official who died in spring of 1962." This address describes how Cherokees must unite to continue traditional ways despite growing Christian influence over the tribe:

October 3, 1901

I just wrote an address upon the way the Keetoowah is organized:
    Now! In a few words I will make plain the way our Keetoowah is organized; for we do not have anything like the law of the Apportioner [the Supreme Being] that they have elsewhere.

Figure 6.8. Page 12 from the first issue of the *Interpreter* (December 1, 1916), the school newspaper of the Cherokee Training School in Park Hill, Okla. The school published in both Cherokee and English. Courtesy of the University of Tulsa, McFarlin Library Archives.

That is what our Apportioner gave to us, the Indians: the White
Pathway that leads to the House. Our Pathway, the White Pathway
of the Apportioner is all that there is to help us. If we understand
and believe in the Keetoowah, it sustains us forever. (53–54)

The belief in the White Pathway is an important continuation of
Cherokee spirituality that still exists today. The syllabary was used
to codify this spiritual movement in 1901. This manuscript reveals
the important role that the writing system played in shaping the
terms of existence and resistance in the face of national policies and
missionary practices meant to extinguish this very understanding
of god and the unity of a people on a spiritual path different from
the ones that the whites had been promoting (see McLoughlin 1984
for further discussion).

Cherokees continued writing in manuscript. Among the social
documents collected and translated by the Kilpatricks was one from
a medicine person who lived near what is today Bunch, Oklahoma,
written in 1909 (Kilpatrick and Kilpatrick 1965: 60):

To find what happened long ago in the year:

The earth shook	1811
The Creek War occurred	1813
They surveyed the land in Georgia	1828
Sequoyah first followed and found them	1831
The stars fell	1833
The people came out here	1837
The people received money	1851
The Government War occurred	1861

The Kilpatricks offer their interpretation of these events, suggesting that the stars that fell might have been the 1835 visit of Halley's
Comet; the 1837 removal from the south and 1851 payment to the old
settlers were memorable events of these times. Interestingly, the
1831 mention of Sequoyah might refer to his work to find and unify
groups of the Cherokees who had chosen to move west to Arkansas,
Texas, and Mexico.

Wahnenauhi (the granddaughter of George Lowrey), who authored a seventy-page history of the Cherokees, sheds some light on
the 1831 reference to Sequoyah. As more land was being ceded to

the United States in the early 1800s, "Companies of Emigrants were very frequently seen, on their way to the Far West. Reluctant, indeed, they were to leave their loved homes, and the 'graves of their Dead.' Love of peace urged them on. And they believed that only by seeking a new Country, they could build up permanent homes for their children. Sequoyah . . . went with that division of his people who emigrated prior to the 'Treaty of 1834–35'" or Treaty of New Echota (Wahnenauhi 1966: 204). These Cherokees were called the Western Cherokees before the Trail of Tears and became known as the old settlers after unification with the Eastern Cherokees after the removal (204). In both Wahnenauhi's and the medicine person's historical sketches of the Cherokees, these dates were important to the history of the tribe. The medicine person might have been prompted to write this chronology in the Cherokee writing system by the exigency of yet another government policy aimed at "civilizing" the Indians to forget their connections to lands, people, and events.

The manuscript and print forms of the syllabary, so abundant during these times of great social upheavals, provided Cherokees with a form of cohesion among the factions and families as well as a means for making sense of these changes, chronicling history from a Cherokee perspective. Note that loss of land and some Cherokees' attempts to find lands that were unoccupied by whites were central aspects in this retelling. Sequoyan made it possible for Cherokees to maintain connections with each other and proved helpful to a tribe continually strained by federal government policies bent upon breaking up the "tribal mass of Indians." The variety of materials and broad range of purposes for which the syllabary was used made possible the establishment and maintenance of Cherokee-based secular and religious institutions.

Images as well as lists of the types of documents indicate the general preponderance of manuscript and print forms of the syllabary. Figures 6.1 to 6.8 present a small selection of print and script examples from this time to illustrate the breadth of Cherokee-sponsored reading and writing. Both manuscript and print versions of the language brought Cherokees through the Civil War, into a second stage of reconstruction, and through the allotment. These documents remain a remarkable testament to the utility of the writing system developed by and for the Cherokees. They contribute to the notion of Cherokee peoplehood by providing content important to the tribe's language, religion, history, and lands. In times of great abundance, materials in Sequoyan proliferated in both manuscript and print forms; in times of great strife, they survived through everyday practices of handwriting. Both forms of Sequoyan proved valuable for the perseverance of the language and offer an abundance of knowledge and linguistic information.

CHAPTER 7

PERSEVERANCE AND CALCULATED INCONSPICUOUSNESS, 1920–1980

Chapter 6 renders a picture of the ways in which Sequoyan came to be widely used in print and manuscript forms during an era of the Cherokee history marked by growth, destruction, and reconstruction. Insofar as the Cherokee writing system moved with great momentum in both print and script material forms, it helped to stabilize the nation and tribe and further develop its identity, despite the difficult historical exigencies of fractionalization of the Civil War, reconstruction, and allotment. Chapters 7 and 8 follow the development of the Cherokee syllabary into its most recent stages of development in order to characterize the ways in which this writing system might be linked to modern technologies, popular media, and histories of perseverance. As the cover of Mort Walker's *Beetle Bailey* in Cherokee (fig. 7.1) suggests, Cherokees continued to map Sequoyan onto mainstream media outlets as they did with newspapers in the early and mid-1800s. Bringing Sequoyan into the modern era, popular media presentations of Sequoyan ensured that in its third stage of evolution this writing system would adapt to the political and social environments that permitted and/or prevented its proliferation.

The evolution of writing systems for Native peoples has been fraught with ideological battles within tribes and between tribes and outsiders. Resistance within the tribe to any type of mediation of spoken language may prevent the development within or imposition of any writing system (Morgan 2009; Hyland 2010). Tribes may

Figure 7.1. *Beetle Bailey* comic used in Cherokee bilingual education. Beetle Bailey © 1975 King Features Syndicate.

adapt writing systems introduced by outsiders to their own languages and purposes (Chuchiak 2010). At other times, as is the case with Sequoyan, the instrumental features of the writing system lead to its continued use by the tribe. The development and uptake of an American Indian writing system has everything to do with the ideological attachments and instrumental uses it may have for the tribes.

If any writing system is to succeed as a permanent instructional and historical resource for Native peoples, anthropologist Willard Walker finds, then the writing system would have to meet several criteria. "The history of the nineteenth century suggests that native literacy is accepted to the extent that it is based on a syllabic writing system, it is available to adults, it is adapted to both sacred and secular contexts, and perhaps most importantly, that it is disseminated independently of White educational institutions" (Walker 1969: 166). Certainly the Cherokee syllabary met all of these demands in its script and print forms. Cherokee reading and writing was disseminated throughout the tribe's educational institutions, even as English was fast becoming the official language of the nation and Cherokee schools. While the Cherokee writing system meets these criteria for acceptance and integration, its contribution to the continued lifeways of the tribe was mitigated by government policies set against, even hostile to, the continued perseverance of this and other American Indian languages, as the early history of the twentieth century reveals.

These policies, destructive as they were, did not deter Cherokees from using their language and writing system and from sustaining a sense of community. This chapter reviews the federal policies of allotment and English-only educational policy that drove what had been an open and abundant use of the Cherokee writing system underground. Despite being bereft of printed materials and strong Cherokee Nation support for Cherokee-language materials, the people continued to persevere in their use of the language between 1910 and 1965 by means of what action anthropologist Albert Wahrhaftig (1998: 96) calls a "calculated inconspicuousness." Cherokees in small towns in Oklahoma, organized around traditional stomp and Cherokee Baptist churches, continued practicing the language, reading and writing in Cherokee. They opted out of white mainstream institutions that failed to support, indeed often violently repressed, the Cherokee language. When external validation of the Cherokee language became more apparent and printed materials became more available to the traditional Cherokees, a groundswell of use and support for the Cherokee print, type, and script emerged in popular culture materials, such as comics, reports, and books.

OVERCOMING THE AFTERMATH
OF ALLOTMENT

The early twentieth century saw a dismantling of all Indian nations after allotment. The state of Sequoyah proposition was defeated in

1905, and the state of Oklahoma was established in 1907 (Debo 1940; Gittinger 1973). Indian commissioners in charge of enrolling Cherokees on the Dawes Roll had assigned a "guardian" to all Cherokees who were determined by self-report or, more often, a commission's quick glance to be full blood (Carter 1999). Many Cherokees claimed partial blood in order to avoid having a guardian assigned to their land, because the guardians were known to turn around and sell the property, giving the original enrollee a fraction of its worth. Another form of embezzlement erupted when oil and coal were discovered on the lands in the northeastern part of the state, where many Cherokees had received their allotments. Historian Angie Debo (1940: 3) incisively describes this trend in treatment of Indians: "It had always been recognized that mentally defective Indians like other defective adults could be placed under guardianship, but it was not until about 1913 that it began to be apparent that all Indians and freedmen who owned oil property were mentally defective." Speculators created other wretched ways to gain land from allottees, sometimes kidnapping orphaned children who had been allotted land to claim guardianship over them and custody of the land rights (Debo 1940; Carter 1999). Land ownership, which policy makers originally argued was the last great measure to assure Indians productive citizenship, turned into yet another ruse to take away their rights to their lands in immoral and unjust but perfectly legal agreements involving the Bureau of Indian Affairs, legal guardians of "incompetent" Indians, and attorneys.

In an effort to stem the tide of fraud, commissioner of Indian affairs F. E. Leupp sent a notice to "[e]very full-blood Indian citizen of the Cherokee Nation, Indian Territory" (fig. 7.2), warning them not to trust anyone who asked them to sign any documents whatsoever.

This warning indicates the extent of the fraud during this time. We can imagine the sense of irony that Cherokees must have felt on hearing the reminder that "the Government is your best and perhaps your only strong friend in these days of difficulty": the days of difficulty were caused by the allotment policy. To his credit, Commissioner Leupp recognized the importance of communicating this friendly advice in Sequoyan, an acknowledgment of the importance and widespread familiarity of the language and writing system in the region at this time.[1]

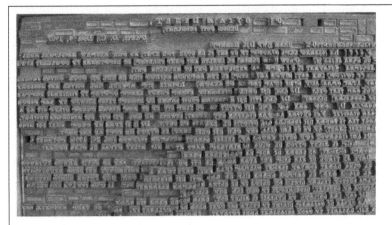

Figure 7.2. Courtesy of Gilcrease Museum, Tulsa, Okla.

Created in 1907 by the U.S. government, this press plate indicates the extent to which Sequoyan was recognized as the writing system favored by many Cherokees. The plate includes a warning to Cherokees from the Department of the Interior, Office of Indian Affairs, issued by commissioner of Indian affairs F. E. Leupp (1905–1909). As a former journalist Leupp might have understood the importance of distributing this warning in print. He chose to do so in Sequoyan, showing respect for the system of writing typically used by the Cherokees who were most often the target of land speculators: those who did not know English and its alphabet. The following translation was kindly provided by Anna Huckaby and the Cherokee Nation translation team by way of Travis Owens, senior project manager for the Cherokee Nation Cultural Tourism Department.

Department of the Interior,
Office of Indian Affairs.
Washington, D.C., March 4, 1907

To every full-blood Indian citizen of the Cherokee Nation, Indian Territory.

My Friend:

You are in great danger of losing the land which you have chosen for a home, unless you carefully follow the instructions which I am giving you. A great many men better educated than you are preparing to take advantage of your ignorance of the law and to steal away from you every acre on which they can lay their hands.

From this time forward, sign no paper of any sort whatever without first consulting the nearest Government representative with whom you are acquainted and in whom you have confidence. I think you can safely go to any of the Government teachers in your neighborhood for advice. The Government Inspector for the Indian Territory at Muskogee is always ready to answer questions and render help to Indians. Government officers generally scattered through the Territory understand their duty. Remember that the Government is your best and perhaps your only strong friend in these days of difficulty.

When a man approaches you with a paper to sign, unless you know that he is a Government officer, always insist on having the advice of a Government officer before signing it. It will not do even to take the word of the man who brings you the paper that he is himself a Government officer unless you know him to be such.

As to any papers you may have signed already, I will tell you what the law of April 26, 1906, says. It provides—

Every deed executed before, or for making of which a contract or agreement was entered into before the removal of restrictions, be declared void and the same is hereby declared void.

From this you will see that any paper affecting your rights to your allotment that you may have signed before the restrictions on your land were removed is of doubtful validity; therefore pay no heed to any man who pretends that he has your agreement to a certain contract until you have consulted your nearest Government friend. The men who have taken unlawful advantage of your ignorance knew that they were breaking the law when they did so. They have no cause for complaint if, after they have tried to cheat you, they find that they are losing their own money.

These are troublesome and perilous times through which the full-blood Indian is passing, and your best helper, the Government, is trying to save you from disaster. Listen well to what it tells you.

Your Friend,

F. E. LEUPP

Mounting evidence of the effects of the Dawes Act and Curtis Act slowly began to come to the attention of the government. Originally titled *The Problem of Indian Administration,* the 1928 Lewis Meriam Report submitted to Hubert Work, the secretary of the interior, presented the results of research on actual conditions of American Indian peoples and pointed to the many failings of the original government policy of allotment. In over eight hundred pages, the report chronicles the deteriorated health, economic, family, legal, and living conditions of Indians around the country, indicts the failed governmental policies, and makes recommendations for future policy. The report's findings were structured around a fundamental premise that the Indian Service should see itself as primarily an educational agency, "devoting its main energies to the social and economic advancement of the Indians, so that they may be absorbed into the prevailing civilization or be fitted to live in the presence of that civilization at least in accordance with a minimum standard of health and decency" (Meriam 1928: 21). Absorption into "the prevailing civilization" would demand an educational agenda wherein the Indian would be viewed as having rights beyond those merely related to property. "Indians are entitled to unfailing courtesy and consideration from all government employees. . . . The Indians have much to contribute to the dominant civilization, and every effort should be made to secure this contribution" (22–23). The Meriam report had the effect of altering federal Indian policy from one based on a presumption that Indians needed to be taught to value individualism and private property ownership to one based on the presumption that policies should be based upon Indians' own perceived needs and feelings about what actions should be taken on their behalf. This fundamental shift would lead to a new era in Indian relations and policy making—and none too soon.

Speculators had purchased much of the land that had been allotted to Indians for pennies an acre when this land went out of trust through the death of the original enrollee or through coercive tactics. Historian Rennard Strickland (1980: 73) lists the extent of deceitful practices used to swindle Indians out of their lands after the allotment:

> Of the thirty million allotted acres more than twenty-seven million passed from Indians to whites. Among the more common devices

used by their fellow Oklahomans were fraudulent deeds signed by others than the owners of the land; purchase prices far below market or actual appraised value of the land; payments of bribes for court approval of fraudulent land sales; excessive administrative and guardianship fees; embezzlement of Indian money and personal expenditure of Indian trust funds; false heirship claims or destruction of Indian wills; and gifts to charities or individual citizens of Indian assets without the knowledge or approval of the Indian or court.

Judges and some attorneys had taken notice of the problem of fraudulent transactions in land sales and began asking citizens to report to the agency any transactions that seemed to be coerced (Debo 1940: 363). By the early 1930s millions of acres of land originally allotted to Indians in Indian Territory had been bought for pennies, leading to the problem of checkerboarding, in which lands owned by Indians become interspersed with non-Indian land, leading to further breakdown in the cohesion of tribal communities. Add to this the wretched living conditions brought on by the Great Depression, lack of health care, and widespread famine: the situation for most Cherokees and Indians in Oklahoma had become dire. In 1930 and 1931 the United States Senate held hearings on the conditions of Oklahoma Indians and learned of the famine and disease in the state.

In the 1930s the Board of Indian Commissioners and the federal government, spurred to action by philanthropists, the results of the Meriam report, and well-publicized cases of cheated, impoverished, and starving Indians, finally undertook an earnest assessment and reflection on the previous three decades of Indian policy. As Debo (1940: 353) notes, "The Board of Indian Commissioners, which was so largely responsible for the breaking up of the communal holdings, admitted in 1929 that the Dawes Severalty Act had been a failure, and that its general effect had been the loss of the Indians' property as soon as it passed under individual tenure." Enter John Collier, a social worker and the former executive director of the American Indian Defense Association. He became the first Indian commissioner who systematically and seriously addressed ways in which the federal government might aid tribes in their cultural, social, and economic perseverance. Taking office in 1933, Collier developed and promoted the Indian Reorganization Act, also known as the Wheeler-Howard Act of 1934.

The allotment had devastated economies, caused destructive fragmentation of landholdings, and deterred tribal organization, but it failed to destroy the tribal government and national institutions of the Cherokees completely. Though tribal government for the Cherokees was scheduled to disappear in 1906, and much of its funding vanished, some vestige of the government remained. Tribal chiefs and attorneys were appointed by the U.S. government to represent the tribe in dealings with the federal government. Among the Cherokees, these appointed officials were little more than businessmen who represented the interests of very few of the tribal members. According to Daniel Cobb (2007: 467), the traditional Cherokees, some of whom resisted allotment, "retained a strong sense of social cohesion and cultural integrity through the Cherokee language, kinship ties, and involvement in the Baptist Church or of the several sacred societies, or both."

The Wheeler-Howard Act reestablished the Cherokee Nation's tribal government and set aside federal government funds to regain the lands lost during allotment. In 1936 the Oklahoma Indian Welfare Act provided the funds necessary to purchase land for Indians, provide economic development loans, and help tribes draw up constitutions and incorporate (Denson 2004: 247). Unfortunately, these laws did little to raise the living standards of Cherokees, who still battled poverty and disease.

These laws did, however, provide for the appointment of a Cherokee Nation chief by the president of the United States and paved the way for the United Keetoowah Band of Cherokees to seek organization and recognition in 1946 (Denson 2004: 248). In 1941 Franklin Roosevelt appointed Jesse Bartley Milam to become the principal chief of the Cherokee Nation. Chiefs who were appointed by the federal government are known as "chiefs for a day" because they would typically serve a day or two in order to sign documents. Under his later appointment terms from 1943 to 1948 Jesse Milam called a national convention in Tahlequah, the capital of the Cherokee Nation, in order to create an executive committee. This became a stepping stone to the current tribal council, to help deal with local and state governments and carry forward legal action on Indian land claims.

When Milam died, W. W. Keeler, a businessman in the oil industry, was appointed by the federal government. In August 1971 he was elected by the Cherokee people to be their chief. Unpopular with traditional Cherokees who believed that he was primarily interested in promoting the interests of a select few of the most prominent families, Keeler nevertheless ushered a functioning Cherokee Nation into the modern era. In the early 1960s the Indian Claims Commission ruled in favor of the Cherokees who sued over the Cherokee Outlet lands being overrun by squatters, boomers, and sooners. The Cherokees won $14 million. Keeler and his associates used "this new capital to invest in numerous tribal projects, among them the Cherokee National Historical Society" (Denson 2004: 249). Other programs included a revitalization of the educational program and language perseverance efforts.

With the reorganization of tribal government, settlements from lawsuits, and strong leadership from subsequent Cherokee Nation chiefs, most notably Ross Swimmer (1975–85), Wilma Mankiller (1985–95), and Chadwick Smith (1999–present), the Cherokee Nation has experienced another cultural, educational, and political renaissance. Funded in part through monies provided by the Indian Self-Determination and Educational Assistance Act (1975), Cherokees continue to promote education about Cherokees and in the Cherokee language and develop economic and cultural initiatives. These initiatives have contributed to materials and programs dedicated to teaching and developing further uses for the Cherokee language in print and manuscript versions as well as in the digital realm.

THE SYLLABARY IN MANUSCRIPT
AND PRINT, 1920–1965

Reading and writing in Sequoyan continued throughout the dark winter and long spring of Oklahoma's initial statehood in 1917 until the Indian Self-Determination and Education Assistance Act of 1975 (Strickland 1980). The number of speakers, readers, and writers of Cherokee during this period did not seem to be promisingly high to the Kilpatricks, though these practices continued to be deeply rooted in aspects of peoplehood, including religion and history. Kilpatrick and Kilpatrick (1965: viii) describe an alarming trend that they observed during their efforts to gather, translate, and archive social documents of Cherokees: "Seldom in print is one reminded of the sad truth that Sequoyah's syllabary and the whooping crane stand in approximately the same relationship to oblivion. Few indeed are the Cherokees who can read and write Cherokee. The spoken language itself faces extinction." The Kilpatricks comment upon the vast number of Cherokee manuscripts that might have been obtained by historians and anthropologists decades earlier but note that in 1965 "the average Cherokee cabin is likely to be devoid of a single scrap of Sequoyan as it is a copy of Catullus" (viii). Despite their grim prognosis for the future of Cherokee language writing and reading materials, the Kilpatricks still managed to gather a number of social documents between 1920 and 1965, thirty-five of which were translated in their book *The Shadow of Sequoyah* (1965).

Taking issue with the Kilpatricks' likening of the life expectancy of the Cherokee language to the whooping crane, anthropologist Willard Walker (1967: 83) lists a number of efforts being undertaken to promote Cherokee language, reading, and writing. Though he acknowledges that the number of speakers and writers of Cherokee has declined, he asserts that language instruction continues in the fifty-nine Cherokee-speaking churches, that a primer was printed and distributed to more than one thousand Cherokees, and that the number of speakers, though low, remains encouragingly strong. "With regard to the rate of Cherokee literacy . . . the percentage of Cherokees over thirty years of age who are literate in Cherokee varies from 36% at Hulbert . . . to 65% at rural Bull Hollow" (83). These data suggest that during the 1960s reading and writing in the Cherokee language in Oklahoma might "very well be retained indefinitely by the adult segment of the population as an integral part of Christian and pagan worship and of native medical practice" (83). Self-sponsored Cherokee-language materials were in use in several Cherokee-populated counties. The statistics that Walker cites were drawn from an advance copy of a report by a research team from the University of Chicago funded by the Carnegie Corporation to study bilingual education (Wahrhaftig 1966).

Albert Wahrhaftig, who was a graduate student at the University of Chicago in 1963, gathered demographic data on Cherokees for this Carnegie initiative. Wahrhaftig was asked to generate the descriptive statistics of Cherokee people living in rural areas where the language and writing system was still practiced. He completed this work with Hiner Doublehead and Fines Smith, both Cherokees fluent in the language and familiar with the families and communities in the hills of northeastern Oklahoma. Together they created a map and detailed counts of families in Oklahoma showing that more than fifty distinct communities of Cherokees still spoke, read, and wrote in the language. As a result of their work, and the work of numerous Cherokees who conducted linguistic research in their communities, they developed a collection of stories, a language primer, and a twice-weekly radio program and increased the circulation of the *Cherokee Nation Newsletter* (Cobb 2007: 473).

Despite the Kirkpatricks' grim forecast, perhaps it is more accurate to say that the Cherokee language, as Margaret Bender (2002: 18) writes, has "been remarkably resilient throughout the last two tumultuous centuries. . . . In Oklahoma in the 1970s the number of monolingual Cherokee-speakers was sufficient to merit a bilingual education program in the schools and translation services at public events and institutions" (18). Indeed, as this chapter demonstrates, the tenacity of the Cherokee people in adapting new technologies to reproduce, use, and foster the learning of Sequoyan is evident in the types of materials available to and circulating between monolingual and bilingual Cherokee speakers.

While the Kilpatricks might have lamented the limited number of manuscripts produced by and for Cherokees between 1920 and 1965, the variety of texts translated for their book alone suggests that use of the language remained consistent for everyday forms of secular and personal communications. Walker (1967: 84) found that these manuscripts "constitute an admirable sample of Cherokee literature." They included translations of documents (most of which were in the private collection of the authors), ranging from notes that a medicine person took on a patient to gospel songs, minutes of a Sunday school meeting, prayers, love letters, social comments on historical events, letters about specific experiences, poetry, observations, diary entries, and instructions on how to use medicines. With so many personal, interpersonal, and communal reasons to write, Cherokee manuscript production maintained itself among the speakers still left in Oklahoma. They were prompted to write for themselves, their loved ones, their communities, and perhaps even the imagined audiences of Cherokees in the future.[2]

Documents relating to the day-to-day workings of the Cherokee Baptist Church are particularly enduring in Cherokee culture. These churches, and the families who attend them, still use Cherokee and English in Oklahoma, while printed materials such as hymnals and the New Testament remain in use in both Oklahoma and North Carolina (Bender 2002). As part of his work with the Carnegie Project in Cross-Cultural Education from 1963 to 1967, Willard Walker (1967: 83) found that "some sort of regular instruction in the syllabary is being carried on in most of the fifty-nine Oklahoma Cherokee speaking churches." These churches worked together in a timeless tradition of creating ᏍᏏᎩ /gadugi/ 'work teams' to help another church's congregation. Gadugi are groups of people who join forces, sometimes with formal rules and officers in charge of certain supplies and duties, to address an immediate need or problem in the community (Kilpatrick and Kilpatrick 1966: 13). A work team can sometimes produce documents outlining its promised work or activities. For example, the Kilpatricks translated an early document written in Wolftown, North Carolina, in 1853 that describes the procedures that a church member would follow for borrowing funds jointly held by the gadugi. Tsali, a church member, was assigned to safeguard and distribute this money (11–13). This Wolftown work team was organized something like a cooperative bank, with ledgers produced to account for the monies taken in and distributed over the year.

As with townships, church communities practiced Cherokee reading and writing in support of gadugi. Unlike the work team in Wolftown, however, a work team in Oklahoma "is composed of unpaid workers called together for a specific task in the interests of a private charity or community welfare" (Kilpatrick and Kilpatrick 1965: 75). The tasks described in social documents of Oklahoma Cherokee Baptists did not have the economic imperative that the work team in the Wolftown documents conveys. When the Echota Sunday school made plans for the coming year in 1926, for example, the Sunday school committee met and planned several stages of preparation for a work team that was to take place for two weeks from July 25, 1926.[3] In the committee meeting minutes, they assigned Ahma and Wadi to find those who would get a cow for the meeting; chose

Unesdala to be in charge of frying the meat; assigned Digugodisgi to carry water and choose his helpers; and set the exact date, two weeks from Wednesday, for the gadugi to take place (76).

In another instance, Etsini Ganiqueyogi, the church secretary, was asked to coordinate church members from the Sycamore Tree Church in Cherokee County and the Echota Church in Adair County in order to organize workers for an upcoming church convention. In an official document from the Sycamore church to the Echota church written on August 21, 1938, she writes that the organization of members has been completed and that eighteen workers would be helping with the baking and "to help all of you in whatever you ask" (Kilpatrick and Kilpatrick 1965: 86). The names of nine women and nine men are listed in the document as workers who would be cooks, bakers, and helpers in general. Organizing work crews, assigning tasks, and securing resources to facilitate a larger common purpose have been central Cherokee cultural practices that demanded their share of Cherokee reading and writing. These practices were common to the everyday functioning of the church, and this document reveals that Cherokee Baptist churches were bringing people together at a time of need, feeding everyone present, and donating the logs, food, and work time to help each other build something better. Importantly, Sequoyan was at the center of these practices at a time when it was largely believed, as Daniel Cobb (2007: 466) puts it, that "a majority of Oklahomans accepted the fiction that . . . Cherokee history and peoplehood were, for all intents and purposes, things of the past." These documents indicate that, rather than being a thing of the past, Cherokee reading and writing was an ongoing, everyday practice used to support long-standing practices of organized, concerted efforts toward the betterment of the people.

Even when not related to gadugi, Cherokee Baptist Church documents reveal the ways in which particular practices of reverence became institutionalized through their codification in Cherokee writing. In a fascinating document dated May 30, 1955, in the collection of the Kilpatricks gathered from Sycamore Tree Baptist Church, the church secretary quotes the chairman reading from an official document produced some forty-six years earlier to set the procedures at the opening of the current ceremony and records the actions taken at the Sycamore Tree Cemetery Decoration on May 30, 1955:

> Chairman Uhyv:dhlo:yi Sdui:sdi opened the meeting at Sycamore Tree Cemetery Decoration:
> "'To begin, there will first be a song, then a prayer, and then the flower-makers will place the flowers here in the Cemetery. May 30, 1909.'
> "Now it is May 30, 1955. That is what we base this upon here to-day when we meet here in Sycamore Tree Cemetery. Now these are the Chairmen:
>> Suda:ni Une:gada
>> Uhyv:dhlo:yi Sdui:sdi
>> Ganv:do:hi Ga:dlinuli:sgi."
>
> May 30, 1955
>
> Old soldiers laid away and memorialized—3 in number.
> New soldiers—4 in number.
> Children buried during the past year—4 in number.
> Adults—1.
> First the ground will be cleared in order to place the flowers.
> 1. La:wan(i) Nuwo:dhvn(a)—preacher for the old soldiers.
> 2. I:nagi Ghu:wv—will afterward talk in English.
> 3. Sali:gug(i) Godé:sgi.
> All of the preachers will offer a dismissal prayer. (Kilpatrick and Kilpatrick 1965: 102–103)

This document served many purposes at once: it linked the current practices of honoring the dead to past practices, quoting from those precedents to establish the validity and authority of the current practices; it made a ceremonial procedure for this honoring by designating the exact steps to be taken by those present in order to honor the dead; it authorized the officers' roles by designating three chairmen of the ceremony as well as authorizing the speakers' roles; and it made room for English to be used in this observance that was officially conducted in the Cherokee language. This document reveals a glimpse into fundamental aspects of peoplehood (history, religion, and language) emerging in everyday procedures for a church ceremony. Most importantly, it reveals how Cherokee writing practices built upon each other over several decades in times when the language and culture of the people were not even believed to exist.

Documents written in Cherokee often referenced other documents, showing the integration and accumulation of various Cherokee-language texts. A document in the Kilpatricks' collection dated August 9, 1959, gives the minutes of a Sunday school meeting in Cherokee. The record keeper described a breadth of Cherokee-language texts being used at this Sunday school meeting. They sang from a Cherokee hymnal and "used the children's prayer book; and also the Chairman read Philippians, Chapter 1, Verses 23 to 28; and then we prayed. And then we began reading our Bibles, and then the Teacher read" (Kilpatrick and Kilpatrick 1965: 104). When the teacher finished reading, the congregation discussed the reading and any questions that they wanted to share about the verse.[4] This simple document chronicles a depth of reading and writing practices in Cherokee taking place in one church on August 9, 1959. The report on the ways in which the Bible was "read," "discussed," "questioned," and "understood" helps reveal the extent to which churches contributed to the tribal language and syllabary use in manuscript form. The Cherokee Baptist Church certainly played a noteworthy role in maintaining Cherokee-language reading and writing practices, as did the Cherokee traditional medicine people and others in their everyday lives.

Of the thirty-five documents dated between 1920 and 1965 included in *The Shadow of Sequoyah*, at least eight were written by medicine people or recorded traditional medicines, including diagnoses, prayers, remedies, prescriptions, notes on patients, recording of dreams, instructions for healing, and letters. These papers, the Kilpatricks (1965: 106) speculate, record "ways that were perhaps already ancient when Moses raised his rod in the wilderness." Medicine people have long been keepers of a vast array of Cherokee reading and writings (Mooney 1900; Bender 2002), and these documents recorded practices and knowledge often not meant for outsiders to see.

The Kilpatricks translated two letters from and to members of the traditional organization of the United Keetoowah Society. A letter from the chief of the Keetoowah Society conveys information about his family. The other letter, written by a Keetoowah Society official, reports on the recovery progress of another official, who plans to attend the next meeting if he can (Kilpatrick and Kilpatrick 1965: 90–93).

The eldest members of this society, represented in stomp grounds around Oklahoma, are said to have archived several hundred pages of tradition, in particular codifying the songs, prayers, and procedures for organizing stomps. Several Cherokees have referred to these documents but have also pointed out that only Cherokees who are fluent in the language and have been trained from a young age in how to run stomp grounds are privy to them. "Letters of the genre of this one," the Kilpatricks surmise, "must have been written by the thousands during the period in which the Sequoyah syllabary was in general use" (93).

Self-sponsored documents included in the Kilpatricks' collection reflect communication between families, recordings of memories, diary entries, and hymns and songs, which remain favorite subjects to record today. The "Hymn Book of Unesdala," a manuscript included in the Kilpatricks' collection, was said to have included hundreds of hymns. Kilpatrick and Kilpatrick (1965: 79) note that the writer, whose name means "Frozen," "had a habit of penciling in a Cherokee text of his own underneath the words in a book of gospel hymns. Many of these books so emended are still borrowed and battered about in his community." They included one of his hymns from the dozens available from him. These hymns could be the creations of their authors, based on melodies and meters from hymns sung throughout Cherokee country.

Circulated handwritten documents such as these referred to additional documents and exemplified many purposes and genres for writing between 1920 and 1965. These documents were written on any materials that Cherokees could find, from brochures to scraps of paper to empty pages and margins of books. In one document a Cherokee recorded the dates when the Cherokees went abroad in 1730: "in a small yellow notebook advertising a brand of snuff is a hodgepodge of entries that one would expect to find: dates of births and deaths, expenditures, names and addresses," and, to the surprise of Kilpatrick and Kilpatrick (1965: 101), a brief history of the Cherokee alliance with Britain in 1730. Certainly the kinds of information recorded in Sequoyan as well as the material nature of these documents are fascinating. Using nearly any materials available to them, Cherokees would write for their own purposes, remaking marketing materials sent to them in English into papers useful for their own ends.

SELF-DETERMINATION, THE CARNEGIE PROJECT, AND BILINGUAL EDUCATION

The average Cherokees' reading and writing efforts were not augmented by outside agencies and a newly constituted Cherokee Nation government until the mid-1960s. The Carnegie Cross-Cultural Education Project that ran from 1963 to 1967 was led by Sol Tax at the University of Chicago. As an action anthropologist, Tax desired to work with community members to author the terms of the change they sought. He assigned his graduate student Robert Thomas, the descendant of Cherokees, to help run the project, based in Tahlequah. Albert Wahrhaftig was in charge of gathering social and demographic data along with several Cherokee colleagues, including David Vann, Calvin Nackedhead, and Fines Smith. Within a year linguist and anthropologist Willard Walker joined the Carnegie Project team in cooperation with noteworthy Cherokee speakers and began producing materials to be distributed throughout the fourteen Cherokee counties. According to Cobb (2007: 473), they gathered and reproduced "a collection of stories and a primer that could be used in formal and informal settings to learn Cherokee." A radio show in Cherokee ran twice weekly, and a *Cherokee Nation Newsletter* was published from 1967 to 1968. This staff also developed an adult literacy course, hired Cherokee speakers, interpreters, and writers, and printed materials in Sequoyan (473).

Several important findings were brought to light as a result of the Carnegie Cross-Cultural Education Project. First, Cherokees were indeed speaking, reading, and writing in the language more than previously believed by outsiders and scholars such as the Kilpatricks. A detailed report (forty-five pages long) titled *The Cherokee People Today: A Report to the Cherokee People* (Wahrhaftig 1966) containing demographic data collected by Wahrhaftig and Cherokees Fines Smith, Wesley Proctor, G. J. Smith, and Hiner Doublehead showed the extent of Cherokee language use.

Alfred Wahrhaftig (2009) described the process by which the report was created. Written in Cherokee and English and illustrated by sixteen-year-old David Vann, the text was created on an IBM electric typewriter for which the team had commissioned a "bounding ball" in a Cherokee typeface with the Cherokee keyboard designed by

Willard Walker. They created 1,500 copies of the report and distributed them through the Tahlequah Printing Company, a shop on the
main street of Tahlequah run by a single person. The report sold for
$1 to English speakers and was free to Cherokee speakers.

In all, the team mapped seventy-four communities in northeastern Oklahoma, asking Cherokees who lived there to indicate who
was included in their communities. As Wahrhaftig (1966: 4) reports,
"Almost always, a Cherokee community consists of a number of
Cherokees living close to a Cherokee church house or stomp ground."
In 1963 they counted 9,491 people living in 1,937 households and
11,232 Cherokees who took part in community worship activities in
the Cherokee Nation (12, 14). Of the 9,491 Cherokees living in these
seventy-four communities, 7,800 spoke Cherokee; of the 11,232 Cherokees taking part in Cherokee life, about 10,500 spoke Cherokee (26).
Most of the children of these Cherokee speakers spoke English, but
"almost all Cherokee children understand Cherokee" (24). The researchers found that "children learn to read English when they are
very young. Some Cherokee children learn to read Cherokee when
they are very young, but most often, Cherokees do not learn to
read . . . until they are more than 30 years old" (26). An average of
47.5 percent of Cherokees in the largest towns who were over thirty
said that they could read Cherokee. Adults learn to read for the purposes of reading the Bible, reading and writing documents related
to traditional medicine, and keeping church records (26). The researchers did not ask who could write Cherokee.

In a report on detailed surveys taken in four Cherokee communities, Wahrhaftig (1970: 20) found that in these communities "the only
printed materials readily available in the Sequoyah syllabary are an
edition of the New Testament and a Cherokee Hymnal." Church records also proved to be a source of continued Cherokee reading and
writing activities, as did " 'medicine books' in which the sacred formulas and prayers for curing are written in Cherokee" (20). People
most commonly learned the writing system from an adult in their
household. "Whereas in the 1920's and 1930's Cherokees taught the
Sequoyah syllabary to children in organized classes at stomp grounds
and at Baptist Sunday schools, such classes" had become rare at the
time of this survey in the mid-1960s (21). In the small towns of Hurl-
bert, Cherry Tree, Marble City, and Bull Hollow, over 340 adults

between the ages of thirty and fifty understood the Cherokee syllabary (21).

This number of Cherokee speakers remaining in the rural Cherokee
communities also reflects the amount of education received. Wahrhaftig (1966: 30) found that 40 percent of "Cherokees living in Cherokee communities have finished 8th grade or gone beyond it." Because
English was and remains the primary language taught in Oklahoma
schools and so many Cherokees who have education move away from
the communities to find jobs, an inverse relationship emerges: the
more education Cherokees received, the less likely they were to remain in the community and speak the Cherokee language. Between
the sheer economic need to leave a small Cherokee community once
education had been obtained and the poorly staffed educational system that was ideologically disinclined to teach bilingual education, it
is unlikely that those Cherokees who went to school continued to have
reasons and materials to maintain their home language. These exigencies might help account for the downward trend in numbers of
Cherokee language users.

Those who did attend school also faced tremendous ideological
pressure to devalue the Cherokee language in favor of speaking,
reading, and writing in English. Wahrhaftig interviewed a Cherokee who had attended school on Black Gum Mountain in the 1890s
who told him that children who were not able to master literacy in
English were whipped:

> After this [the whippings] had gone on for some time, a group of
> Cherokee adults entered the school with whips of their own and
> wrote words on the blackboard in the Sequoyah syllabary. They
> told the teacher to read the words. When he could not, they told him
> that if he intended to whip their children for being unable to read
> words in *his* language, then they intended to whip him for being
> unable to read words in *their* language . . . and they did. (Cherokee
> informant quoted in Wahrhaftig 1970: 25; emphasis in the original)

Such pride in reading and writing Cherokee would remain in
Cherokee communities, though people often decided to opt out of
the educational system altogether in lieu of compromising their linguistic perseverance. A chosen alienation and the safety of seclu-
sion in small cohesive communities allowed Cherokees in these

communities to continue practicing the language. By the time the Carnegie Foundation funded this study in the 1960s, Cherokees were among the least-educated groups of people in Oklahoma, though many may have been able to read, write, and speak in the Cherokee language.

The idea of the Carnegie Project was to promote Sequoyan in order to encourage greater ease in the transition to schools and the English-speaking world's language and institutions. For Sol Tax, the director of the project, the goal was to learn something from this study that would allow Native peoples around the world to become more developed, presumably through a greater facility of interacting with white institutions (Cobb 2007: 469). Wahrhaftig (1998: 95) explains that the Carnegie Project in Cross-Cultural Education was in response to an alarmingly low English literacy and educational attainment rate for Cherokees, the lowest of any American Indian group according to the 1950 census. "Cherokees had obviously withdrawn from schools, education, and English literacy in general," the researchers' logic went, so the problem "lay with negative definitions of literacy and education which were themselves the product of inequities in social structure. . . . The thrust of the Carnegie project in Tahlequah was to test the proposition that "people will more rapidly become literate in a national language if they first become literate in their own language" (95). So the point of the Carnegie Project was to help Cherokees value their own language more, seeing it as something that could be useful in working with white mainstream institutions, such as schooling and government. In other words, the purpose of getting Cherokees to value their language more was so that they would ostensibly value English more, placing the onus to change language ideologies squarely on the shoulders of Cherokees who ironically already secretly harbored esteem for the Cherokee language and writing system.

The problem was not Cherokees who valued Sequoyan and the language but white schoolteachers, Oklahomans in general, and the national government, which all held the Cherokee language in low esteem. The children raised in Cherokee-speaking households had increasingly felt the ways in which the white public stigmatized the Cherokee language. These children stopped using Cherokee in the home and were less likely to practice it when speaking with their younger siblings, creating a schism between generations in households where children sometimes used a language different from that of their parents (Wahrhaftig 1970: 17–18). Hence by the mid-1960s Cherokees who spoke, read, and wrote the language understood well that Cherokee language use had been discouraged in schools. The bilingual education policies at this time reinforced this negative valuation of Native languages and emphasized instead the need for Cherokees to lose their language in order to learn English and attend school.

As a result of the 1968 Bilingual Education Act, bilingual programs were spearheaded by Northeastern State University and public schools in the fourteen-county area in the jurisdiction of the Cherokee Nation. Dr. Neil Morton, the former director of Education Services for the Cherokee Nation and one of its longest-serving employees, clarified the initial missions of bilingual education programs in an audiotaped interview (Morton 2009):

> Those programs were designed primarily to ease the transition from the home to public school because of the child's lack of facility in the English language. It was not uncommon in 1970 for students to come to school for first grade or kindergarten, if the school happened to have a kindergarten, without the ability to speak a single word of English. So the bilingual program was not really designed to promote Cherokee. It was designed as a bridge, or really not even that, a crutch, to aid the transition from Cherokee speaking to English speaking classrooms. . . . But the bilingual effort was spearheaded by Northeastern State University. . . . It was a method to advance English, not Cherokee.

In 1969 the Cherokee Bilingual Education program was funded by the U.S. government and began operation in four rural Oklahoma schools. The students who were enrolled in the federally sponsored Bilingual Education program, developed for the elementary classes in 1971, showed significant increases in reading abilities in English by 1982 (Bacon et al. 1982). But their abilities to read and write in Cherokee were not surveyed. While the Carnegie Project did not achieve its goal to create greater valuation of the Cherokee language among Cherokee elders, who already valued their language, and did not help Cherokees ease into English-speaking schools, it (along with the federal bilingual education program) might inadvertently have prompted an increased appreciation for the Cherokee language.

The numbers of readers and speakers of Cherokee in the early 1960s, while somewhat more encouraging than had been expected by scholars and outsiders, demonstrated a need for more materials printed and distributed in Cherokee, for more materials for children in Cherokee, and for a consolidated effort to increase the numbers of speakers, readers, and writers. Institutional and governmental support for Cherokee language use also began in the mid- and late 1960s. These efforts would dovetail well with the continued use of Sequoyan and the Cherokee language in small communities.

LANGUAGE PERSEVERANCE, THE
NATION, AND THE TRIBE

Without an elected leader and official Cherokee Nation from 1906 to 1971, the Cherokee people still continued to speak, read, and write in Cherokee, to value their language, and to find ways to use it, if in secret and in isolation from outsiders. Chief Keeler was not always sympathetic and indeed was often suspicious of the Carnegie Project team, though the team hoped to influence federal Indian policy to move away from the destructive termination ideas to a more promising ideology of self-determination (Cobb 2007: 474–78). The politics regarding who should run the Cherokee language revitalization efforts and the creation of the Cherokee heritage center and village were fractious indeed (Cobb 2007). When all was said and done, however, Keeler was duly elected chief by the people in 1971 and the Carnegie team moved on to take up different initiatives. The Cherokee government was reestablished, and in 1976 the Constitution was ratified.

The Cherokee Nation with W. W. Keeler as the appointed chief began running the *Cherokee Nation News* as an offshoot of the *Newsletter* from 1967 to 1977. This newsletter was printed primarily in English, though it did include selected pieces in Sequoyan developed by the Cherokee Nation Bilingual Education program, including a traditional story of the Ukten or Uktana (fig. 7.3). The April 3, 1973, issue of the *Newsletter* also listed the types of materials made

THUNDER AND THE UK'TEN'

By Willie Chopper, with translation by the Cherokee Bilingual Program, Tahlequah, Okla.

This is the story of when an Uk'ten' and Thunder had a fight. Some people tell it a little bit different. When I hear other people tell it, sometimes it (their version) seems better. This one (version) I know is a little bit similar (to the version of Yansa) and others have told it before. The older men used to tell this one (version). This one tells about how the Uk'ten' and Thunder first found each other.

In olden times there were two boys. They used to hunt all the time with bows and arrows. Sometimes they killed birds and squirrels, sometimes rabbits and many (other) smaller animals.

Once the two boys were walking in a deep valley where it was very rugged and rocky. As they were walking among big rocky crags, they found a large snake lying upon a rock. This snake was very lean and hungry. He told the boys to stop, that he wanted to ask them something.

"I'm very hungry," he said to them. "Would you find me some food? I'll eat birds or squirrels. When I become strong again, you can use me, or I'll help you in whatever you are doing in any way that I can for as long as we live."

DBLꭲGꙅY Dꝏ ᎣY'Ꮟh

ᎪDZ ꙡZᏢᏉ θ ᎣYꙏh Dꝏ DBLꭲGꙅY ᎣꝏCᏋT.
TSꙆZ DhZᏢꙅE ꙡꙆYꙆ ꝗꙆꝏ θᎣΛᏏT. DhꝼTZ Dh-
ZᏢꙅE ꙅYꝏSθ, ꜧꙆYꝯ ꜧθᎣΛꝼ ChZᏢꙅA θꝲᏢꙅLΛꝼT.
ᎣꝯꙆꙅ GꙅꙆ DhꝼT ᎣhZᏢᏢT ᎭD. ꝯθꝏꙅꙆZ ᎣhZᏢᏢ
ᎭD Cꭲhꟽ. ᎪDZ ꙡZᏢꙅY θ ᎣYꙏh Dꝏ DBLꭲGꙅY
TEꙅ SθꙆGꝏ@T.

ᎪꙅYZ ꜧꝼR DhᏔᏢᏉ DᎪᏢT. ꜧᎪꙅꝗZ DhZᏉꝼ-
VᏢ ꙆSCꙆ EꙆ. TBꙆᏉZ ꜧꙅꭲ Dꝏ ᎤGᏢ ꙆhꜧᎪᏢT,
TBꙆᏉZ ꜧꙅS Dꝏ ꝯꙆꝏᎣꙆ AꝲꙅꙆ TᎣꝼ RꙆT.

ᎤꙅZ GGYꙆ ᎭD DhꝯC DθTᏉ ᏉᎾh SꝼꙆᏢB
Ꭳꜧꙅꝏ Dꝏ Ꭳꜧꙅ FR, ᎣᎾZ DθTR ꞀᏔθ ꙡAꙅꙆꙅ Ꭳꙅ
SSWꝼB ᎣhGꝏᏢ TᎾꙆ ᎣᏔθ ShE Ꭳꜧ SST. ᎤGᏢZ
ꙆEGꙅꙅꙆ TYꙆ ꜧRY. ᎣꝏꝼꙆ Dꝏ ᎣꜧꙅꙅY ꝼᏉ TᎾꙆ.
ꝯθꝏᎾꙅVꙆ SᎣᏉꝏ DhꝯC. AꝲꙅꙆZ ꝯꝏꙆ ᎣSᏢꙅꝼ,
ᎭD TᎾꙆ.

TS DYꜰꙅᏉ, SᎣᏉꝏT. RᏢꙅꙅ TꙅYhꜰꙅ
AꝲꙅꙆ DYYꙅꙆ ꜧꙅꭲ Dꝏ ᎤGᏢ ꙅY TSꜧꙅS. DG-
ꝇhYꙆ TꝗᏢꙅꟽθ, ꙅꙅᏢꙅY ꙅY. ꜧSꙆꙅ AꝲꙅꙆ ꙅꙆ-
ꝏꙡꙅ ᎾYYꙅ TSꭲ TꙅꙅꙅꙅᏢ TSꙅ TAᎠꙆ, SᎣᏉꝏ ᎭD
TᎾꙆ.

Continued Next Week

available by the Cherokee Bilingual Program, including a syllabary primer in which "each lesson is devoted to a character and reviewed and drilled again in later lessons so one doesn't forget"; Cherokee oral language programs in Roman script; conversational tapes; a calendar "completely typed in the syllabary with illustrations by a local Indian artist"; and, of course, Cherokee songbooks, "typed in three different ways, English, Roman script, and translated into the Cherokee syllabary" (3). The Cherokee Nation stood behind efforts to persevere in the language, history, and spiritual aspects of people-hood, as it does today. Sequoyan was at the center of these efforts, which indicates the key role that this writing system plays in facili-tating language learning.

Perhaps the single most important work that the Cherokee Nation Bilingual Education program produced was Durbin Feeling's *Cherokee-English Dictionary* (1975), edited by William Pulte. The Au-gust 21, 1973, issue of the *Newsletter* describes this important work undertaken by a committee and commissioned by Chief W. W. Keeler. "For many years, the Cherokees have needed, longed for and wanted a dictionary of their language. It was to be a special dictionary that could be used by speakers of Cherokee and those unable to speak but the desire to learn Cherokee. That dream is now coming true" (2). The dictionary opens with a dedication by Chief Keeler, who clearly links continued use of Sequoyan and the language as central aspects of Cherokee peoplehood: "I believe that if the Cherokee people are to retain their heritage, it is necessary for them to also preserve their culture by continuing the use of the language" (fore-word). Connecting language, culture, and identity in this way, Chief Keeler manifests an underlying notion of peoplehood and a clear understanding of one of the most important ways in which tribes can maintain the mutually supporting relationships of language, history, place, and spirituality.

In 1973 Agnes Cowen took up the Cherokee Nation Bilingual Ed-ucation Program as a nonprofit initiative after the national bilingual education program had run its course at Northeastern University. As Dr. Morton explains,

> Since Mrs. Cowen was a first language speaker of Cherokee and held an M.A. in elementary education, this made her a natural fit for

the program to expand. So her methodology was to use the bilingual program as this transition and to promote the Cherokee language. It worked wonderfully because at first the language was viewed as a novelty by the students. "How do you say red in Cherokee?" And it became popular to speak Cherokee among non-Cherokees as well as Cherokee students, so it's a complete reversal. . . . So Agnes Cowen did a great deal to reverse that prejudice, and for me it became so refreshing to go into a classroom and see an entire bulletin board with the Cherokee syllabary describing the items on the bulletin board. And to have Cherokee children and non-Cherokee children say: "How do you say this? How do you say that?" So Cherokee became popular. . . . I'd say it became popular by 1985.

The Cherokee Nation Bilingual Education program began providing materials and opportunities and stressing positive values attached to the Cherokee language. Cherokee children saw non-Cherokee kids in their class becoming interested in the language, appreciating it, and wanting to learn phrases. Agnes Cowen's educational efforts reinscribed the mission of the national bilingual education program with an ideology that valued Cherokee as much as English.

This positive valuation of Cherokee also contributed to the development of new technologies and educational resources to engage readers and popularize the Cherokee language. The nonprofit organization commissioned the creation of a Cherokee typewriter from the Paillard Corporation. Two manual typewriters had been created for the Cherokee Nation (fig. 7.4), but Cowen's typewriter was the first electric one. As the *Cherokee Nation News* (April 10, 1973) reported in the caption under a picture of Adalene Smith: "Adalene Smith, Cherokee translator, Cherokee Bilingual Education Program, Tahlequah, said it took her three months to learn how to type on this unique typewriter. She presently types 30 wpm." The keyboard has eighty-five keys in an arrangement that shows no relation to either the script syllabary or the printed order. In fact, the logic of the keyboard arrangement remains a mystery. The *Cherokee Nation News* report on the new electric typewriter also included a freshly typed hymn (a favorite genre among Cherokees, as noted). "America" was "translated by Agnes Cowen and typed on the Cherokee typewriter

Figure 7.4. One of two manual typewriters created for the Cherokee Nation. The keyboard layout matches the layout of the Cherokee electric typewriter with one exception. The electric typewriter switched the fourth key from the left top row (ᏥᎦ) with the third key from the left in the third row (iσ'). The typewriter is on display at the Sequoyah Cabin in Sallisaw, Okla. Courtesy of the Research Division of the Oklahoma Historical Society.

by Adalene Smith." The Cherokee translation was typed with a phonetic spelling of the syllables in the Roman alphabet.

By 1975 the Cherokee Bilingual Education Program was producing bilingual materials for all ages. Led by Agnes Cowen and Faynell Mills, Cherokee/English bilingual speakers, readers, and writers created a host of materials. Martin Cochran and Agnes Cowen (1972) published a young-adult book called *Life of Famous Cherokee Men* in which they profiled Sequoyah, William Wirt Hastings, Will Rogers, Joseph Thornton, and Elias Boudinot. The stories were created for teachers and bilingual assistants at the middle-school level to help in developing units on all of the men in the book. Each unit begins with a three- to five-page biography in Sequoyan, followed by several pages of loose interpretations in English and illustrations. The opening story of Sequoyah introduces English speakers to the writing system as it appeared in print: "Sequoyah used many living things to form his characters. Some were based upon the walking stick and other insects. Some came from worms and snakes. On the following pages are sources for some of these characters" (5–6).

These hand-lettered pages were obviously meant to provide a visual mnemonic for many of the eighty-six printed characters. Although it is likely that Sequoyah developed a visual mnemonic for learning the manuscript form and developing it into shorthand for print, the mnemonic in this book seems to come from the script version of the characters. In any case Cochran and Cowen believed that a visual mnemonic for the glyphs might have been useful for the bilingual education teachers who had learned to write using the alphabet.

Agnes Cowen and Martin Cochran also published a series of comics in conjunction with King Features in both Cherokee and English, including Mort Walker's *Beetle Bailey* (fig. 7.1), Chic Young's *Blondie* (fig. 7.5), and Mort Walker and Dik Browne's *Hi and Lois*.

The comic book seems to have been produced in English print first, with talk bubbles and space left blank for the Cherokee to be handwritten. Then the whole comic was compiled into one master copy and printed by Charlton Publications, Inc. The inside cover explains the unique way to read the comic, which was compiled in Cherokee for the first half and in English for the second half. Clearly intended for Cherokee readers of all ages, these comics had an important impact in making the Cherokee writing system popular and accessible again in manuscript form, which was then printed and distributed.

The Cherokee Phoenix and Indian Advocate resumed printing in 1977 in the Cherokee Nation and still features the Cherokee syllabary in its masthead. The paper publishes mostly stories related to the government and general interest stories in both Cherokee and English. These newspapers, a visible manifestation of the newly formed Cherokee Nation, provided even more impetus for a revaluation of the Cherokee language in the larger society.

Dr. Morton describes the complexity of these changing value systems in relation to the new Cherokee language classes that were instituted for adults between 1970 and 1980. "These were taught by Cherokee speakers who were not teachers. . . . But oddly enough many of the first enrollees in the classes were not Cherokees who missed out in that generation but were shopkeepers, storekeepers. They saw this as a way to increase their clientele. . . . The general Cherokee isolated community residents were rather hesitant to accept this newfound interest in the language because they had been

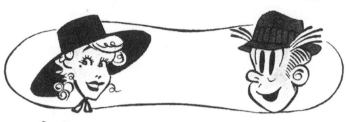

ᏣᎳᎩ / GWY

ᎠᏗ ᏣᎯᎢ ᎤᏩᏓ ᏯᏁᏥᏍᎪᏍ.
ᏔᎦ ᎠᎦᏟ ᏣᏯᏫ ᎠᏣᏲᎠᏍ.
ᏫᎾᏃ ᎠᎦᏟ ᏔᏍ ᎦᎾᎦᏫ ᎠᏣᏲᎠᏍ
ᏣᏯᏃ ᏬᏍᎦᎢᎠ Ꮎ ᏣᏯᏫ ᎠᏬᏝ
ᏔᎦ ᏇᎦᎦᎠᏲᎠᏍ ᏣᎷᏍᎢᏔ. ᏔᏍᏃ
ᏇᏟᎠᏟᏯᏲᎠᏍ �YᏫ ᎦᎾᎦᏫ ᎠᏬᏝ
ᎠᎳᏲᎠᏲᎠᏍ. ᏓᏃ ᏤᎠᏋ ᏯᎷᎬ
ᎤᏣᎦ ᏛᎮᏁ ᎠᏬᎦᏔ, ᎠᏝᏃ
ᎡᏍᏬ ᎦᏟᏴ ᎾᏍᏭᏲᎠᏔ.
ᎦᎾᏍᏃ ᏬᏍᎦᎢᎠ ᏊᏲᎢ Ꮎ
ᏍᎢᏍᏚᏗ ᎤᏦᎢᏋ
ᎮᏣᏯᏲᎠᏍ. ᏔᎦ ᎠᎦᏟ
ᎠᎠᏍᏬ ᏣᏍᎹᏝᏬᎡ ᏔᏍ
ᎵᎮᏔ.

ᏃᏍᏃ Ꭰ ᎸᎮᏍᎡᎾ ᎠᎠᏗ ᏍᏙᎲᏊᎢᏔ
ᏇᏁᏍᏚ ᏔᏣᎡᎵᏣᏔ.ᎾᎲ. 31;32;33

• ENGLISH

This is a special comic book. The first half of the book has stories written in Cherokee. The second half has the same stories in English.

If you are learning Cherokee try reading that part first. If there are words that puzzle you check the same page in the English section. The words may not be exactly the same, but you will understand the thought.

If you are learning English, start with the stories on page 17 and use the first half of the book to check your understanding of it.

Translated by Martin Cochran, Materials Development Assistant

Prepared under the direction of Agnes Cowen and Faynell Mills, Co-Directors of the Cherokee Bilingual Education Program

Figure 7.5. Inside cover of *Blondie* in Cherokee and English, explaining how the comic is to be read. Blondie © King Features Syndicate.

discouraged for three generations not to use the language." Cherokees had experienced having their mouths washed out with soap for speaking Cherokee, losing their recesses and lunch hours for refusing to speak English, and being punished for not speaking English fluently. "So this new turnaround happened rapidly, but in some areas. It didn't happen too rapidly in the isolated communities. The isolated communities . . . by 1980 had stopped teaching children Cherokee." The Cherokee communities that practiced the language in "calculated inconspicuousness" until the 1965 Carnegie Project had nearly stopped teaching their children to speak Cherokee, because the language had been so stigmatized in schools and by the public. When children began to perceive that their parents' language use was "backward," they too started relying more on English (Wahrhaftig 1970).

Cherokee adults did not trust this newfound interest because generations of Cherokees had experienced oppression, brutality, and humiliation for not speaking English. They had witnessed the ways in which their language use was stigmatized and therefore, understandably, practiced it only in places and through means that they knew were safe and secure. In this context, Cherokees understood that the purposes in using the language would become bounded by private needs. Because Cherokee language use was so stigmatized until the 1980s, the reasons for Cherokee language use became less frequent, more private, and thus harder to generate. Despite the writing system's power to codify linguistic information, Cherokees faced the threat of language extinction on two fronts. First, young people in the tribe showed a decreased willingness to learn and use the language. Second, outside pressures for generations had stigmatized and punished the use and learning of the language.

The Cherokee Nation Bilingual Education Program helped generate broader appeal for the language by producing instructional materials for readers and speakers in Sequoyan as well as through its clever adaptation of the language to mainstream publishing, language classes, and new technologies. This newfound interest slowly permeated the limestone of public belief about the importance of the Cherokee language, recharged the wellspring of its value, and at last flowed clearly into the murky waters of mainstream opinion, at precisely the time when the language faced alarmingly low numbers of speakers. This remarkable coalescence of outward value by shop-keepers, the resurgence of the Cherokee Nation through newspapers and educational programs and materials, and a higher profile for the speakers of the language contributed to a rebirth of interest in the Cherokee syllabary and the language it so closely represents.

While this brief history demonstrates the often-unseen persever-ance of the tribe, the material forms that the Cherokee syllabary took during this long winter and welcomed spring suggest that its flexi-bility contributed to its continued use. Manuscript forms of the Chero-kee language circulated in isolated communities among adults who used them to record histories, church procedures, and medicines; organize work groups at stomp grounds; communicate with distant friends and relatives; and serve as a mnemonic for important dates. Handwritten into comic books in the 1970s, printed in reports and newspapers, and typewritten in educational resources, the material forms of this flexible writing system can be adapted for almost any communication technology.

This ability to adapt to many media while retaining crucial links to linguistic information has proven especially important for the proliferation of Sequoyan in modern times. It is worth pointing out that each new medium does not replace a former medium but builds upon it, extending its reach and social value without compromising its visual and linguistic integrity. As chapter 8 describes, the Chero-kee writing system in digital forms has taken center stage in recent secular and national efforts to ensure that this aspect of Cherokee peoplehood remains strong.

PEOPLEHOOD AND PERSEVERANCE

The Cherokee Language, 1980–2010

To this point, I have been arguing that the Cherokee syllabary has played a crucial role in facilitating Cherokees' efforts to maintain a sense of peoplehood through profound social and cultural change. Sequoyan has been a flexibly adaptive tool that codifies meaningful units of language in script, print, and digital media (as this chapter demonstrates). Whenever the syllabary is present, the four aspects of peoplehood can potentially be present as well: language, sacred history, religion, and place. Like any tool endowed with various meanings by the people who use it, the Cherokee writing system has been a central part of language perseverance efforts in secular and national initiatives.

The proliferation of the Cherokee language and Sequoyan in print fluctuated with the historical fortunes of the Cherokee Nation. Times of peace and prosperity allowed the nation to focus on developing materials, classes, and initiatives that promoted continued use of the Cherokee language and writing system; times of war, poverty, short-sighted federal policies, and social stigmatization had a negative impact on the types of materials, learning situations, and initiatives available for Cherokees to continue practicing the language publicly. Cherokees in small towns, however, kept use of the language alive in churches and stomp grounds, in daily communications, and through a legacy of religious literature printed in the syllabary. The language was stigmatized outside of the home until the mid-1960s, but it would take another twenty years until Cherokee elders who lived in these small towns began to trust this newfound interest in the language. With self-determination and newly established tribal governments in the 1970s, Cherokees elected their first chief since allotment: W. W. Keeler. The nation itself was poised to address the abject poverty, need for health services, and erosion of language use and began to prioritize its efforts.

Educational projects of the Cherokee Nation have addressed the need for more purposes and material forms for use of the Cherokee language on multiple fronts. These efforts have been prompted by an increased urgency on the part of traditional speakers and the nation's representatives to address perhaps the single most important cultural issue for Cherokees today: impending language loss. As one of the four pillars of peoplehood, language is absolutely essential to a shared cultural and social identity. The Cherokee Nation recognized the growing problem of language erosion and passed legislation in 1991 to address the problem. Under the Act Relating to the Tribal Policy for the Promotion and Preservation of Cherokee Language, History and Culture (Cherokee Nation 1991), Cherokee and English were finally recognized as the official languages of the tribe, providing even more validity and impetus for the use of Cherokee. Cherokees from rural communities might again begin to see the nation's valuing of the language through its use in official functions. The Cherokee Nation would try to use both Cherokee and English when providing services, resources, and information and communicating concerns to members of the tribal council.

Officially sanctioning the use of Cherokee, the act recognizes the necessity for more materials to be produced by the nation in official communications. The act provides a policy whereby the political arm of the nation will maintain Cherokee as a living language:

A. Efforts to involve tribal members to the greatest extent possible in instruction in Cherokee language.

B. Establishment of a permanent Cherokee Language Program within the Tribal Education Department. . . .

C. Encourage the use of Cherokee language in both written and oral form to the fullest extent possible in public and business settings.

D. Encourage creation and expansion of the number, kind, and amount of written materials in the Cherokee language. (702)

Cherokee Nation employees were charged with learning Cherokee language, history, and culture as part of their hiring and to "promote pride and tribal identity and respect for the tribal government and Cherokee people" (703). Use of the Cherokee language and syllabary was to be supported in everyday work with the nation's citizens, in outreach to educational institutions, and in the internal development of employee skills in representing the language, culture, and history. At the same time, the act provides for an explicit, public, and open valuation of the language, to be shared by the 6,500 employees of the Cherokee Nation. The extent to which Cherokee is used in day-to-day national functions, publications, and educational initiatives is slowly becoming more apparent.

In addition to creating more Cherokee-language materials, developing the knowledge base of employees, and promoting a positive view of Cherokees and Native peoples, the act also calls for increased attention and devotion of time, energy, and efforts to reach out to educational institutions. These provisions address the need to recognize and employ Cherokee elders who are fluent in the language, to oppose negative and biased depictions of Cherokees and American Indians in educational institutions, and to provide instruction in many settings before and after school, in the evening, and on weekends for adults interested in the Cherokee language.

In his interview Dr. Neil Morton (2009), who served as director of Education Services for the Cherokee Nation, credits this act and Chief Smith with the development of the plethora of educational initiatives currently undertaken by the nation, many of which rely on Sequoyan in multiple forms. In order to develop these programs, Education Services first needed to judge how many people speak the Cherokee language in Oklahoma today. Dr. Morton explained that determining this was not at all easy. What the nation learned about the number of speakers and learners is alarming:

> We actually do not know. We find that there is hesitancy for persons . . . the elderly persons who speak the language, it's not uncommon for them to say, "Well, I do not speak it well." We find so

few that will say, "Yes, I speak it and I can read and write." Even
those who can read and write, by very careful study and trial and
error, will indicate on a survey that they cannot. So . . . we did a
survey in 2002 within the jurisdictional area of the Cherokee Nation.
The survey found that—in other words, they may have been there,
but we didn't find them—found that no one under the age of forty
was fully conversant in the language. We found that about fifty out
of three hundred spoke the language in the homes. And the most
damaging thing that we found is that most children of fluent speakers did not speak [Cherokee]. . . . In 1991 Chief Smith signed the
Cherokee National Language and Cultural Preservation Act. And
there was a gradual, methodical process until the opening of the
immersion schools [in 2001].

Dr. Morton refers to a survey undertaken by the Cherokee Nation
that was the first step in an initial phase of developing a robust
language-renewal plan. While Cherokee speakers might still be reluctant to admit their fluency when taking a survey, it may be close
to accurate that no one under the age of forty was fully conversant
with the language. According to Will Chavez (2009: 1), this same
survey of Cherokee citizens "showed nearly 64 percent of Cherokee
citizens do not speak or understand the language. About 5 percent
understand the language but cannot speak it, 17 percent understand
and have some speaking ability, 3 percent are conversational, 10 percent are highly fluent, and only 1 percent have mastery of the language." It is even more disturbing that so few children raised in
homes where Cherokee is the primary language spoken are retaining their language once they enter English-speaking schools. Importantly, though, 95 percent of the respondents surveyed agreed
that ensuring the vitality of the language was important to Cherokee identity and heritage (Simmons 2009). This suggests that the language is valued as part of identity and heritage, that language loss is
an important issue to address in order to maintain Cherokee peoplehood, and that those Cherokees who still speak, read, and write
the language are valued assets.

The "gradual, methodical process" of addressing the alarming attri-
tion rates of speakers that Dr. Morton refers to has involved the development of a host of educational programs run by and for the Cherokee
Nation and funded primarily by the Department of the Interior and

the Cherokee Nation. Infrastructure was established and a staff was hired to direct several arms of the Education Services at the Cherokee Nation, including Cultural Resources, which does translating and online language classes; the Cherokee Heritage Center, which provides education and archival resources; higher education, Sequoyah High School, and Early Childhood and Head Start programs; and Co-Partner, Learn and Serve, and immersion programs that develop collaborative efforts to bolster Cherokee language, history, and culture education in summer and after-school programs.

With an operating budget of over $43 million and 329 employees, the programs run by these groups in the Cherokee Nation Education Services Team have touched every level of educational advancement for citizens inside Oklahoma and around the country. These programs support 842 Head Start children, 87 students in the Cherokee Immersion School, 20,198 Johnson O'Malley students, 389 Sequoyah High School students, and 3,600 online language program participants (Cherokee Nation 2007: 2). This coordinated effort addresses several problems in Cherokees' overall education and schooling in Oklahoma: the need for more curricular materials to address the history of Oklahoma accurately and fully; the need for access to language speakers and opportunities to learn, practice, and immerse in the Cherokee language; and the need for careful and accurate cultural representations of Cherokee life and traditions.

Although an extensive portrayal of these efforts is beyond the scope of this book, some discussion of the materials produced using the Cherokee syllabary is warranted. The Cherokee syllabary can codify so much linguistic information that it makes sense to use it whenever possible in these classes. Many of the resources developed by the Cherokee Nation's Education Services group recognize the important cultural work that the Cherokee writing system does. The teachers and translators in the Education Services group must rely upon the Roman alphabet to varying degrees, however, depending on the audiences for these educational resources. When and where Sequoyan and the Cherokee language can be used extensively, the learners seem to garner deeper experience and stronger relationships to Cherokee history, culture, and place. When English and transliterations of Cherokee into the Roman alphabet must be relied upon, it is much harder to gauge the depth of experience.

THE CHEROKEE IMMERSION SCHOOL

The Cherokee Immersion School was created in 2001 to ensure that the Cherokee language was being taught to youths in order to address the problems revealed in the 2001 survey. The Cherokee language would not survive another generation, because most of the speakers were over the age of fifty and the children were not learning and using the language. The school boasted a 2009 budget of $2.6 million and is funded completely by the Cherokee Nation general fund. This translates to roughly $43,000 per student spent each year to help ensure that youths are learning the language (Good Voice 2009). Dr. Morton describes the current organization and five-year plan for the school. The first class was enrolled in 2001: "we add a class each year. We started with three-year olds . . . the preschoolers, the kindergarteners, first graders, second graders, third graders. We graduated third graders last year. We have a fourth grade this year. We add a grade each year." The long-range plan for the Immersion School students follows this step-by-step progression, adding a new class each year, with some instruction in English in later years.

> We'll go preschool, in other words age three, through grade six with immersion. With a gradual implementation of English primarily in an after-school mode, but with some in school as the grades progress. And then for those students that desire to go into the seventh and eighth grade at Sequoyah [High School], we will have a regular English curriculum and will have one class in Cherokee. . . . Then for the High school, we will offer Cherokee each of the four years of high school with progressive difficulty. By the time the students finish twelfth grade, they will be at the mastery level in Cherokee and will be translators actually.

All of the students enrolled in this Immersion School come from English-speaking homes, though the majority of students and parents are citizens of the Cherokee Nation. Some of the students are citizens of other tribes, and a few are not enrolled in any tribe. Despite the limited amount of Cherokee used in the home, the success of the school is attributable to a single statistic: "Our third graders are fully fluent in reading and writing, in other words, they have begun to think in Cherokee. They keep their journals and so forth"

in Cherokee. The ability of the students to read and write in Sequoyan and speak Cherokee is important because it reverses the trend
of a generation earlier: "So now we have eighty-seven students in
the immersion program. . . . but none of the parents of the eighty-
seven students speak the language." Parents of these students may
have grown up in households in or near Cherokee communities, but
this generation did not benefit from programs designed especially
for continuation and deep immersion in the Cherokee language.
The children of these parents, however, are already fluent in the
language.

This remarkable achievement can be attributed to a well-resourced,
well-educated staff that tries to hold steadfastly to the explicit value
of the Cherokee language and process of education in which students never hear and rarely see English and the alphabet in the curriculum. The Cherokee-only rule is ostensibly applied in this school
every day, except, of course, when speaking to the parents of the
children. "To have the opportunity to place young Cherokee students
from preschool to grade one in a setting where they enter school at
8:30 in the morning until they leave school at 3:30 in the afternoon,
never having seen or heard any language other than Cherokee. Now
that has not been done before. That is brand new. So we're taking
the genius of Sequoyah into this century. And that is exciting" (Cherokee Nation 2009a). Of course the students live in an English setting
outside of school; but during school hours Cherokee in all forms is
privileged, explicitly excluding English and the alphabet in much
the same way that Sequoyah himself privileged the Cherokee language and his own writing system and excluded English and the
alphabet.

This policy, initially supported by the parents of the students,
proved more difficult to sustain than originally hoped. Some of the
students in this school, though able to read and write in Cherokee to
an age-appropriate degree, apparently went through testing in English and were found to be behind in their math and science rates.
This caused concern among the parents, who successfully lobbied
the school administrators to offer extended classes at the end of the
day in English in math and science. The two teachers from the school
with whom I spoke were frustrated with the parents and their colleagues who taught in English, especially during the main part of

the day, due to their willful ignorance of the initial Cherokee-only policy. They believed that the parents should have taken more responsibility for their children's learning outside of school and knew when they enrolled their children that this would be required of them. These teachers were adamant that the Cherokee-only curriculum had achieved impressive success in developing Cherokee speakers, the ostensible goal for the school in the first place.

Part of this success is because the eighty-seven youths who are enrolled in the Cherokee Immersion School learn the syllabary with no references to English phonetic spellings of the glyphs.[1] Most of the curricular materials produced for these classes are solely in Sequoyan, although some provide English transliterations. When produced in digital media the sounds of the glyphs are always written in the syllabary and not in English transliterations. Because these students are deeply immersed in the language, they do not need to have literal translations for each of the phrases.

For example, in a document that instructor Ed Fields provided to his online language classes and Dr. Morton provided to me during our interview as part of the Immersion School curriculum, a young boy is pictured with the parts of his body identified in Cherokee (fig. 8.1). The Cherokee words for anatomical features take prefixes to identify their person: first person (my), third person (his/her/its), or second person (your). On the top left of the right-hand image, DᏬᎪᏞ /asgoli/ literally translates as 'his/her head.' The alphabet never needs to appear in the curricular materials for immersion classes because the Cherokee writing system contains all the linguistic information that the teachers and students need, due to the genius of Sequoyah. The syllabary never relied upon the English alphabet in its original manuscript form and may have borrowed only a few designs of letters for the print version. The omission of English elements as well as the remarkably complex meaning-making potentials of the syllabary allow its exclusive use in these immersion classes just as it has been used exclusively in some Cherokee communities since 1821.

The flexibility of the Cherokee language and syllabary is particularly evident when coining new words for these curricular materials. Dr. Morton described how the language instructors and translators in both the Cherokee Nation and the Eastern Band meet four

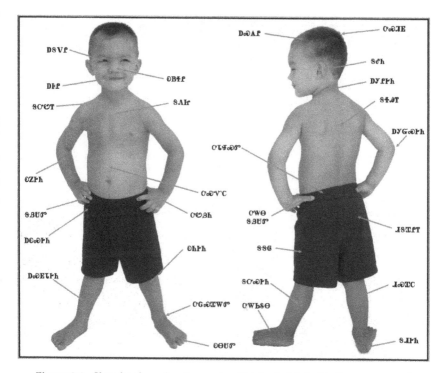

Figure 8.1. Cherokee boy, showing parts of his body labeled in Sequoyan, used in the Cherokee Immersion School. Courtesy of the Cherokee Nation Education Services.

times annually in part to coin new terms for language materials. The Cherokee Nation has also established an informal "speakers' bureau" in which elders and Cherokee speakers from the community are invited to Tahlequah every month to meet students, review and give their blessings to new words that are coined, enjoy a meal, and talk, read, and write with the children in the immersion classes. The one rule for these meetings is to speak only Cherokee at all times. All of these meetings and discussions about how best to represent new knowledge in the Cherokee language culminate in curricular materials that reflect the sound system of Cherokee and some of the history of the tribe.

Coining new terms for the states, for instance, allowed the educational resource team to create a U.S. map in Cherokee (fig. 8.2). Some

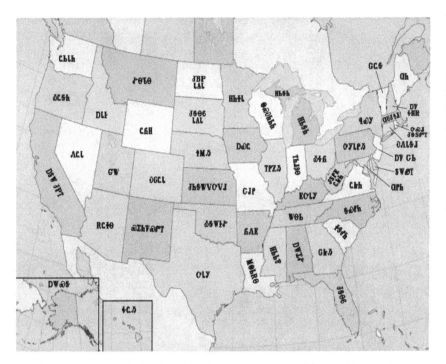

Figure 8.2. Map of the United States showing the names of the states in Sequoyan (some are phonetic spellings of the English state names in Sequoyan and others are traditional Cherokee words for the states). Courtesy of the Cherokee Nation Education Services.

of these states' names were simply Cherokee phonetic spellings of their English names: for instance, Michigan is ᎻᏏᎦᏂ /mi-si-ga-ni/; Minnesota is ᎻᏂᏐᏓ /mi-ni-so-da/; New York is ᏄᏯᎩ /nu-ya-gi/; and Oklahoma is ᎣᎦᎵᎰᎹ /o-ga-li-ho-ma/. Some states retained names that they earned in recent Cherokee history. Arkansas is ᏲᏁᎬ /yo-ne-gv/ 'place of whites,' as the boundary state of Oklahoma, the 'place of red people,' and California is ᎠᏕᎳ ᏧᏢᎢ /a-de-la tsu-tlv-i/ 'money in the ground,' as it was called during the gold rush. Tennessee, of course, took its name from a Cherokee word to begin with: the ᏔᎾᏏ /tanassi/ or ᏔᎾᏏ /tanasi/ villages located on the Tanasi River.

These immersion materials have in common the understanding that the Cherokee syllabary itself carries meaning beyond merely representing the sound of the language. The syllabary is indeed a code (Bender 2002), which carries with it constellations of meaning, the history of the tribe, and understandings of place and location.

Reading and writing in Cherokee often recalls the ways in which Cherokee used to be spoken and thus becomes an important act of perseverance. For instance, I visited with John Ross, former principal chief of the United Keetoowah Band and currently a Cherokee Nation translator specialist in the Education Department, who kindly agreed to check over language materials I had developed (see tables 2.8 and 2.9). During the visit he mentioned how important reading and writing in the syllabary was for continuing Cherokee ways of viewing the world. He offered a copy of a Cherokee word list that he had helped develop, which the language consortium approved in April 2010. This list referenced state names, including one for Florida that Ross had heard in his family: DCfiMⱮꙨᎩT ꙨSSᎩ /atliyoluh-vsgii sgadugi/ roughly 'it floats state,' describing the place where Cherokees would go to gather rice. The word for "state" draws upon the word SSᎩ /gadugi/, which refers to organized teams of people working collectively for a commonly shared goal (see chapter 7). While the English word "state" describes a political organization that grew from regionalism, the Cherokee word more closely matches a historical tradition of collective action.

The map currently has the name JSΘ6 /tsuganawv/ 'south' for Florida. Both words are descriptive of the place in relation to the location where Cherokees had lived, but the one Ross remembered also included information about some Cherokees' practice of traveling south to enjoy wild rice. Florida is south of the original homeland, but it was also remembered as a place where Cherokees found sustenance and accurately described as an environment that they had seen and experienced. Sequoyan affords the possibility of indicating linguistic, historical, and cultural practices with each character, especially in verb phrases such as Ross's example.

As these examples indicate, Cherokee can be used to approximate English words, to recall specific events and relations, and to remember practices and values from long ago. This is in part because of its remarkable instrumentality, with the potential to describe sound and meaning at once. The Cherokee writing system is not just a syllabary that codifies sound but can also codify meaning. As such, it marks knowledge; entire cultural logics at many levels of meaning are systematically represented with each glyph. The latent meaning potentially residing in each glyph becomes apparent when it is slotted into noun and verb phrases. When asked about this remarkable representational power of the syllabary, Dr. Morton remarked with a chuckle: "And as you get deeper and deeper into it, you continue to wonder more and more, how did one person figure this out?" This powerful writing system reveals so much about Cherokee language, history, and identity that learning it first in these immersion classes helps ensure the perseverance of the language and people.

When learners use the syllabary and begin to understand the cultural and linguistic logics behind it, they see the world more completely contextualized with fewer words than they might use in the atomistic sound system of the alphabet. "Think about it this way," Dr. Morton began. "Let's take the English language. . . . We are taught when we're taught to read, teachers make us focus on a letter or a small word, . . . so that's a flashlight, we're shining a flashlight, that's all we see, we don't see the rest of it. Well, when the immersion student is using the syllabary, it will not be a flashlight, but more of a table lamp with a diffused light. They will see all, they will see more of it." Dr. Morton developed this anecdote based on his experience with the school and offered a comparison to a hypothetical English alphabet learner who is taught to focus on a letter or a small word. The learner is asked to choose the letter "a," when the flashcard "a" is placed in the middle of the table, then the "b" and "c" flashcards are placed nearby on the table. If you take away the cards and ask what the card in the middle was, the learner will tell you "a" but can't tell you what the other cards were because each letter is being learned only as a sound and in isolation from the other letters.

Returning to his experience with the immersion students, Dr. Morton continued: "Now, a Cherokee student, if you put one syllabary character in the middle and then put the two over here, and you ask them what was the syllabary character in the middle of the table, they'll tell you [the character asked about] after the cards are removed, but they'll also tell you those two [pointing to where the other two characters were placed]." The other two help make meaning. "It's something about the way the Cherokee student approaches language. They approach it like this [gestures widely]: and when we teach the English language, we approach it like this [putting hands together to form a small circle]." Teachers in the Immersion School, though, point out that not all students are able to understand the meaning of verb phrases as they are sounding them out. Though the students know the syllabary and have a wide array of sight recognition words already learned, they are only beginning to learn and understand that more complicated verb phrases can potentially carry meaning with each character. These teachers have been trying to develop educational materials that present Sequoyan verb phrases in the wider light of meaning that Dr. Morton described to help move students into the deep levels of meaning potentially present in each character. Because the syllabary affords this encompassing perspective on language and understanding, it is the sole writing system taught in the main part of the day in the Immersion School and given a place of prominence in the additional educational efforts of the Cherokee Nation.

The privileged position of Sequoyan relates primarily to its robust representational properties, though it also has symbolic value as a marker of Cherokee identity (Bender 2002). The point is that in the Immersion School the Cherokee writing system can and does stand alone as the writing system of choice precisely because it represents so much linguistic and cultural knowledge, even as it represents the sound system.

For all its merits as a representational system, linguists hasten to point out that the Cherokee syllabary, like all other writing systems, is an imperfect representation of the sound system (phonetics) of the language. The syllabary does not indicate the aspirated /h/ sound in particular words, the tonal system, or the ways in which some consonants are read. "While the syllabary does not express some crucial distinctions," linguist Brad Montgomery-Anderson (2007: 18) writes, "it does often provide information as to the underlying structures of words before the application of phonological changes." When words are spoken in Cherokee, elisions of interior vowel sounds and omissions of final vowel sounds are common; but the writing system preserves these important indicators of meaning even as the pronunciations are shortened or forgotten across time in everyday speech.

Importantly, digital remediation of the Cherokee syllabary allows learners to see and practice with the writing and sound system together. The Immersion School uses digital media differently than other language classes offered by the Cherokee Nation, in which the alphabet and English must be relied on more for instruction. The immersion program offers students interactive see-and-say games written solely in Cherokee. In one DVD that includes stories, kids' shows, songs, and animated books, young students are taught numbers as they view illustrations of Cherokees doing everyday things (such as fixing cars and cooking) and traditional activities (such as grinding hickory nuts, cooking, dancing at a stomp, and hunting). One slide shows eight men and women appropriately arranged and dressed, dancing in a circle around a small fire as they might see at a stomp dance. The Cherokee subtitle reads ᏚᏁᎳ ᏎᎯᏘᏘ ᎠᎾᎳᏍᎦᏯᏗ /tsunela yenii analasgia/ 'eight there are of them they are dancing,' as guitar music plays and the words are spoken aloud. The numbers one through nine are first said in Cherokee then repeated in the sentence that describes what is happening in the picture. In every digital educational resource produced by the education program, carefully timed interplays of motion in the visuals, the syllabary subtitle, and the voiceover work together to link the sound system of the Cherokee language to the written and visual action, thereby reinforcing and highlighting the meaning-making potentials of the syllabary.

Though many of the Immersion School materials privilege the syllabary to the exclusion of the alphabet and English, some materials do draw upon Romanized transliterations of words and phrases and alphabetically influenced learning materials. A 264-page interactive language program offers everyday Cherokee words and phrases accompanied by audio files. Each page includes a picture with its English name directly underneath, followed by the Romanized spelling of the Cherokee word in a slightly larger font and then by the Cherokee syllabary in the largest font on the page, in color. When clicked, the individual syllables in the Romanized transliterations play an audio file of that single sound. When the orange Cherokee word in the syllabary is clicked, the audio file plays for the entire word.

Figure 8.3 shows the word for dove, which translates literally as 'acorn it cries for.' Though this interactive book uses English, the design indicates to the youths and parents whose language might be English in the home that the Cherokee syllabary is the most

Dove

gu-le di-s-ko-ni-hi

Figure 8.3. Page 11 from an interactive language program, *Common Words and Phrases,* showing the word "dove" with design emphasis placed on the syllabary. Audio files hot-linked to the word demonstrate how to pronounce these words for parents of Immersion School students. Courtesy of the Cherokee Nation Education Services.

important. The English words for these items are least emphasized, though perhaps the first to be recognized. The Romanized spelling is a scaffolding device, a stepping stone to move the learner to the Cherokee writing system, which is visually most emphasized.

The English word was included in this interactive DVD because of the amount of Cherokee that students' families spoke at home. Jeff Edwards (2009), who now works in the Methods and Advancement Department of the Educational Services division of the Cherokee Nation and was one of the authors of the book, points out that its primary audience was the parents of the Immersion School students. "Most of our parents at the immersion program are not speakers. So in turn they did not know if their children were saying the words right when reading stories at home or spelling them correctly. So that was the primary purpose of the interactive book [DVD], to promote the language outside of the immersion program and to help non-speaking parents. Once word got out that there was an interactive Cherokee computer program that spoke the Cherokee language I could not produce enough of them!" Cherokees enrolled in the online language classes and K–12 students involved in the Cherokee challenge bowls, many of whom speak English as their primary language, asked for copies of this DVD. Translations needed to be included because English is their first language, but the design emphasizes Sequoyan coupled with sounds.

The Cherokee syllabary is sung glyph-by-glyph on another interactive DVD used in the immersion classes, to the tune originally created for the alphabet song. As each syllable is sung, its corresponding character appears for a short time on the screen. English speakers who know the alphabet song, and many do, will recognize the tune. This song in Cherokee is sung using the syllabary chart that was popularized for print (see chapter 4) and has been used extensively since then, even though its arrangement centers upon alphabetic ordering of the glyphs based on English vowel sounds. This DVD offers learners visual representations of the syllabary with each sound, however, even though it draws upon the tune of the alphabet song. This design choice deemphasizes the influence of the alphabet, even though it draws upon educational tropes used to teach the alphabet. This choice also appears in the interactive language program discussed above. Though this interactive language lesson uses the ubiquitous syllabary chart, it omits the title of the original chart: "The Cherokee Alphabet."

The Cherokee Nation Educational Department creates materials that promote the importance of the Cherokee writing system, by removing the influence of the alphabet whenever possible and giving the syllabary a place of prominence in the curriculum. This choice is not only instructionally sound (given the instrumental ways in which the syllabary works to impart cultural logics of the Cherokee language) but also ideologically important. It privileges the syllabary and Cherokee language to the near exclusion of the alphabet whenever possible. Such a move is crucial for learners because it helps make them aware of the ways in which writing systems work, the ways in which they help establish and maintain peoplehood, and the ways in which they are ideologically loaded tools for meaning-making.

ONLY WHEN NECESSARY

In addition to the Immersion School, the Cherokee Nation Educational Services group creates materials and presents resources for k–12 students and adults whose first language is English. These materials must use the alphabet because their learners already see the Cherokee language through the alphabetic lens. But using letters to mediate reading and writing hinders English speakers from learning the cultural logics inherent in the Cherokee syllabary and language. The alphabet works so differently as a writing system because it atomizes the sound system and requires many more glyphs to create a sentence. On the surface, the alphabet appears easier to use, because it has only twenty-six letters. Knowing that English speakers rely on the alphabet and how imperfect it is, the Cherokee-language materials created for learners whose first language is English often include transliterations of the Cherokee syllabary, followed by translations of the pronunciation in English phonetics, followed by a loose translation of the Cherokee word or phrase in English. In the screenshot from the talking leaf Cherokee language interactive website (figure 8.4), the fluent Cherokee language speaker and language development specialist Sue Thompson, who works in the Cherokee Nation Co-Partner Johnson O'Malley (JOM) Program, says the

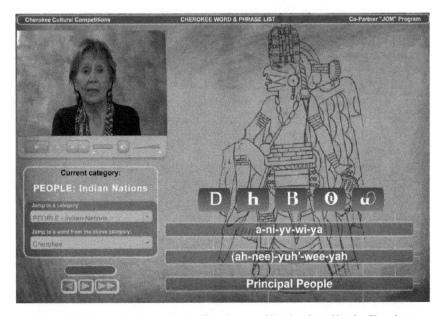

Figure 8.4. Interactive see-and-say Cherokee word list developed by the Cherokee Nation's Co-Partner JOM Program for use in language bowl competitions across the fourteen-county jurisdiction of the Cherokee Nation. Courtesy of the Cherokee Nation Education Services.

Cherokee word slowly first, by syllable, then quickly in its daily spoken form. Video of Thompson plays on command in the upper left corner as the Cherokee syllabary most prominently displays "Ꭰꮒ ꮾꮻꮍ" /ani yvwiya/, the name we Cherokees call ourselves. The Romanized transliteration "a-ni-yv-wi-ya" and phonetic pronunciation with diacritics "(ah-nee)-yuh'-wee-yah" follow underneath this, with the English translation "Principal People" last.

These materials were developed for the thousands of Cherokee citizens and Oklahoma students in the k–12 public school systems who participate in annual Cherokee language and challenge bowls. These Cherokee cultural competitions are one facet of the comprehensive Cherokee Nation Co-Partner JOM Program that serves more than 20,000 students, the most of any Cherokee Nation educational efforts. The program was legislatively enacted from the federal program developed during the Indian New Deal of the 1930s to subsidize American Indians' education, health, and housing services. Today tribes across the country use JOM educational funds to offset the educational costs of developing language and culturally relevant educational materials for their citizens and the public schools attended by large numbers of American Indian students.

With seventy-two public school and community partners, the Cherokee Nation Co-Partner JOM Program provides "multiple opportunities for JOM students in grades k–12 to exercise their use of the Cherokee language, increase their knowledge of Cherokee history and tribal government, and expand their cultural knowledge" (Cherokee Nation 2007: 4). In addition to language and challenge bowl competitions during the school year, the program hosts an annual art and creative writing contest and a summer youth leadership institute. The students are primarily English speakers and have varying degrees of access to and understanding of the Cherokee writing system and language in their homes. Though the JOM program privileges the syllabary by placing it at the top of the words listed on the screen and in the largest font, the JOM program leaders must necessarily include Romanized transliterations and English translations because these students' primary language is English. This should not be taken as an indication that program leaders value the alphabet more than the syllabary, however, but rather as a concession to the reality that most of their students must come to the Cherokee language through the English language and literacy.

The same problem exists in the online Cherokee language classes that begin with single words and phrases using English transliterations. Cherokee 1 teaches students basic vocabulary, pronunciation of the syllables in the syllabary, and short conversational exchanges. Cherokee 2 students learn short phrases and more complex verb phrases, and by the end of the class most of the slides are presented in the Cherokee syllabary with English transliterations (see fig. 8.5). Ed Fields, the instructor of these classes, speaks Cherokee as his first language and has taught these online courses since 2004. The chat questions, statistics, and roster are posted under the video feed.

As the class progresses, Ed begins by pronouncing the Cherokee first, underlining each glyph on the right as he says the words (fig. 8.5). Then he provides a literal translation of the words in English phonetic spellings (on the left part of the slide in the figure). Again

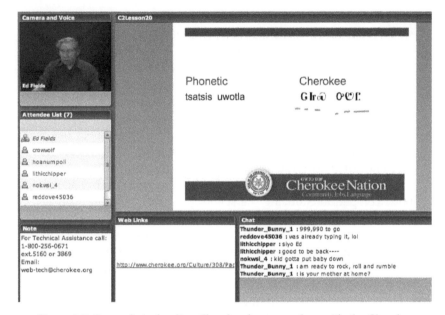

Figure 8.5. Screenshot of online Cherokee language class with the Cherokee syllabary underlined as Ed Fields says each glyph individually then together in everyday speech. Courtesy of the Cherokee Nation.

the Cherokee syllabary is treated as a primary indicator of linguistic knowledge: it is featured in the advanced classes, with the English phonetics as a bridge back into the English translations. If the words have multiple meanings, Ed translates these as well and writes the other English meanings of the phrase. The slide in figure 8.5 shows ᏣᏥᏏ ᎤᏬᏝ /tsatsis uwotla/, meaning 'is your mother home or sitting down?'

The problem, of course, is that adults and youths who have learned English as their first language have a difficult time seeing the cultural logics that the syllabary imparts, so the alphabet and English must be used as a bridge into the Cherokee language. This makes the Cherokee language even more difficult to learn because the alphabet and syllabary work differently. The syllabary, with more than three times the number of characters, appears to be cumbersome and needlessly complex, as it did to linguist John Pickering over a century ago when he tried to adapt the Cherokee language to the alphabet (see chapters

4 and 5). English-speaking students at times have a hard time matching what they hear in the pronunciation of the syllabary with what they see, having difficulty with connecting the glyphs, phonetic translations, and actual phonetics of the language. But the digital form offered in these language classes provides the needed bridges for students to see these connections. In the same lesson from advanced Cherokee 2 shown in figure 8.5, the students ask about elisions and aspirated /h/ sounds in the word for school, ᏙᏁᎶᏆᏍᏗ /tsunadeloquasdi/ roughly, 'place where they go to learn.' Ed uses the interactive feature to draw on the English phonetic spellings to show where the syllable is elided and an aspirated "h" sound should be inserted to make the spelling sound more like everyday spoken Cherokee, /tsun(a)del(h)(o)quasdi/, using the parentheses to show sounds that have been added and/or elided. The final evolution of the syllabary into digital media allows audio files to play along with the Cherokee syllabary in real time with an instructor, providing a close link between spoken and written Cherokee, even if the alphabet and phonetic spellings must also be relied upon.

STANDARDIZATION OF THE
SYLLABARY AGAIN

Digital remediation of the Cherokee syllabary offers users some connections between sound and glyph along with the English phonetics, and the web presence of the Cherokee Nation has been an important clearinghouse for digital-language materials. The Cherokee Nation website, run by webmaster Tonia Williams, has done much to standardize the Cherokee writing system. Foremost among these efforts was the creation of a digital font to be used in all national documents, cultural resources, and language materials. The font was created by Tonia Williams in the Information Systems Division of the Cherokee Nation and was designed by the Cherokee Nation Cultural Resource Center: Dr. Gloria Sly (former director), Anna Huckaby (language training coordinator), and Lisa LaRue (literature review coordinator). The creators of this typeface standardized the many versions of the Cherokee font into one version that has become widely used and most closely matches the one found in the 1828 syllabary chart.

The keyboard map for the Cherokee font (fig. 8.6) differs completely from the keyboard layout mapped for the Cherokee typewriters, which is completely understandable. Because so few typewriters were actually produced with the Cherokee font, it made little sense to map the computer keystrokes to the typewriter keystrokes. Unlike the QWERTY keyboard layout for English typewriters, which translated completely to the keyboard for computers, the Cherokee keyboard completely changed the layout of the keystrokes from one development to the next. This keyboard map and font were graphics, as opposed to Unicode, an internationally standardized numeric designation for each character that invisibly tells all computers what characters should be displayed. This caused the font to fall out of favor with the Cherokee Nation because all computers had to have this font installed to be able to read the images of each glyph. Unicode Cherokee font formats were developed for the tribe by Chris Harvey of LanguageGeek.com and have since been adopted by the

Figure 8.6. Recently made obsolete by the Cherokee Unicode font, this chart for the Cherokee font keystroke layout for a computer keyboard was the first ever designed.

tribe as the standard for all computer output in Sequoyan. Unicode fonts can be read across platforms and software and on social networking software. Roy Boney and Joseph Erb are at the forefront of making sure that Cherokee Nation employees, citizens, language learners, and social media users are aware of and able to utilize unicode-based fonts in everyday life.

Chapter 3 presents evidence of the visual mnemonic that emerged from the original arrangement of glyphs in manuscript form; seven key forms govern the structure of all subsequent shapes of the glyphs. Cherokees who knew those forms would only have needed to learn the flourishes and embellishments that made the subsequent shapes unique. Though the manuscript form might have been easier to learn given these design features, a shorthand for the script emerged from the longhand. Chapter 4 uses both visual and historic evidence to make the case that the design for printed Cherokee was probably developed by Cherokees and was in use as a shorthand for at least two years before the fonts were commissioned. The design for printed Cherokee seems to have been based upon the shorthand for the syllabary that was already in use by Cherokees by the time the first type was cast. These design features of the script and printed Cherokee would have facilitated the ease of learning and standardization of the syllabary. They were drawn from designs created by Sequoyah, who eschewed any links with English sound systems and transformed as many as eleven letters of the alphabet to create the designs used today in print. Though a number of the glyphs today resemble alphabetic letters, many of these glyphs were borrowed because their design features retained some element of the original manuscript shape. This was a system of, by, and for Cherokees, standardized and modernized by Cherokees, despite the credit often given to Samuel Worcester for his role in designing and arranging the manuscript form of the glyphs into print. What then became of the arrangement and design logics of the print fonts as the computer keyboard layout was created for the syllabary?

Traces of the characters' shorthand designs remain in the individual glyphs used for the computer keyboard. The most frequently used Cherokee syllables are placed on the lowercase level, with less frequently used syllables on the uppercase level. The Cherokee font keystroke layout (fig. 8.6) shows that locations for Cherokee glyphs were based largely upon relations to English sounds and alphabetic designs. All of the Cherokee vowels were paired with their corresponding English vowels. If the Cherokee sound began with a consonant sound in English, for instance, the font keystroke was paired with that letter (e.g., Ꮚ /yo/ was paired with uppercase "Y" and Ꮹ /ya/ was paired with lowercase "y"; ꮪ was paired with lowercase "s," while Ꮞ /se/ was paired with uppercase "S"; and Ꮃ /ta/ was paired with lowercase "t," while Ꭷ /ti/ was paired with uppercase "T"). Sometimes a visual link was made between the Cherokee glyph design and its apparently corresponding letter: for example, the glyph Ꮋ /lu/ was linked with the uppercase "M"; the glyph Ꮓ /no/ was linked with uppercase "Z," and the glyph Ꮃ /la/ was linked with lowercase "w." Where no match could be found with either a corresponding English sound or an alphabetic design, a key was simply assigned. Four keys were designated for an accent mark and three sight recognition words: the number 1 corresponds to ᏣᎳᎩ /tsalagi/, 'Cherokee'; 2 corresponds to ᎣᏏᏲ /osiyo/, 'hello'; and 3 corresponds to ᏩᏙ /wado/, 'thank you.'

The Cherokee font keystrokes were very difficult to learn: it would take months of everyday use to be able to locate all the keys. Because so many Cherokee speakers and writers who use the computer keyboard have English as their primary language, the ways in which the keyboard bridges into English make some sense. It relies on sound and visual relations to the alphabet-based layout of the QWERTY keyboard. This is perhaps the keyboard map's greatest strength and weakness. The way in which the original syllabary linked to Cherokee sounds was of utmost importance to Sequoyah, who chose not to link any of the glyphs to the English sound system (see chapters 1 and 2).

Though the overall design of the Cherokee font keystroke layout was meant to make the most frequent Cherokee sounds the easiest to find, it had to map onto the QWERTY design. In other words, the Cherokee language had to be mediated through the alphabetic layout because a Cherokee keyboard had not been created. These shortcomings were addressed in two important ways through online resources developed shortly after the font. The first is a syllabary chart with a prerecorded voiceover done by Cherokee translator and Living Treasure basket weaver Anna Huckaby (Cherokee Nation 2009b).

The second is a Cherokee converter that accepts words typed in English phonetic spellings of Cherokee and translates them into the correct syllabary characters (Cherokee Nation 2009c:). The converter bypasses the need to learn the keyboard layout altogether because all the text can be written in English phonetics. Unfortunately, this means that Cherokee learners may not see any advantage to learning the Cherokee glyphs by heart, separate from the crutch of English phonetic spellings. They would simply rely on the English alphabet to spell out the sounds of the Cherokee language. Thus the converter is an imperfect tool for Cherokee writers, who must rely on visible transliterations; the converter might seem to support continued use of the syllabary but in effect makes it more remote.

The Cherokee syllabary was mapped onto the QWERTY keyboard in ways that divorced it from the instrumental and visual qualities that may have made it so learnable in the first place (see chapters 2 and 3). While the digital reproduction of the Cherokee syllabary can potentially recontextualize the Cherokee language with its sounds and the visual design of the glyphs, as many of the language materials do, the QWERTY keyboard has forced the syllabary into a closer relation to English than it ever had. This relationship might seem to have helped English speakers bridge to Cherokee more easily, but instead it has had the effect of making the Cherokee writing system more opaque, reducing it to a font that mimics English sounds and letter designs.

Another limitation of the Cherokee font became apparent in the age of Web 2.0 when collaboratively authored sites such as Wikipedia and social networking sites such as Myspace and Facebook became common. Because the first Cherokee font was based in part on images rather than on numerical input that computers could recognize, it often appeared as gibberish to end users: a random collection of boxes and numbers. The Cherokee font had not been standardized using Unicode. Without a Unicode designation for each character, Cherokee language users on computers at both ends had to have the graphic font installed. Potential avenues for learning and using Sequoyan were being missed, and users (representing many generations) who read and wrote in these social networking and collaboratively authored sites were not able to post in the Cherokee font.

Cherokee Nation cultural specialist Joseph Erb, curriculum specialist Roy Boney, and Chris Harvey, a researcher and developer at the Indigenous Language Institute, have promoted a Unicode font system for Sequoyan. Harvey, who runs the Language Geek website (LanguageGeek.com), a clearinghouse for Unicode fonts for all languages, developed the Unicode designations and the now standard Cherokee font, Digohweli. He examined several samples of handwriting from manuscripts housed in the Cherokee Heritage Center in Tahlequah and checked the utility and accuracy of his character's designs with several Cherokees fluent in Sequoyan. Harvey paid particularly close attention to the serifs because these were important to the Cherokees fluent in Sequoyan and appeared consistently across the several writing samples he analyzed. He gave the example of the character i /v/, which to the eye untrained in Sequoyan appears to be like the lowercase "i" in the Roman alphabet. His font design emphasizes the serif at the bottom of the letter because it was an essential design feature in the handwriting he analyzed (Harvey 2010). The shorthand character i /v/ in Digohweli retains the essential design elements seen in Sequoyah's own hand in figure I.1 (fifth row down, sixth cell from the left).

The Unicode font system can be downloaded and installed in two ways: the first allows those who have already mastered the former keyboard layout to continue using it to write in Cherokee. This is the preferred choice of a number of Cherokee translators. The second way of downloading the Unicode font allows users to assign Sequoyan characters to English letters and uses the QWERTY layout.

For Cherokee learners this has the benefit of mapping onto the sound system of the language: as they type the transliterations, the correct character appears. If they are already familiar with the English keyboard and don't need to hunt and peck, the transliterations are no longer visible: the sounds of the words and the visual display of the character are once again seamlessly connected. The alphabetic transliterations correspond to those on the standardized syllabary charts (fig. 4.1). For example, when I type /ageyu tsalagi/ 'Cherokee woman' with the caps lock on using the Cherokee linguistic keyboard layout, the transliteration appears. When I type the same transliterated spelling with the caps lock off, the Cherokee font appears: D-Ᏺ-Ꮐ Ꮐ-Ꮃ-Ᏸ. Because I touch-type, without using looking down to find the keys, I'm not as aware of the transliteration as I am aware of the sound of the syllables. In other words, the alphabet recedes as primary mediation for the typing: Cherokee sounds attached to the spellings and visible Cherokee characters once again connect sound to the visual design of the character. The Unicode system and Cherokee font nearly remove the alphabetic influence when typing Sequoyan.

Another important benefit of the Unicode-based fonts accrues as users type: a good amount of visual information from the original shorthand designs is retained in the shape of the characters, depending on the font chosen. Plantagenet Cherokee and Digohweli Old Do, for instance, retain the original orientation of the Λ /do/ character, correcting Worcester's arbitrary decision to change its orientation. These fonts restore six additional glyphs to their former manuscript shorthand designs that were illustrated by Sequoyah on the right side of each cell in figure I.1: Ꮑ /li/, Ꮒ /mo/, Ꮵ /yi/, Ꮣ /le/, Ꮿ /ha/, and Ꮩ /lv/. Yet both fonts retain six designs that lost visual links to the manuscript shorthand when developed into print and thus do not honor the visual heritage as well, perhaps because these designs had become standardized in handwriting: S /du/, C /tli/, Z /no/, Ꭴ /que/, Ꮥ /de/, and Ɛ /quv/. Overall, though, these font designs respect the original shorthand manuscript forms demonstrated by Sequoyah because they recoup visual information in the majority of their characters' designs. Using a Unicode-based font, Cherokee language learners can potentially reinforce the visual with the aural in ways that the original syllabary did so well. Depending on the fonts chosen, the design integrity of the characters can also be reinforced again, allowing the genius of Sequoyah to enter the twenty-first century.

THE CHEROKEE SYLLABARY:
PEOPLEHOOD AND PERSEVERANCE

Digital reproductions of Sequoyan and the Cherokee language bring the evolutionary story of the Cherokee syllabary to the present day. As it developed from script to print to digital media, Sequoyan has proved instrumentally flexible and has accrued several layers of cultural value. Importantly, every material form that the Cherokee syllabary has taken since its invention has provided linguistic and visual information that guarantees some measure of integrity with the original manuscript designs, manifesting the brilliance and ingenuity behind its creation. Whatever its material form, Sequoyan has lent itself equally well to any genre, any communicative need, and any delivery form. The syllabary has secured valuable semantic knowledge of the language for generations, has ensured a legacy of meaning-making for Cherokees, and has become a cornerstone of continued language perseverance efforts.

Although the syllabary's design and arrangement appear to be based on English print and ordered around English vowel sounds, this relationship was never present in Sequoyah's original. The system was taught in manuscript version and developed into shorthand by Cherokees, and Samuel Worcester's influence in its development into print largely has been overstated. Sequoyah apparently intentionally developed this writing system to be separate and separable from English and the Roman alphabet. The tribe put up outright resistance to any influence of an alphabetic-based orthography for the Cherokee language, forever securing a place for Sequoyan in the hearts and minds of the people. In its earliest stages of development, Sequoyan became inextricably linked to Cherokee identity, highly valued in the tribe, and important for everyday use.

Many English-speaking students try to develop visual and/or oral mnemonics to aid memorization of the glyphs, as Cowen and Cochran (1972) did with their insect mnemonics invented for English speakers. But these visual mnemonics differ completely from Sequoyah's arrangement and design of the Cherokee glyphs. As an artist himself, trained in observation of form, he found a way to organize eighty-six distinct shapes into the seven forms. These forms, mostly ornamental, were reduced, transformed, and rescaled into Cherokee shorthand, which became the basis for the printed glyphs widely used today.

When it moved into print forms, Sequoyan accrued even more weight by becoming a symbol of civilization to outsiders and a marker of national and tribal identity to insiders. Indeed, the Cherokee Nation and tribe became recognizable as distinct and mutually supportive entities through the development of print and a national newspaper in both English and Sequoyan. Though the

English language and literacy have certainly been one means through which the nation has been able to exist and interact with outside governments, the Cherokee language and Sequoyan have also been central to the maintenance of a continued and richly adaptive notion of peoplehood. Sequoyan in print delivered to Cherokees and the world a set of materials that codified the tribe's sovereignty, culture, and knowledge. The cultural logics that made the Cherokee syllabary so easy to learn and use remained deeply and widely employed until the allotment era (see chapter 6) and were sponsored at both the national and tribal level.

The depth and breadth of Sequoyan is beginning to resurface in the language materials developed by the Cherokee Nation for the immersion classes and educational programs. These educational resources use online and printed materials to ensure that the sounds of the language are linked to the visual design of the writing system. Students hear, see, and experience the Cherokee language and writing system as complementary and mutually sustaining. They also learn something of the Cherokee worldview implicit in each word and phrase written in the language.

The evolutionary story of the Cherokee writing system from script to print to digital forms reveals several facets that make up the brilliance of the system. The syllabary codifies more than just sound; it often represents meaningful units of language. Every Cherokee language teacher and speaker asked about this point confirms that important finding: this is not just a syllabary but works at times like a morphographic system as well. The Cherokee writing system can potentially represent sound units and meaning with each glyph; the meaning generated depends on its order in the noun and verb phrase. Chapter 2 presents the results of a linguistic analysis of each glyph to provide concrete linguistic evidence for some of the potential meanings latent in each character. The cultural logic of Cherokee peoplehood is written into every word.

The story of the development of Sequoyan also provides clues to the best ways to approach the learning of this system. Adults and teens whose primary language is English who are trying to learn Cherokee face the challenge of becoming aware of the alphabetic lens and working to move beyond it. When the Cherokee syllabary can be understood as the instructional resource that it is, the cultural logics of the writing system can emerge for learners. These logics include many levels of potential meaning in each glyph, a sound system that closely if imperfectly matches day-to-day spoken Cherokee, and a design that is largely and purposely distinct from the alphabetic influence. The alphabet and the syllabary work in completely different ways instrumentally and linguistically. The syllabary is more of a morphographic system than previously understood: while obviously based on sound units, it can also link each character to larger meanings.

Because these systems work so differently, the terms used to describe Cherokee reading and writing also need to shift. Historians and literacy scholars should learn this lesson from the story of the Cherokee syllabary's development told in these pages. Literacy (abilities with the letter) belongs strictly to the alphabet. The instrumentality and meaning-making practices to which literacy lends itself are not those that make sense when reading and writing in Cherokee. Rather, the Cherokee writing system has an instrumentality that is remarkably rich phonetically, semantically, syntactically, and logically. Reading and writing with the Cherokee syllabary can best be described as having fluency in Sequoyan.

These findings suggest that adult learners whose primary language is English might develop fluency with the Cherokee language by using the writing and sound system immediately. Literal translations of each glyph can be provided in order to make apparent which meaning, order, and/or function is attached to it. These literal translations may not make immediate sense to the English-speaking ear, but they make perfect sense when seen in and through Cherokee logics. The sounds of the words pronounced and then translated literally work as scaffolding: students can begin to predict what type of linguistic information is potentially carried in each glyph as it is ordered in particular words.

Practice with Sequoyan can be facilitated by using the Unicode fonts and taking advantage of the abundant online and print materials that the Cherokee Nation offers. Facebook pages and text messages can be written in Sequoyan, and digital stories in Cherokee and Sequoyan are also available. The more Sequoyan is used, the more Cherokee language, history, reverence for place, and religion can be secured.

A central part of Cherokee peoplehood is enacted through a variety of technologies, from basket weaving to blowguns, crystals, and beadwork, all of which can be meaningful even if not apparently symbolic or based upon a writing system. As with any technology that has become a central facet of peoplehood, the material form of the tool matters less than the relationships it embodies. The Cherokee syllabary has taken several material forms, some more adaptable to daily use than others. But these variations matter less than the ways in which it inscribes the four aspects of peoplehood: language, history, place, and spirituality. Because the Cherokee syllabary can mark all of these aspects simultaneously and with such efficiency, due to its ease of use for native speakers and its transportability, it has been key to the tribe's syncretic change. It overwrites outsider influence, bending it into a Cherokee mindset. Thus Cherokees can quickly understand, adapt, and overcome through continued meaning-making in and on Cherokee terms. Not surprisingly, given the syllabary's instrumentality in continuing Cherokee peoplehood and perseverance, it has accrued considerable symbolic importance as an outward sign of Cherokee identity. It has immense ideological weight within the tribe and nation.

The instrumentality of Sequoyan is surely rich and important, and it has helped shape Cherokee identity. The perseverance of Cherokee people has much to do with how this writing system has come to be valued, the way in which it is attached to identity, and its embodiment of spirituality, land, history, and language. The proliferation of printed materials in the Cherokee language and by Cherokees has coincided with peace and prosperity in the tribe. Cherokee writing has been fostered by nationalistic movements that simultaneously serve a tribal core and present a "civilized" face to outsiders. It has been sustained in small towns through organized work groups, Baptist churches, stomp grounds, and daily communications. While it is frightening to consider that the 2001 survey found no one under the age of forty who could speak, read, and write Cherokee fluently in these small towns, such speakers may exist. National efforts to intervene in language loss are certainly showing returns on the investment, slowly, incrementally, and with a shared vision that includes a place of privilege for the Cherokee writing system. Hope remains so long as these efforts continue.

NOTES

Introduction: Peoplehood, Tools, and Perseverance

1. See Street 1984; Harris 1986, 2009; Finnegan 1988; and Heath 2001 for critiques of these great divide theories.

2. To be certain, inventing traditions can be problematic, especially when weighing the evidence, or lack thereof, presented in support of the identity claims of self-identified Indians and newly formed state-sanctioned tribes (Thornton 1985, 1997; Sturm 2002; Garroutte 2003; Tall Bear 2003; Allen 2005; Cushman 2008). In these instances where tribal identities are claimed with little supporting evidence, Hobsbawm's idea of inventing traditions has more traction.

3. For explanations of the development of ethnohistorical methods, see Krech 1991; Trigger 1986; Wood 1990.

1. Sequoyah and the Politics of Language

1. The Gilcrease Museum has four documents that Jack Kilpatrick attributed to Sequoyah, including the syllabary in figure I.1. The second of these documents demonstrates the numeric system and the shorthand of the syllabary in Sequoyah's arrangement and is signed by him: ᏍᏏᏉᏯ /ssiquoya/. The top of this document includes a penciled note: "George Gist's Alphabet & numerals in his own handwritten west of Arkansas year 1839–for J. H. P. [John Howard Payne]." If the first note served as a cover letter for these four documents, it would have been written between 1832 and 1839.

2. At the bottom of this handwritten artifact is a penciled note from a librarian: "The original and copies of this letter moved from Ross to Payne and finally to Sequoyah file."

3. John Howard Payne's 1835 interview of Sequoyah tells a different story of his father and mother, but the endings are typically the same. When Sequoyah is very young, his father leaves. He is raised by his mother and her family in Will's Town on the Tennessee River in what is today Alabama (Bass 1932).

4. Since diacritics would not have been used in the English literacy models that Sequoyah had access to, it is not likely that he would even have seen a model of a writing system that uses diacritics to indicate subtle differences in pronunciation. In any case diacritics such as accent marks probably would not have been useful in these instances, because the semantic change in one syllable would have needed to be marked. In other words, Sequoyah would have had to draw a completely different image for one subtle yet noteworthy change in the word.

5. It is possible to create a logographic system based at least in part upon images, as the Chinese did, where a character represents a word. This process required hundreds of scribes, however, who worked methodically together over thousands of years. The Chinese used such a method to develop their writing system, "clearly set out in Han times by the author of the first dictionary of Chinese characters, the great lexicographer Xu Shen (ca. 57–ca. 147)" (Vandermeersch 2002: 68).

2. The Syllabary as Writing System

1. The Moravian Mission published the *Cherokee Messenger* between 1844 and 1846 in Indian Territory.

2. Ironically, by the late 1880s Sequoyah had become a legend for bringing an "alphabet" to Cherokees, thus helping the tribe reach an advanced state of "civilization." George Foster (1885) wrote a book describing Sequoyah as an American Cadmus and modern Moses because he gave an "alphabet" to Cherokees. Cadmus was credited with introducing the Phoenician writing system to the Greeks that would later become their alphabet.

3. My own experiences in taking online Cherokee language classes as well as speaking with numerous Oklahoma Cherokees confirm Bender's findings about the North Carolina Cherokees in this regard.

4. Bender stops short of providing a linguistic analysis of the glyphs and their potential meanings that would further have supported her claims. This chapter extends her important findings by providing linguistic evidence that might also be useful as an instructional resource for Cherokee language learners.

5. I am indebted to Cherokee National Living Treasure Sue Thompson for her translations and teachings here.

6. Many thanks to John Ross, who double-checked these tables for accuracy.

7. Oxford linguist Roy Harris (1986, 2009) provides a useful overview of the ways in which linguistics has failed to give an adequate account of how writing systems work because of the alphabetic bias. See also Cushman 2011a and 2011b for a detailed discussion of the alphabetic bias that has gotten so many scholars off on the wrong foot when approaching Sequoyan.

8. Many thanks to the anonymous reviewer of the manuscript of this book for insights in this regard.

9. Rogers (2005: 14), a linguist, finds that Chinese is morphographic, "where the primary relationship of glyphs is to morphemes." Most writing systems scholars, however, call it logographic: glyphs are related to words and ideas. The term "morphographic" retains the sound and idea relationship represented by each glyph. Yet the Cherokee writing system can potentially use sounds to show relation to many levels of meaning.

10. As writing systems go, the syllabary has advantages. "Much has been made of the economic advantage of syllabic writing over word writing, which stems from the fact that the number of the speech syllables of a language is closed while that of words is open. Typically, syllabic writing reduces the burden on memory, as compared to word writing" (Coulmas 2003: 146–48). In this way Sequoyah developed a system that takes advantage of the economy of the syllabary and the cultural and linguistic depth of an ideographic system.

3. The Syllabary's Design

1. I am grateful to Richard Allen, policy analyst of the Cherokee Nation, for drawing my attention to this footnote.

2. The syllabary has only six rows with initial characters, but one of the characters has two forms, resulting in seven primary forms.

3. Seven is an incredibly important number to Cherokees for at least seven reasons. The star in the middle of the Cherokee Nation seal symbolizes its importance.

4. The Syllabary from Script to Print

1. James Mooney includes a reproduction of this particular syllabary chart as plate 5 in his *Myths of the Cherokees* (Mooney 1900: 112).

2. Mooney (1900: 111–12) found that the creation of fonts and the purchase of a press for the Cherokee Nation allowed an expansion of the kinds of artifacts in both Oklahoma and North Carolina. The proliferation of genres published by the nation in the Cherokee writing system is one indicator of continued reading and writing after print was developed. Elias Boudinot (1832), editor of the *Cherokee Phoenix*, offers another indication of the Cherokees' interest in seeing their language in print: "About 200 copies of this newspaper are circulated weekly, in the nation. . . . At the same press have also been published in Cherokee, the Gospel of Matthew, and a Hymnbook; and a tract containing portions of Scripture. It is found that these publications are read with great interest, and weekly meetings are held in some neighborhoods, to read the *Cherokee Phoenix*" (quoted in Perdue 1983: 58). Boudinot estimates that about one-half of the Cherokees could read and write in 1830 (Perdue 1983: 58), with the census of 1835 showing that 43 percent of households had Cherokee-language readers (63). Taken together, Cherokee reading and writing practices remained steady or increased as a result of print.

3. Grant Foreman (1938: 44–46) quotes excerpts of this interview.

4. James Mooney (1900) offers a description of how Sequoyah might have gone about borrowing the designs of the seven letters. Though he attributes this information to "author's personal information" (Mooney 1900: 220), it bears a striking resemblance to the account offered by Elias Boudinot in his 1832 essay "Invention of a New Alphabet." Mooney (1900: 219) writes that Sequoyah tested a symbol for each character. "For this purpose he made use of a number of characters which he found in an old English spelling book, picking out capitals, lower-case, italics, and figures, and placing them right side up or upside down, without any idea of their sound or significance as used in English." Sequoyah seems to have purposely

avoided the influence of letter-sound correspondences and the workings of the alphabet, so it makes sense that he would chose the designs of letters and disregard the sound system. Boudinot (1832) also mentions a spelling book and quotes Knapp's interview with Sequoyah as a primary source. Mooney also does not seem to be aware of the syllabary produced for John Howard Payne that was created in 1839.

5. Though both Perdue (1994: 122) and Walker and Sarbaugh (1993: 85, 91) mention Pickering's orthography and the tribe's rejection of it, they do not explore the political and ideological social processes and implications of rejecting Pickering's orthography and demanding that Sequoyan be seen in print. In "The Cherokee Syllabary from Script to Print," I take up this idea in greater detail (Cushman 2010).

5. Elias Boudinot and the Cherokee Phoenix

1. All issues of the *Cherokee Phoenix* are now available in electronic form based on print reproductions from the Georgia Newspaper Project, Digital Library of Georgia (Farmington Hills, Mich.: Thomson Gale, 2006; available at http://dlg.galileo .usg.edu/meta/html/dlg/zlgn/meta_dlg_zlgn_chph02.html?Welcome; access limited by licensing agreements).

2. In these respects, this chapter adds dimension to regional histories of American literate lives (Brandt 1998, 2001; Royster 2000; Powell 2007; Graff 2007; Rumsey 2009a, 2009b). Regional histories are indeed useful in providing unique vantages on American lives at particular times and under a variety of circumstances. "From a regional perspective, historians are able to demonstrate how unequal distributions of literacy related to unequal distributions of other things—wealth, roads, schools, trade, political privilege. . . . Regional histories also illuminate the value of literacy as a resource. In the early days of mass literacy, the worth of individual literacy would rise with the rates of literacy in a region" (Brandt 2001: 28). Defined along geographical boundaries, regional histories connect places and populations to economies of exchange and literacy. They reveal the unevenly distributed wealth, opportunities, and infrastructural resources of homesteads, farms, towns, and cities and by doing so provide a useful place to begin mapping individual literacy achievement against a national backdrop of various economies of literacy. This chapter provides insight into the types of cultural and linguistic perseverance that intersect with the political and economic mappings of literacy achievement.

3. Walker (1985) provides useful clarification on the roles that Samuel Worcester and Elias Boudinot played in the publication of this newspaper. Though it is not clear that Boudinot knew the Cherokee writing system, he was certainly bilingual.

4. McLoughlin (1986: chapter 19) makes a detailed comparison of the Cherokee Constitution and the United States Constitution to show where the two overlap and diverge. Suffice it to say that the Cherokee Constitution worked remarkably well to advance three aspects of peoplehood: language, history, and land. Thornton (1993: 364–65) describes how the Cherokees codified a governmental structure that reflected Cherokee ways, though calling it a "civilized tribe." "In 1808 Cherokees

recorded their first formal laws and established a national police force, the Light-horse Patrol. They created a bicameral legislature in 1817, and a Supreme Court in 1822. In 1827–28 state building reached its climax when the Cherokee wrote and adopted a republican constitution." He adds: "This established a tripartite form of government like that of the United States, with a Principal Chief, National Council, and Supreme Court, and created the Cherokee 'Nation.' " Thornton makes no mention of the ways in which the Cherokee syllabary in print aided in the continued renewal and revitalization of the Cherokee Nation even as it continued to codify the national institutions, laws, and government. This omission elides the importance of writing and print in sustaining the revitalization of the tribe and making transparent the tools and media through which these revitalizations were at least in part codified.

5. This translation was made by John Miller for Hugh Montgomery (Ross, "To the Cherokee People," July 1, 1829, in Moulton 1985: 1:166).

6. The Breadth of the Cherokee Writing System, 1840–1920

1. See McLoughlin (1974, 1984) for a discussion on the antimissionary movement among the old-settler Cherokees.

2. At this time, Indian affairs involving tribes and the U.S. federal government were handled through the War Department.

7. Perseverance and Calculated Inconspicuousness, 1920–1980

1. It is not clear where this type was secured or who constructed this type plate. The plate was brought to my attention by a volunteer at the Gilcrease Museum who knew of it, though the piece had not been catalogued. The librarian allowed me to photograph it in the hope of finding more information about it. When I showed this to Travis Owens, cultural tourism senior project manager for the Cherokee Nation, he had it translated. Together he and Duane King, director of the Gilcrease Museum and Cherokee historian (Fitzgerald and King 2006; King 2007), agreed to display it in the Cherokee National Supreme Court Museum along with the last printing press for the *Cherokee Advocate*.

2. Frans Olbrechts and Will West Long collected hundreds of pages from countless Cherokee authors of not yet translated manuscripts in Sequoyan from North Carolina, which are archived at the National Anthropological Archives (MS 4600 folders 34–47). Dates on these documents range from the early 1900s to as late as 1921. Among these papers are two notebooks in Cherokee, several medicine formulas, and various social documents, including a tally of voters who took part in an election. These papers indicate that Sequoyan was widely used by Eastern Cherokees, just as it continued to be central to the daily life of individual Cherokees in Oklahoma communities during the early 1900s.

3. While the Kilpatricks are not clear about what event may be represented by the ᏍᏲ /gadugi/, the document seems to suggest that a gathering would be for the purpose of flooring a church and its porch.

4. The script of this Sunday school class reflects the structure of services held in many of the Cherokee Baptist churches around the present-day fourteen-county

Cherokee Nation. Hymnals in Cherokee are provided by the churches, some with phonetic spellings of Cherokee in English. Many of those in attendance read from the Cherokee New Testament, from a book that may have been in the family for generations.

8. Peoplehood and Perseverance: The Cherokee Language, 1980–2010

1. Margaret Bender found that the Cherokee teachers in North Carolina were inconsistent in their use of English phonetic translations of the Cherokee glyphs. Some relied solely on the syllabary, she speculates, because they believed that "the syllables are actually syllable-long morphemes with stable semantic meanings" (Bender 2002: 122). Some used the English alphabet as a crutch in learning the Cherokee language.

References

Allen, Richard. 2005. "Creating Identity at Indian Expense: Public Ignorance, Private Gain." Sequoyah Research Center Symposium, Little Rock, University of Arkansas, October 20–22, 2005.

———. 2007. Personal communication, June 18.

———. 2010. "Number of Cherokee Citizens." Personal communication, June 24.

American Board of Commissions of Foreign Missionaries (ABCFM). 1826. "Cherokees, Syllabic Alphabet, Invented by a Native." *Missionary Herald* 22(2) (February): 47.

———. 1827a. "Cherokees: Progress of Religion." *Missionary Herald* 23(7) (July): 212.

———. 1827b. "Printing Press and Types for the Cherokee Nation." *Missionary Herald* 23(12) (December): 382.

Anderson, Benedict. 2006. *Imagined Communities: Reflections on the Origin and Spread of Nationalism.* London: Verso.

Arnheim, Rudolf. 1954. *Art and Visual Perception: A Psychology of the Creative Eye.* Berkeley: University of California Press.

Axtell, James. 1979. "Ethnohistory: An Historian's Viewpoint." *Ethnohistory* 26(1) (Winter): 1–13.

Baca, Damian. 2008. *Mestiz@ Scripts, Digital Migrations and the Territories of Writing.* New York: Palgrave Macmillan.

Bacon, H., G. Kidd, and J. Seabarg. 1982. "The Effectiveness of Bilingual Instruction with Cherokee Indian Students." *Journal of American Indian Education* 21(2): 34–43.

Barbour, James. 1826. *Letter from the Secretary of War, to the Chairman of the Committee on Indian Affairs, Accompanied by a Bill for the Preservation and Civilization of the Indian Tribes within the United States.* Document No. 102, 19th Cong., 1st Sess. Washington City: Gales and Seaton.

Bass, Althea. 1932. "Talking Stones: John Howard Payne's Story of Sequoyah." *Colophon: A Book Collectors Quarterly* 9(3) (unpaginated).

———. (1936) 1996. *Cherokee Messenger.* Foreword by William Anderson. Norman: University of Oklahoma Press.

Bender, Margaret. 2002. *Signs of Cherokee Culture: Sequoyah's Syllabary in Eastern Cherokee Life.* Chapel Hill: University of North Carolina Press.

Boudinot, Elias, ed. 1828a. "Constitution of the Cherokee Nation." *Cherokee Phoenix* 1(1) (February 21).

———. 1828b. "New Echota." *Cherokee Phoenix* 1(37) (November 12).

———. 1828c. "Prospectus." *Cherokee Phoenix* 1(2) (February 28).

———. 1828d. "To Cherokee Correspondents." *Cherokee Phoenix* 1(11) (May 6).

———. 1832. "Invention of a New Alphabet." *American Annals of Education* (April 1). Reprinted in Theda Perdue, ed., *Cherokee Editor: The Writings of Elias Boudinot,* 48–63. Knoxville: University of Tennessee Press, 1983.

Brandt, Deborah. 1998. "Sponsors of Literacy." *College Composition and Communication* 49(2) (May): 166–85.

———. 2001. *Literacy in American Lives.* Cambridge: Cambridge University Press.

Brokaw, Galen. 2010. "Indigenous American Polygraphy and the Dialogic Model of Media." *Ethnohistory* 57(1): 117–33.

Carter, Kent. 1999. *The Dawes Commission and the Allotment of the Five Civilized Tribes, 1893–1914.* Orem, Utah: Ancestry.com.

Chavez, Will. 2009. "Long-Range Language Preservation Plan in Progress." *Cherokee Phoenix,* http://www.cherokeephoenix.org/6/Article.aspx (accessed September 14, 2009).

Cherokee Nation. 1972. "Thunder and the Uk'ten." *Cherokee Nation News,* September 5.

———. 1973a. "Layout of the Cherokee Electric Typewriter Keyboard." *Cherokee Nation News,* April 10.

———. 1973b. "Materials Developed by & Available from the Cherokee Bilingual Program." *Cherokee Nation News,* April 3.

———. 1991. "Legislative Act Relating to the Establishment of the Tribal Policy for the Promotion and Preservation of Cherokee Language, History and Culture." Tahlequah, Oklahoma. http://cherokee.legistar.com/LegislationDetail .aspx?ID=266941&GUID=C8EC5F0A-E523-49A0-92BD-42041FCE32EA&Options =ID|Text|&Search=10+91 (accessed June 2011).

———. 2007. "Cherokee Nation Education Services." http://www.cherokee.org /Services/Education/Default.aspx (accessed July 29, 2010).

———. 2009a. "Cherokee Nation Annual Report." Tahlequah, Okla.: Cherokee Nation, 2009.

———. 2009b. "Syllabary Activity." http://www.cherokee.org/AboutTheNation /Kid'sArea/KidsGames/Default.aspx (accessed June 2011).

———. 2009c. "ᎦᎵᏏᏹ /kaliquadegi/ or 'Converter.' " http://www.cherokee.org /AboutTheNation/Kid'sArea/KidsGames/Default.aspx.

Christin, Anne-Marie, ed. 2002. *A History of Writing: From Hieroglyph to Multimedia.* Paris: Flammarion.

Chuchiak, John. 2010. "Writing as Resistance: Maya Graphic Pluralism and Indigenous Elite Strategies for Survival in Colonial Yucatan, 1550–1750." *Ethnohistory* 57(1): 87–116.

Clifford, James. 2001. "Indigenous Articulations." *Contemporary Pacific* 13(2) (Fall): 468–90.

Cobb, Daniel. 2007. "Devils in Disguise: The Carnegie Project, the Cherokee Nation, and the 1960's." *American Indian Quarterly* 31(3): 465–90.

Coiro, Julie, Michelle Knobel, Colin Lankshear, and Donald Leu. eds. 2008. *Handbook of Research on New Literacies*. New York: Lawrence Erlbaum Associates/Taylor & Francis Group.

Collins, James. 2003. *Literacy and Literacies: Texts, Power, and Identity*. Cambridge: Cambridge University Press.

Coulmas, Florian. 2003. *Writing Systems: An Introduction to Their Linguistic Analysis*. Cambridge: Cambridge University Press.

Cowen, Agnes, and Martin Cochran. 1972. *Life of Famous Cherokee Men*. Tahlequah, Okla.: Cherokee Bilingual Education Program.

Cushman, Ellen. 1998. *The Struggle and The Tools: Oral and Literate Strategies in an Inner City Community*. Albany: SUNY Press.

———. 2005. "Face, Skins, and the Identity Politics of Rereading Race." *Rhetoric Review* 24: 378–82.

———. 2008. "Toward a Rhetoric of Self Representation: Identity Politics in Indian Country and Rhetoric and Composition." *College Composition and Communication* 60(2): 321–65.

———. 2010. "The Cherokee Syllabary from Script to Print." *Ethnohistory* 57(4) (Fall): 625–50.

———. 2011a. "The Cherokee Syllabary: A Writing System in Its Own Right." *Written Communication* 28(3) (July): 255–81.

———. 2011b. "New Media Scholarship and Teaching: Challenging the Hierarchy of Signs." *Pedagogy* 11(1) (Winter): 63–80.

———. 2011c. " 'We're Taking the Genius of Sequayah into This Century': The Cherokee Syllabary, Peoplehood, and Perseverance." *Wicazo Sa Review* 26(1) (Spring): 67–83.

Cushman, Ellen, Eugene Kintgen, Barry Kroll, and Mike Rose, eds. 2001. *Literacy: A Critical Sourcebook*. Boston: Bedford St. Martin's.

Daniels, Peter, 2009. "Grammatology." In *The Cambridge Handbook of Literacy*, ed. David Olson and Nancy Torrance, 25–45. Cambridge: Cambridge University Press.

Debo, Angie. 1940. *And Still the Waters Run*. Princeton, N.J.: Princeton University Press.

DeFrancis, John. 1989. *Visible Speech: The Diverse Oneness of Writing Systems*. Honolulu: University of Hawaii Press.

Deloria, Vine, and Daniel Wildcat. 2001. *Power and Place: Indian Education in America*. Golden, Colo.: Fulcrum Publishing.

DeMallie, Raymond. 1993. " 'These Have No Ears': Narrative and the Ethnohistorical Method." *Ethnohistory* 40(4) (Autumn): 515–38.

Denson, Andrew. 2004. *Demanding the Cherokee Nation*. Lincoln: University of Nebraska Press.

Drucker, Johanna. 1997. *The Visible Word: Experimental Typography and Modern Art, 1909–1923*. 2nd ed. Chicago: University Of Chicago Press.

Edwards, Jeff. 2009. E-mail to author, September 17.

Edwards, Jeff, and Sherry Holcomb. 2005. *Common Cherokee Words and Phrases*. Tahlequah, Okla.: Cherokee Nation.

Ellison, George. 1992. "James Mooney and the Eastern Cherokees." Introduction in *James Mooney's History, Myths, and Sacred Formulas of the Cherokees*, 1–25. Ashville, N.C.: Bright Mountain Books.

Faigley, Lester. 1999. "Material Literacy and Visual Design." In *Rhetorical Bodies: Toward a Material Rhetoric*, ed. Jack Selzer and Sharon Crowley, 171–201. Madison: University of Wisconsin Press.

Feeling, Durbin. 1975. *Cherokee-English Dictionary*. Ed. William Pulte. Tahlequah, Okla.: Cherokee Nation.

Fink, Kenneth. 1998. "Riding Behind with a Pillow Strapped On." In *A Good Cherokee, A Good Anthropologist*, ed. Steve Pavlik, 119–27. Berkeley: University of California Press.

Finnegan, Ruth. 1988. *Literacy and Orality: Studies in the Technology of Communication*. Oxford: Blackwell.

Fischer, Steven. 2001. *A History of Writing*. London: Reaktion Books.

Fitzgerald, David and Duane King. 2006. *The Cherokee Trail of Tears*. Portland, Ore.: Graphic Arts Center Publishing Company.

Foreman, Grant. 1934. *The Five Civilized Tribes*. Oklahoma City: University of Oklahoma Press.

———. 1938. *Sequoyah*. Norman: University of Oklahoma Press.

Foster, George. 1885. *Se-Quo-Yah: The American Cadmus and Modern Moses*. Philadelphia: Office of Indian Rights Association.

Fries, Adelaide L., ed. 1947. *Records of the Moravians in North Carolina*. 7 vols. Raleigh, N.C.: Edwards and Broughton.

Gaines, W. Craig. 1989. *Confederate Cherokees: John Drew's Regiment of Mounted Rifles*. Baton Rouge: Louisiana State University Press.

Garroutte, Eva Marie. 2003. *Real Indians: Identity and the Survival of Native America*. Berkeley: University of California Press.

Gelb, I. J. 1963. *A Study of Writing*. 2nd ed. Chicago: University of Chicago Press.

Gittinger, Roy. 1973. *The Formation of the State of Oklahoma (1803–1906)*. New York: Kraus Reprint.

Glassner, Jean-Jacques. 2003. *The Invention of Cuneiform: Writing in Sumer*. Baltimore, Md.: Johns Hopkins University Press.

Good Voice, Christina. 2009. "Cowan Watts Calls for Policy Changes at Cherokee Immersion School." *Cherokee Phoenix*. http://www.cherokeephoenix.org/3554/Article.aspx (accessed September 15, 2009).

Goody, Jack. 1977. *The Domestication of the Savage Mind*. Cambridge: Cambridge University Press.

Graff, Harvey. 2007. *Literacy and Historical Development: A Reader*. Carbondale: University of Illinois Press.

Hardt, Michael, and Toni Negri. 2000. *Empire*. Cambridge, Mass.: Harvard University Press.

Harris, Roy. 1986. *The Origin of Writing*. London: Duckworth Ltd.

———. 2009. *Rationality and the Literate Mind*. New York: Taylor and Francis, Routledge.

Harvey, Chris. 2010. Personal communication, July 15.

Havelock, Eric. 1986. *The Muse Learns to Write: Reflections on Orality and Literacy from Antiquity to the Present*. New Haven, Conn.: Yale University Press.

Heath, Shirley Brice. 2001. "Protean Shapes of Literacy." In *Literacy: A Critical Sourcebook*, ed. Ellen Cushman, Barry Kroll, Eugene Kintgen, and Mike Rose, 209–45. Boston: Bedford/St. Martin's.

Hicks, Charles. 1825. "Letter dated 14 Jan. 1825 to Thomas McKenney." Bureau of Indian Affairs, RG75, M-234, roll 71; frames 553–58. Letters Received by Office of Indian Affairs, 1824–81. Washington, D.C.: National Archives.

Hill, Archibald. 1967. "The Typology of Writing Systems." In *Papers in Linguistics in Honor of Leon Dosert,* ed. William Austin, 92–99. The Hague: Mouton.

Hobsbawm, Eric, and Terence Ranger, eds. 1983. *The Invention of Tradition.* Cambridge: Cambridge University Press.

Hoig, Stan. 1995. *Sequoyah: The Cherokee Genius.* Oklahoma City: Oklahoma Historical Society.

Holm, Tom, Diane Pearson, and Ben Chavis. 2003. "A Model for the Extension of Sovereignty in American Indian Studies." *Wicazo Sa Review* 18(1): 7–24.

Holmes, Ruth, and Betty Sharp Smith. 1976. *Beginning Cherokee.* Norman: University of Oklahoma Press.

Houston, Stephen, ed. 2004. *The First Writing: Script Invention as History and Process.* Cambridge: Cambridge University Press.

Hyland, Sabine. 2010. "Sodomy, Sin, and String Writing: the Moral Origins of Andean Khipu." *Ethnohistory* 57(1): 165–73.

Inali (ᏔᎯ). 1848–81. Syllabary Chart. National Anthropological Archives, Smithsonian Museum Support Center, Suitland, Md. NAA MS 2241-a. http://collections.si .edu/search/slideshow_embedded?xml=%22http://sirismm.si.edu/naa/viewer /MS2241a_Gallery/MS2241a.xml%22 (accessed July 19, 2009).

Kilpatrick, Anna Gritts, and Jack Kilpatrick. 1965. *The Shadow of Sequoyah: Social Documents of the Cherokees, 1862–1964.* Norman: University of Oklahoma Press.

———. 1966. *Chronicles of Wolftown: Social Documents of the North Carolina Cherokees, 1850–1862.* Bureau of American Ethnology Bulletin 196, Paper 75. Washington, D.C.: Smithsonian Institution.

———, eds. 1968. *New Echota Letters: Contributions of Samuel A. Worcester to the Cherokee Phoenix.* Dallas: Southern Methodist University Press.

Kilpatrick, Jack. 1966. *The Wahnenauhi Manuscript: Historical Sketches of the Cherokees.* Bureau of American Ethnology Bulletin 196, Paper 77. Washington, D.C.: Smithsonian Institution.

King, Duane, ed. 2007. *The Memoirs of Lt. Henry Timberlake.* Cherokee, N.C.: Museum of the Cherokee Indian.

King, Duane, and Laura King. n.d. "Old Words for New Ideas: Linguistic Acculturation in Modern Cherokee." Unpublished paper.

Knapp, Samuel Lorenzo. 1829. *Lectures on American Literature, with Remarks on Some Passages of American History.* New York: Elam Bliss.

Krech, Shepard. 1991. "The State of Ethnohistory." *Annual Review of Anthropology* 20: 345–75.

Littlefield, Daniel, and James Parins. 1984. *American Indian and Alaska Native Newspapers and Periodicals, 1826–1924.* Westport, Conn.: Greenwood Press.

Mankiller, Wilma. 2002. "To Persevere as Tribal People." *Native Americas* (Ithaca) 19(3–4) (December 31): 55.

McKenney, Thomas. 1825. "Report to the War Department." 19th Congress, 1st session. U.S. Serial Set 135, docs. 102–104, 1826. Microprint.

McLoughlin, William. 1974. "Cherokee Anti-Mission Sentiment, 1824–1828." *Ethnohistory* 21: 361–70.

———. 1975. "Thomas Jefferson and the Beginning of Cherokee Nationalism, 1806 to 1809." *William and Mary Quarterly* 32(4): 548–80.

———. 1984. *Cherokees and Missionaries, 1789–1839*. New Haven, Conn.: Yale University Press.

———. 1986. *Cherokee Renascence in the New Republic*. Princeton, N.J.: Princeton University Press.

———. 1993. *After the Trail of Tears: The Cherokees' Struggle for Sovereignty, 1839–1880*. Chapel Hill: University of North Carolina Press.

McLuhan, Marshall. 1994. *Understanding Media: The Extensions of Man*. Boston, Mass.: MIT Press.

McLuhan, Marshall, with Eric McLuhan. 1988. *Laws of Media: The New Science*. Toronto: University of Toronto Press.

Meriam, Lewis. 1928. *The Problem of Indian Administration: Report of a Survey Made at the Request of Honorable Hubert Work, Secretary of the Interior, and Submitted to Him, February 21, 1928*. Baltimore: Johns Hopkins Press.

Montgomery-Anderson, Brad. 2007. "A Reference Grammar of Oklahoma Cherokee." Ph.D. diss., University of Kansas.

Mooney, James. 1892. "Improved Cherokee Alphabets." *American Anthropologist* 5(1) (January): 63–64.

———. 1900. *Myths of the Cherokees*. Washington, D.C.: Bureau of American Ethnology.

Morgan, Mindy. 2009. T*he Bearer of This Letter: Language Ideologies, Literacy Practices, and the Fort Belknap Indian Community*. Lincoln: University of Nebraska Press.

Morton, W. Neil. 2009. Personal interview with the author, audiotaped on September 4, Tahlequah, Oklahoma.

Moulton, Gary, ed. 1985. *The Papers of Chief John Ross*. 2 vols. Norman: University of Oklahoma Press.

Olbrechts, Frans. 1931. "Two Cherokee Texts." *International Journal of American Linguistics* 6(3) (April): 179–84.

Olson, David. 1994. *The World on Paper*. Cambridge: Cambridge University Press.

Ong, Walter. 1982. *Orality and Literacy: The Technologizing of the Word*. London: Methuen.

Payne, John Howard. (1835) 1932. "The Life of George Gist." Edited by Althea Bass. *Colophon: A Book Collectors Quarterly* 9(3) (unpaginated).

Penn, William. 1829. "Present Crisis in the Condition of the American Indians." *Cherokee Phoenix and Indians' Advocate* (New Echota, Ga.), November 4 (30): col. A, 1.

Perdue, Theda. 1977. "Rising from the Ashes: The Cherokee Phoenix as Ethnohistorical Source." *Ethnohistory* 24(3): 207–18.

———. 1983. *Cherokee Editor: The Writings of Elias Boudinot*. Knoxville: University of Tennessee Press.

———. 1994. "The Sequoyah Syllabary and Cultural Revitalization." In *Perspectives on the Southeast: Linguistics, Archaeology, and Ethnohistory*, ed. Patricia Kwachka, 116–25. Athens: University of Georgia Press.

Phillips, W. A. 1870. "Se-Quo-Yah." *Harper's Monthly Magazine* 41 (June): 542–48.

Pickering, John. 1830. *Grammar of the Cherokee Language*. Boston: Mission Press.

Pickering, Mary Orne. (1887) 2009. *Life of John Pickering*. The Making of Modern Law, Farmington Hills, Mich.: Gale, Cengage Learning. http://galenet.galegroup .com.proxy2.cl.msu.edu/servlet/MOML?af=RN&ae=F3700413477&srchtp=a& ste=14 (accessed July 3, 2009).

Powell, Katrina. 2007. *The Anguish of Displacement: The Politics of Literacy in the Letters of Mountain Families in Shenandoah National Park*. Charlottesville: University of Virginia Press.

Pulte, William. 1985. "The Experienced and Nonexperienced Past in Cherokee." *International Journal of American Linguistics* 51(4) (October): 543–44.

Reyburn, William. 1953a. "Cherokee Verb Morphology 1." *International Journal of American Linguistics* 19(3) (July): 172–80.

———. 1953b. "Cherokee Verb Morphology 2." *International Journal of American Linguistics* 19(4) (July): 259–73.

———. 1954. "Cherokee Verb Morphology 3." *International Journal of American Linguistics* 20(1) (January): 44–64.

Rodríguez, Ileana. 2001."The Places of Tradition: Modernity/Backwardness, Regionalism/Centralism, Mass/Popular, Homogeneous/Heterogeneous." *CR: The New Centennial Review* 1(1) (Spring): 55–74.

Rogers, Henry. 2005. *Writing Systems: A Linguistic Approach*. Malden, Mass.: Blackwell.

Roosevelt, Theodore. (1901) 1910. "First Annual Message." December 3. In *Presidential Addresses and State Papers*, vol. 2 (unpaginated). New York: Review of Reviews Company.

Rosaldo, Renato. 1989. *Culture and Truth: The Remaking of Social Analysis*. Boston: Beacon Press.

Ross, John. 1828. "Annual Message." New Echota, Cherokee Nation: October 13, 1828. In Moulton 1985: 1:140–45.

———. 1829a. "To the Cherokee People." July 1. In Moulton 1985: 1:166–67.

———. 1829b. "To the National Committee and National Council." November 4. In Moulton 1985: 1:176–77.

———. 1832. "Letter to Sequoyah." January 12. In Moulton 1985: 2:234–35.

———. 1836. "To Lewis Cass." April 22. In Moulton 1985: 1:417–18.

———. 1842a. "Memo for Provisions for a New Treaty." August 24. In Moulton 1985: 2:146–47.

———. 1842b. "To David Greene." September 22. In Moulton 1985: 2:148–49.

———. 1842c. "To John C. Spencer." August 12. In Moulton 1985: 2:145–46.

———. 1843. "Annual Message." October 3. In Moulton 1985: 2:176–81.

———. 1861. "Address to the Cherokees." August 21. In Moulton 1985: 2:479–81.

Routh, E. C. 1937. "Early Missionaries to the Cherokees." *Chronicles of Oklahoma* 15(4): 449–65. http://digital.library.okstate.edu/chronicles/v015/v015p449.html (accessed August 1, 2009).

Royster, Jacqueline Jones. 2000. *Traces of a Stream: Literacy and Social Change among African American Women*. Pittsburgh: University of Pittsburgh Press.

Rozema, Vicki. 2002. *Cherokee Voices*. Winston-Salem, N.C.: John Blair Publishers.

Rumsey, Suzanne. 2009a. "Cooking, Recipes, and Work Ethic: Passage of a Heritage Literacy Practice." *Journal of Literacy and Technology: An International Online*

Academic Journal 10(1) (April). http://www.literacyandtechnology.org/volume10 /jlt_v10_1_rumsey.pdf (accessed September 19, 2009).

———. 2009b. "Heritage Literacy: Adoption, Adaptation, and Alienation of Multimodal Literacy Tools." *College Composition and Communication* 60: 573–86.

Salomon, Frank, and Sabine Hyland. 2010. "Guest Editor's Introduction." *Ethnohistory* 57(1): 2–9.

Scancarelli, Janine. 1992. "Aspiration and Cherokee Orthographies." In *Linguistics of Literacy,* ed. Pamela Downing, Susan Lima, and Michael Noonan, 135–52. Amsterdam: John Benjamins.

———. 1994. "Another Look at a 'Primitive Language.'" *International Journal of American Linguistics* 60(2): 149–60.

Scribner, Sylvia, and Michael Cole. 1991. *The Psychology of Literacy.* Cambridge, Mass.: Harvard University Press.

Sebba, Mark. 2006. "Ideology and Alphabets in the Former USSR." *Language Problems and Language Planning* 30(2): 99–125.

———. 2007. *Spelling and Society: The Culture and Politics of Orthography around the World.* Cambridge: Cambridge University Press.

———. 2009. "Sociolinguistic Approaches to Writing Systems Research." *Writing Systems Research* 1(1): 35–49.

Simmons, Gregg. 2009. "Programs Promote Language Revitalization." *Cherokee Phoenix* (September). http://www.cherokeephoenix.org/1793/Article.aspx (accessed September 14, 2009).

Simmons, William. 1988. "Culture Theory in Contemporary Ethnohistory." *Ethnohistory* 35(1) (Winter): 1–14.

Starr, Emmet. 1921. *History of The Cherokee Indians.* Oklahoma City: Genealogical Publishing Co.

Street, Brian. 1984. *Literacy in Theory and Practice.* Cambridge: Cambridge University Press.

———, ed. 1993. *Cross-Cultural Approaches to Literacy.* Cambridge: Cambridge University Press.

———. 1995. *Social Literacies: Critical Approaches to Literacy Development.* London: Addison Wesley Publishing.

Strickland, Rennard. 1980. *The Indians of Oklahoma.* Norman: University of Oklahoma Press.

Stuart, John. 1837. *A Sketch of the Cherokee and Choctaw Indians.* Little Rock, Ark.: Woodruff and Pew.

Sturm, Circe. 2002. *Blood Politics: Race, Culture, and Identity in the Cherokee Nation of Oklahoma.* Berkeley: University of California Press.

Tall Bear, Kimberly. 2003. "DNA, Blood, and Racializing the Tribe." *Wicazo Sa Review* 18: 81–107.

Thomas, Joseph. 2008. "Creating Cherokee Print: Samuel Austin Worcester's Impact on the Syllabary." *Media History Monographs* 10(2): 1–20.

Thompson, Peter. 2003. "'Judicious Neology': The Imperative of Paternalism in Thomas Jefferson's Linguistic Studies." *Early American Studies* 54 (Fall): 187–224.

Thornton, Russell. 1985. "Nineteenth-Century Cherokee History." *American Sociological Review* 50(1): 124–27.

———. 1993. "Boundary Dissolution and Revitalization Movements: The Case of the Nineteenth-Century Cherokees." *Ethnohistory* 40(3): 359–83.

———. 1997. "Tribal Membership Requirements and the Demography of 'Old' and 'New' Native Americans." *Population Research and Policy Review* 16: 33–42.

Trigger, Bruce. 1986. "The Unfinished Edifice." *Ethnohistory* 33(3) (Summer): 253–67.

Tuchscherer, Konrad, and P. E. H. Hair. 2002. "Cherokee and West Africa: Examining the Origins of the Vai Script." *History of Africa* 29: 427–86.

United States Census Bureau. 1994. "Table 18. American Indian and Alaska Native Languages Spoken at Home by American Indian Persons in Households, by Sex and Age: 1990." In *Characteristics of American Indians by Tribe and Language*, 874. Washington, D.C.: Government Printing Office. http://www.census.gov/population/www/socdemo/race/cp-3-7.html (accessed July 25, 2009).

———. 2003. "Table 1. American Indian and Alaska Native Languages Spoken at Home by American Indians and Alaska Natives 5 Years and Over: 2000." In *Characteristics of American Indians and Alaska Natives by Tribe and Language: 2000*, 1. Washington, D.C.: Government Printing Office. http://www.census.gov/census2000/pubs/phc-5.html (accessed July 25, 2009).

Vandermeersch, Leon. 2002. "Writing in China." In *A History of Writing*, 66–86. Paris: Flammarion Press.

Wahnenauhi. 1966. "Historical Sketches of the Cherokees: Together with Some of Their Customs, Traditions, and Superstitions." In *The Wahnenauhi Manuscript*, ed. Jack Kilpatrick, 179–214. Bureau of American Ethnology Bulletin 196, Paper 77. Washington, D.C.: Smithsonian Institution.

Wahrhaftig, Albert. 1966. *The Cherokee People Today: A Report to the Cherokee People.* Pittsburgh: Carnegie Corporation Cross-Cultural Education Project.

———. 1970. *Social and Economic Characteristics of the Cherokee Population of Eastern Oklahoma: Report of a Survey of Four Cherokee Settlements in the Cherokee Nation.* Washington, D.C.: American Anthropological Association.

———. 1998. "Looking Back to Tahlequah: Robert K. Thomas' Role among the Oklahoma Cherokee, 1963–1967." In *A Good Cherokee, a Good Anthropologist*, ed. Steve Pavlik, 93–105. Los Angeles: UCLA Press.

———. 2009. E-mail to author, August 27, 2009.

Walker, Willard. 1967. Reviewed work(s): *The Shadow of Sequoyah: Social Documents of the Cherokees, 1862–1964* by Jack Frederick and Anna Gritts Kilpatrick. *International Journal of American Linguistics* 33(1): 82–84.

——— 1969. "Notes on Native Writing Systems and the Design of Native Literacy Programs." *Anthropological Linguistics* 11(5) (May): 148–66.

———. 1985. "The Roles of Samuel A. Worcester and Elias Boudinot in the Emergence of a Printed Cherokee Syllabic Literature." *International Journal of American Linguistics* 51(4): 610–12.

Walker, Willard, and James Sarbaugh. 1993. "The Early History of the Cherokee Syllabary." *Ethnohistory* 40(1) (Winter): 70–94.

White, John. 1962. "On the Revival of Printing in the Cherokee Language." *Current Anthropology* 3(5): 511–14.

Witthoft, John. 1948. "Will West Long, Cherokee Informant." *American Anthropologist* 50(2) (April): 355–59.

Wood, Raymond. 1990. "Ethnohistory and Historical Method." *Archeological Method and Theory* 2: 81–109.

Worcester, Samuel ["W."]. 1827. "Letter to Jeremiah Evarts, 2 September." *Papers of the American Board of Commissioners for Foreign Missions* 18.3.1, vol. 5, part 2, no. 232. Microfilm reel 739, frames 609–10. Woodbridge, Conn.: Research Publications.

———. 1828a. "Cherokee Alphabet." *Missionary Herald* 24(5) (May): 162.

———. 1828b. "The Invention of the Cherokee Alphabet." *Missionary Herald* 24(10): 330.

———. 1835. Letter to David Greene, August 26. In Althea Bass, *Cherokee Messenger,* 187–90. Norman: University of Oklahoma Press, 1936.

Young, Mary. 1981. "The Cherokee Nation: Mirror of the Republic." *American Quarterly* 33(5): 502–24.

INDEX

CPSIA information can be obtained
at www.ICGtesting.com
Printed in the USA
LVHW031933281021
701807LV00001B/2